CW01064907

Applied DAX with Power BI

From zero to hero with 15-minute lessons

Teo Lachev

Applied DAX with Power BI

From zero to hero with 15-minute lessons

Published by:
Prologika Press
info@prologika.com
https://prologika.com

ISBN 13	978-1-7330461-0-7
ISBN 10	1-7330461-0-0

Author:	Teo Lachev
Technical reviewer:	John Layden
Cover designer:	Zamir Creations
Copyeditor:	Maya Lachev

The manuscript of this book was prepared using Microsoft Word. Screenshots were captured using TechSmith SnagIt.

contents

preface

DAX is growing in popularity thanks to the momentum surrounding Microsoft Power BI, Excel Power Pivot, and Analysis Services Tabular. Whether you are a business analyst or a BI pro, a good working knowledge of DAX is important for extending your models with custom business logic. You won't get far in Microsoft BI without DAX.

This book was born out of necessity and I've been working on it for a while. In my consulting practice, I had been teaching and implementing Power BI and Analysis Services Tabular, and people were constantly asking for DAX book recommendations. Indeed, DAX is not an easy topic and has its ways to humble even experienced practitioners. There are a few good reference books out there, but they could be somewhat overwhelming for novice users. So, I turned my classroom and consulting experience into this book and designed it as a self-paced guide to help you learn DAX one lesson at a time.

As its name suggests, the main objective of this book is to teach you the practical skills of how to take the most of DAX from whatever angle you'd like to approach it. You'll learn DAX methodically with self-paced lessons that progress from simple topics, such as calculated columns, to more advanced areas, such as time intelligence, joins, and security. Most lessons are five to six pages long, and it should take no more than 15 minutes to complete the lesson's exercises. And if you do one lesson per day, you'll be a DAX expert in a month!

With the growing popularity of Power BI, I decided to use this technology for the exercises. However, although this book teaches you DAX with Power BI, a nice bonus awaits you ahead because you're also learning how to program Excel Power Pivot and Analysis Services Tabular. So, if one day you find yourself working on a self-service model in Excel or an organizational model powered by Analysis Services Tabular, you'll find that you already have the knowledge.

Although this book is designed as a comprehensive guide to DAX, it's likely that you might have questions or comments. As with my previous books, I'm committed to help my readers with book-related questions and welcome all feedback on the book discussion forums on my company's web site (https://prologika.com/daxbook). Consider also following my blog at https://prologika.com/blog and subscribing to my newsletter at https://prologika.com to stay on the Microsoft BI latest.

Now, turn to the first lesson and get from zero to DAX hero at your own pace!

Teo Lachev
Atlanta, GA

about the book

The book doesn't require any prior experience with DAX, but it assumes that you have experience in Power BI data modeling. If you don't, I recommend you start with my "Applied Microsoft Power BI" book, which teaches you how to create self-service data models. To get the most out of this book, read and practice the lessons in the order they appear in the book. That's because each lesson builds upon the previous ones, to introduce new concepts and reinforce them with step-by-step exercises.

Part 1, *Introduction*, starts with the fundamentals. It introduces you to the DAX origin and main constructs. You'll learn important data modeling techniques, including star schemas and relationships. You'll also learn about the Power BI storage engine and how storage affects DAX.

Part 2, *Calculated Columns and Tables*, teaches you to extend your tables with basic and advanced calculated columns, including columns for looking up, aggregating, and filtering data. You'll understand how calculated columns are evaluated and how to change the evaluation context. And you'll discover how calculated tables can help you implement role-playing dimensions, date tables, and summarized tables.

Part 3, *Measures*, explains how measures give you the needed programmatic power to travel the "last mile" and unlock the full potential of Power BI. After learning the measure fundamentals and filter context, it shows you how to create basic measures. Then, it moves to more advanced concepts, such as restricting and ignoring the filter context, as well as grouping and filtering data.

Part 4, *Time Intelligence*, further expands your knowledge of measures and teaches you how to implement time intelligence. It starts by teaching you how to work with built-in and custom date tables. After revisiting quick measures for time intelligence, it teaches you how to implement custom formulas for more advanced requirements, such as custom date filters and semi-additive measures. You'll learn how to centralize time intelligence formulas by using calculation groups.

Part 5, *Queries*, covers creating custom queries to test measures outside Power BI Desktop, exploring the model data, and implementing reports with other tools that require you to specify a dataset query, such as Power BI Report Builder. You'll also discover how to identify and address performance bottlenecks.

Part 6, *Advanced DAX*, starts by showing you how you can use DAX to implement different types of joins, including recursive (parent-child), many-to-many, inner, outer, and other joins. It explains how to implement row-level security (RLS) by applying DAX row filters. You'll also learn how to handle more complicated security policies, such as by externalizing secured policies in a separate table.

acknowledgements

Welcome to the Applied DAX with Power BI book! Writing books is difficult and DAX doesn't make it any easier. Fortunately, I had people who supported me. This book (my eleventh) would not have been a reality without the help of many people to whom I'm thankful. As always, I'd like to first thank my family for their ongoing support. My daughter, Maya, contributed the most by polishing the manuscript.

Thanks to my technical reviewer John Layden, whom I had the privilege to work with previously on consulting engagements, for reviewing the manuscript, and providing valuable feedback. Thanks to Shay Zamir for another great cover design.

As a Microsoft Most Valuable Professional (MVP), Gold Partner (Data Analytics and Data Platform), and Power BI Red Carpet Partner, I've been privileged to enjoy close relationships with the Microsoft product groups. It's great to see them working together! Special thanks to the Power BI and Analysis Services teams.

Finally, thank *you* for purchasing this book!

conventions

This book uses different typefaces to differentiate between code and regular English, and to help you identify important concepts. Code that you type is presented in this font:

EVALUATE DimSalesTerritory

Referencing columns follows the DAX Table[Column] notation. For example, DimEmployee-[FullName] refers to the FullName column in the DimEmployee table. Table relationships also follow the DAX syntax. For example, FactResellerSales[OrderDateKey] ⇨ DimDate[DateKey] denotes a many-to-one relationship between the OrderDateKey column in the FactResellerSales table and the DateKey column in the DimDate table. The relationship direction (many-to-one) is indicated by the direction of the arrow.

Exercises typically have the following sections although sections can be omitted:

Practice
This section identifies the steps you need to take to complete the exercise, such as the DAX code that you type in.

Output
This section highlights the result from the practice, such as a screenshot from a report that uses DAX calculations or results from a query.

Analysis
The Analysis section provides the author's explanation about the practice and output sections, such as line-by-line analysis of a DAX formula.

source code

Applied DAX with Power BI doesn't require much to get you started. You can perform all practices with free software, and you don't need a Power BI license. **Table 1** lists the software that you need for all the exercises in the book. As you can see, most of the software is not required.

Table 1   The software requirements for practices and code samples in the book

Software	Setup	Purpose	Lessons
Power BI Desktop	Required	Implementing self-service data models	All
DAX Studio (https://daxstudio.org)	Recommended	Testing DAX queries	Part 5
Power BI Service (powerbi.com)	Optional	Testing data security	Part 6
SQL Server Management Studio (SSMS)	Optional	Testing DAX queries	Part 5
Power BI Report Builder	Optional	Creating a paginated report	Part 5
SQL Server Analysis Services Tabular 2019	Optional	Implement calculation groups	Part 4
Tabular Editor (https://tabulareditor.github.io/)	Optional	Implement calculation groups	Part 4

You can download the source code for the practices from the book page at https://prologika.com/daxbook. After downloading the zip file, extract it to any folder on your hard drive (I recommend C:\DAX\Source\). Once this is done, you'll see a folder for each part of the book. In each part folder, you'll typically find a file for each lesson and the file name matches the lesson name. This file includes the DAX formulas if you prefer to copy and paste them.

Start with the Adventure Works.pbix file in the \Source\Practice folder and keep on extending it as you go through the lessons. For your convenience, the Adventure Works.pbix file in each part folder includes the changes you need to make in the exercises in the corresponding part of the book, plus any supporting files required for the exercises. For example, the Adventure Works.pbix file in the \Source\Part2 folder includes the changes that you'll make during the Part 2 practices.

(Optional) Installing the AdventureWorksDW database

Extending the Adventure Works model with DAX doesn't require reimporting the data. However, Lesson 4 shows you how you can implement custom columns in Power Query, and this requires reimporting the affected tables. If you decide to do this exercise, you need to install the Adventure-WorksDW database. This is a Microsoft-provided database that simulates a data warehouse. You can install the database on an on-prem SQL Server (local or shared) or Azure SQL Database. Again, you don't have to do this (installing a SQL Server alone can be challenging).

 NOTE   Microsoft ships Adventure Works databases with each version of SQL Server. More recent versions of the databases have incremental changes and they might have different data. Although the book exercises were tested with the AdventureWorksDW2017 database, you can use a later version if you want. Depending on the database version you install, you might find that reports might show somewhat different data.

Follow these steps to download the AdventureWorksDW2017 database:

1. If you don't have a SQL Server, download and install the free developer edition from https://microsoft.com/sql-server/sql-server-downloads.

2. Download the AdventureWorksDW2017 backup file from https://github.com/Microsoft/sql-server-samples/releases/download/adventureworks/AdventureWorksDW2017.bak.

3. Install SQL Server Management Studio (SSMS) from https://docs.microsoft.com/sql/ssms/download-sql-server-management-studio-ssms.

4. Open SQL Server Management Studio (SSMS) and connect to your SQL Server database instance. Restore the AdventureWorksDW2017 backup file. If you're not sure how to do so, read the instructions at https://github.com/Microsoft/sql-server-samples/releases/tag/adventureworks.

 NOTE The data source settings of the sample Power BI Desktop models in the source code have connection strings to the AdventureWorksDW database. If you decide to refresh the data, you must update the AdventureWorksDW data source to reflect your specific setup. To do so in one step per file, open the *pbix file in Power BI Desktop, and then expand the Edit Queries button in the ribbon's Home tab, and click "Data source settings". Click the "Change source" button and change the server name to match your SQL Server name.

Reporting errors

Please submit bug reports to the book discussion list on https://prologika.com/daxbook. Confirmed bugs and inaccuracies will be published to the book errata document. A link to the errata document is provided in the book web page. The book includes links to web resources for further study. Due to the transient nature of the Internet, some links might no longer be valid or might be broken. Searching for the document title is usually enough to recover the new link.

Your purchase of APPLIED DAX WITH POWER BI includes free access to an online forum sponsored by the author, where you can make comments about the book, ask technical questions, and receive help from the author and the community. The author is not committed to a specific amount of participation or successful resolution of the question and his participation remains voluntary. You can subscribe to the forum from the author's personal website https://prologika.com/daxbook.

PART 1

Introduction

I f you imagine a layered Power BI model, where the bottom layer is Power Query (for data shaping and transformation) and the middle layer is the data model (where your tables and columns are), then DAX calculations will be the top layer. Therefore, DAX is dependent on the model schema and data quality. If you don't get these layers right, you won't be successful with DAX either. Therefore, the book starts with important fundamentals.

The first lesson introduces you to DAX, its origin, and main constructs. In the second lesson, you'll learn important data modeling techniques, including star schemas and relationships. Lastly, it's important to have at least a high-level understanding of the storage engine to better understand how DAX formulas work.

When going through the exercises, start with the Adventure Works.pbix file in the \Source\Practice folder. If you need to refer to the completed exercises and reports for this part of the book, you'll find them in the Adventure Works model in the \Source\Part1 folder included in the book source code.

Lesson 1

Introducing DAX

Power BI promotes rapid personal business intelligence (BI) for essential data exploration and analysis. Chances are, however, that in real life you might need to go beyond the raw data and simple aggregations. Business needs might necessitate extending your model with calculations. DAX gives you the programmatic power to travel the "last mile" and unlock the full potential of Power BI.

This lesson introduces you to DAX and how it's used in Power BI. You'll use DAX to implement a simple calculated column, measure, and a query with the provided Adventure Works Power BI Desktop file in the \Source\Part1 folder.

1.1   Understanding DAX

Data Analysis Expressions (DAX) is a powerful formula-based language included in Microsoft Power BI, Excel Power Pivot, and Analysis Services Tabular that allows you to add custom business logic with Excel-like formulas. DAX has two main design goals:

- Simplicity – To get you started quickly with implementing business logic, DAX uses the Excel standard formula syntax and, in fact, inherits many Excel functions. If you're a business analyst, you may already know many Excel functions, such as SUM and AVERAGE. When you use Power BI, you will find the same (or similar functions) in DAX.

- Relational – DAX is designed with data models in mind and supports relational artifacts, including tables, columns, and relationships. For example, if you want to sum up the SalesAmount column in the FactResellerSales table, you can use this formula:

    =SUM(FactResellerSales[SalesAmount])

Although this book teaches you DAX with Power BI, a nice bonus awaits you ahead because you're also learning how to program Excel Power Pivot and Analysis Services Tabular. So, if one day you find yourself working on a self-service model in Excel or an organizational model powered by Analysis Services Tabular, you'll find that you already have the knowledge!

1.1.1   A Short History of DAX

Realizing the growing importance of self-service BI, in 2010 Microsoft unveiled an Excel add-in called PowerPivot (renamed to *Power Pivot* in 2013 because of Power BI rebranding). Since the tool needed an expression language, the natural choice was building upon and extending the Excel formulas. This revised formula language was named Data Analysis Expressions (or DAX for short) to emphasize its role as a programming language for data analytics.

NOTE Given the relational nature of a data model, you might wonder why Microsoft didn't opt for SQL instead of Excel-like formulas. Although this scenario was strongly considered, SQL is a standard of the American National Standards Institute (ANSI). Therefore, introducing new extensions turned out to be a difficult proposition. Moreover, back then Microsoft believed that Excel would become the Microsoft premium tool for data analytics.

On the professional side of things, Microsoft SQL Server Analysis Services 2012 introduced a new implementation path called *Tabular,* side by side with the traditional Multidimensional path for designing OLAP cubes. BI pros use Analysis Services Tabular to implement scalable organizational models, such as in the case where they need to import hundreds of millions of rows. Tabular is also the workhorse behind Power BI Service (powerbi.com) and Power BI Desktop. For example, every Power BI Desktop instance has a corresponding Tabular service running in the background that hosts the data model and processes DAX queries from Power BI reports.

Because Tabular uses the same storage engine (called xVelocity) as Power Pivot, DAX made its way to the professional toolset. SQL Server 2012 extended DAX as a query language to allow external tools to query Tabular models in its native language.

In 2015, Microsoft unveiled Power BI as their next generation BI platform for organizational and self-service data analytics. Because Power BI is also powered by xVelocity, it inherited DAX. Given the large momentum and adoption behind Power BI, DAX now plays a more prominent role than ever.

 NOTE Although having its roots in Excel formulas, DAX formulas are designed to operate on data models and thus reference tables and columns. Excel cell and range references have no relevance in data models and can't be used in DAX.

1.1.2 What Can You Do with DAX?

In a nutshell, you can use DAX expressions to extend your models with custom business logic and to query external models. There are three main ways you can leverage the programming prowess of DAX: calculated columns, measures, and queries.

Introducing calculated columns

A calculated column is a table column that uses a DAX formula to produce the column values. This is conceptually like a formula-based column added to an Excel list. The formulas of calculated columns are evaluated for each row so they are useful if you want add custom columns that do something with other columns in the same row. Consider a calculated column called FullName that's added to the Customer table. It uses the following formula to concatenate the customer's first name and last name:

FullName=[FirstName] & " " & [LastName]

Because its formula is evaluated for each row in the Customer table (see **Figure 1.1**), the FullName calculated column uses a DAX expression to return the full name for each customer by concatenating the FirstName and LastName columns. DAX refers to this by-row evaluation context as *row context*. Again, this is very similar to how an Excel formula works when applied to multiple rows in a list.

When a column contains a formula, Power BI computes the value for each table row and saves it. And from that point, a calculation column is just like a regular column. Therefore, calculated column values are immutable, meaning that they can't change as a result of runtime conditions. For example, the formula won't produce different results when the end user applies a filter. Speaking of reporting, you can use calculated columns to group and filter data, just like you can use regular columns. For example, you can add a calculated column to any area of the Power BI Desktop's Visualizations pane when it makes sense to do so.

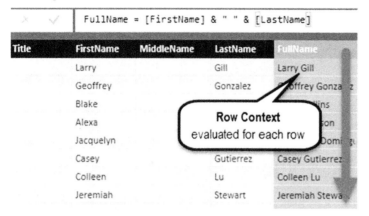

Figure 1.1 Calculated columns are expression-based columns added to a table and are evaluated for each table row.

Introducing measures

The true power of DAX is realized by implementing measures. Measures are also expression-based but their formulas are evaluated at runtime, that is when the report is run. Specifically, DAX measures are evaluated *at runtime* for each report *cell* as opposed to once for each table row. DAX measures are always dynamic, and the result of the measure formula is never saved. Moreover, measures are evaluated in the filter context of each cell, as shown in **Figure 1.2**.

Figure 1.2 Measures are evaluated for each cell, and they operate in filter context.

This report summarizes the SalesAmount field by countries on rows and by years on columns. The report is further filtered to show only sales for the Bikes product category. The filter context of the highlighted cell is the Germany value of the DimSalesTerritory[SalesTerritoryCountry] field (on rows), the 2008 value of the DimDate[CalendarYear] field (on columns), and the Bikes value of the DimProduct[ProductCategory] field (used as a filter).

If you're familiar with the SQL language, you can think of the measure filter context as a WHERE clause that's determined dynamically and then applied to each cell on the report. When Power BI calculates the expression for that cell, it scopes the formula accordingly, such as to sum the sales amount from the rows in the ResellerSales table where the SalesTerritoryCountry value is Germany, the CalendarYear value is 2008, and the ProductCategory value is Bikes.

NOTE Unlike calculated columns, which might be avoided by using other implementation approaches, measures typically can't be replicated in other ways – they must be written in DAX. That's because any other approach would produce static values that don't change as a result of the user filtering data on the report. For example, you may pre-calculate year-to-date (YTD) sales as of the most current date, but this will not allow the user to see YTD sales as of a prior date.

Introducing DAX queries

Lastly, you can use DAX to query Power BI, Power Pivot, and Analysis Services Tabular models. A DAX query is centered on the DAX EVALUATE statement. For example, this simple DAX query returns all data from the DimSalesTerritory table in the Adventure Works Power BI model.

EVALUATE DimSalesTerritory

Although not officially supported by Microsoft outside Power BI on the desktop, client tools can send DAX queriers to the Analysis Services Tabular instance that is behind every Power BI model (they can also send MDX queries). For example, when you interact with a report, Power BI generates DAX queries and sends them to the Analysis Services Tabular instance that hosts the model. If you are tasked to create reports using tools that require you to specify a query when you connect to Tabular or Power BI, such as Microsoft Reporting Services, you can create your own DAX queries.

NOTE While only Power BI Desktop is officially supported to interact with the Analysis Services Tabular instance on the desktop, any client can interact with the Tabular instance behind a Power BI Premium workspace and query a published Power BI model. To learn more, read the article "Connect to datasets with client applications and tools" at https://docs.microsoft.com/power-bi/service-premium-connect-tools.

Another practical implication of a DAX query is creating and testing DAX measures outside Power BI Desktop. Suppose you are working on a complex DAX measure and you prefer to test it and profile its performance in the DAX Studio community tool. You can define the measure in DAX Studio and use a DAX query to test the measure.

1.1.3   Understanding DAX Syntax

As I mentioned, one of the DAX design goals is to look and feel like the Excel formula language. Because of this, the DAX syntax resembles the Excel formula syntax. The DAX formula syntax is case-insensitive. For example, the following two expressions are both valid:

=YEAR([Date])
=year([date])

That said, I suggest you have a naming convention and stick to it. I personally prefer the first example where the function names are in uppercase and the column references match the column names in the model. This convention helps me quickly identify functions and columns in DAX formulas, and so this will be the convention that I'll use in this book.

Understanding expression syntax

A DAX formula for calculated columns and explicit measures has the following syntax:

Name=expression

Name is the name of the calculated column or measure. The expression must evaluate to a scalar (single) value. Expressions can contain operators, constants, or column references to return literal or Boolean values. The FullName calculated column that you saw before is an example of a simple expression that concatenates two values. You can add as many spaces as you want to make the formula easier to read.

s can also include functions that perform more complicated operations, such as aggregat-
r example, back to **Figure 1.2**, the DAX formula references the SUM function to aggre-
;Amount column in the FactResellerSales table. Functions can be nested. For example,
formula nests the FILTER function inside the COUNTROWS function to calculate the
ems associated with the Progressive Sports reseller:

⌐UNTROWS(FILTER(FactResellerSales, RELATED(DimReseller[ResellerName]) = "Progressive Sports"))

Referencing columns

One of DAX's strengths over regular Excel formulas is that it is designed to work with data model constructs, such as table columns and relationships. This is much simpler and more efficient than referencing Excel cells and ranges with the Excel VLOOKUP function that you might have used in the past. Column names are unique within a table. You can reference a column using its fully quali-fied name in the format <TableName>[<ColumnName>], such as in this example which references the SalesAmount column in the FactResellerSales table:

FactResellerSales[SalesAmount]

If the table name includes a space or is a reserved word, such as Date, enclose it with single quotes:

'Reseller Sales'[SalesAmount] or 'Date'[CalendarYear]

When a calculated column references a column from the same table, you can omit the table name. The AutoComplete feature in the Power BI Desktop formula bar helps you avoid syntax errors when referencing columns. And of course, DAX has many formulas to help you tackle simple and complex requirements, but this is all you need to know for now to get started with DAX.

 TIP The official DAX documentation by Microsoft can be found at https://docs.microsoft.com/dax. Another useful ref-erence resource maintained by the community is the DAX Guide at https://dax.guide/.

1.2   Practicing Basic DAX

Next, you'll practice working a basic calculated column, a measure, and a DAX query to get a taste of programming with DAX. Because Power BI Service (powerbi.com) doesn't currently support modeling features, you can't extend a published model directly in Power BI Service. Instead, you must use Power BI Desktop to extend your data model with calculated columns and measures.

1.2.1   Implementing a Calculated Column

DAX includes various operators to create basic expressions, such as expressions for concatenating strings and for performing arithmetic operations. You can use them to create simple expression-based columns.

Practice

Let's create a calculated column that shows the customer's full name:

1. Double-click the \Source**Practice**\Adventure Work.pbix file to open it in Power BI Desktop.
2. In the left black navigation bar, click the Data View tab to open the Data view that lets you browse the content of the tables in the model.
3. In the Fields list on the right, click the DimCustomer table to select it. In the data preview grid that shows the data in the table, scroll to the right and observe that the table has FirstName and Last-Name columns, but it doesn't have a column for the customer's full name. If you have two or more

customers with the same first name, the report will group them together. This could be avoided by using the customer's full name on the report.

4. In the Modeling bar, click the New Column button. This adds a new column named "Column" to the end of the table and activates the formula bar.

5. In the formula bar (only available in the Data View and Report View tabs), enter this formula (see **Figure 1.3**):

FullName = DimCustomer[FirstName] & " " & DimCustomer[LastName]

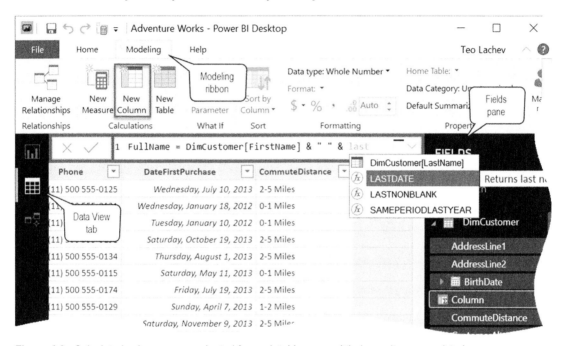

Figure 1.3 Calculated columns are evaluated for each table row and their results are persisted.

6. Press Enter or click the checkmark button to the left of the formula bar.

Analysis
This formula defines a calculated column called *FullName*. Then, the DAX expression uses the concatenation operator to concatenate the FirstName and LastName columns in the DimCustomer table and to add an empty space in between them. As you type, AutoComplete helps you with the formula syntax, although you should also follow the syntax rules, such as that a column reference must be enclosed in square brackets.

Output
Once you commit the formula, Power BI evaluates the expression and adds the calculated column as a last column in the table. Power BI propagates the formula to all rows in the DimCustomer table. Power BI adds the FullName field to the DimCustomer table in the Fields pane and prefixes it with a special *fx* icon so you can quickly tell the calculated columns apart.

 NOTE What's the difference between a column and a field anyway? Besides physical columns, a table in the Fields pane can include additional fields, such as calculated columns, measures, groups and bins. For the most part, however, you can refer to columns and fields interchangeably.

1. (Optional) Click the Report View tab in the navigation bar. Create a visual that uses the DimCustomer[FullName] column (or refer to the Calculated Column visual in \Source\Intro\Adventure Works).

2. Press Ctrl+S (or File ⇨ Save) to save the Adventure Works file. Remind yourself to use this file from this point forward for practices.

1.2.2 Creating a Quick Measure

Quick measures are Power BI prepackaged DAX measures for common analytical requirements, such as time calculations, aggregates, and totals. Quick measures are a great way to get you started with common DAX measures and learn DAX along the way.

Practice
Suppose you want to implement a running sales total across years.

1. Right-click the FactResellerSales table in the Fields pane and then click "New quick measure". Alternatively, right-click FactResellerSales[SalesAmount] in the Fields pane and then click "New quick measure".

2. In the "Quick measures" window, expand the Calculation drop-down. Observe that Power BI supports various quick measures.

3. Select "Running total" under the Totals section (see **Figure 1.4**).

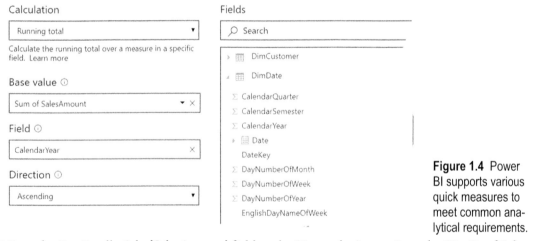

Quick measures

Figure 1.4 Power BI supports various quick measures to meet common analytical requirements.

4. Drag the FactResellerSales[SalesAmount] field to the "Base value" area. Drag the DimDate[CalendarYear] to the Field area. Click OK.

Analysis
Power BI adds a new "SalesAmount running total in CalendarYear" field to the FactResellerSales table in the Fields pane.

1. Make sure that the Report View tab or the Data View tab is selected (you can't see the measure formula in the Model View tab).

2. Double click this field in the Fields pane. Rename it to *SalesAmount RT*.

3. Notice that the formula bar shows the DAX formula behind the measure:

```
SalesAmount RT =
CALCULATE(
    SUM('FactResellerSales'[SalesAmount]),
    FILTER(
        ALLSELECTED('DimDate'[CalendarYear]),
        ISONORAFTER('DimDate'[CalendarYear], MAX('DimDate'[CalendarYear]), DESC)
    ))
```

This formula uses the CALCULATE function to overwrite the context of the expression passed as a first argument. Specifically, the second argument uses the FILTER function to filter the DimDate table to return only dates that are before than or equal to the current year on the report. It does so by using the DAX ISONORAFTER function. When the third argument of this function specifies a descending order, it compares the second argument to the first, and returns TRUE if the second argument is less than or equal to the first. So, if the report year is 2012, the FILTER function will return all dates from DimDate whose year is less than or equal to 2012.

 TIP Love it or hate it, the formula bar is the only editor Microsoft provided to work with formulas of calculated columns and measures. If you hate it, I'll show you in the "Queries" part of this book how you can create and test measures outside Power BI Desktop using the DAX Studio community tool. If you love it, take a look at these keyboard shortcuts to get the most out of it (https://docs.microsoft.com/power-bi/desktop-formula-editor).

Once you create the quick measure, it's just like any explicit DAX measure. You can rename it or use it on your reports. However, you can't go back to the "Quick measures" window. To customize the measure, you must make changes directly to the formula, so you still need to know some DAX.

Output
Let's create a report to test the new measure (or refer to the Quick Measure report in \Intro\Adventure Works.pbix file).

1. Add a Table visual to the report with the DimDate[CalendarYear] and FactResellerSales-[SalesAmount] fields in the Values area. To prevent Power BI from summarizing CalendarYear by default since it's a numeric field, expand the drop-down next to CalendarYear in the Values area and select "Don't summarize".

TIP Some numeric fields, such as CalendarYear, CalendarQuarter, shouldn't be summarized at all as doing so produces non-sensical results. To tell Power BI not to summarize a numeric field again, select the field in the Fields page, click the Modeling ribbon, expand the Default Summarization dropdown, and select "Don't summarize". This removes the sigma (Σ) icon in the Fields pane in front of the field to indicate that the field won't be summarized by default.

2. Add FactResellerSales[SalesAmount RT] field to the Table visual. Notice that it accumulates across years, as shown in **Figure 1.5**.

CalendarYear	SalesAmount	SalesAmount RT
2010	$489,328.5787	$489,328.57
2011	$18,192,802.7143	$18,682,131.2
2012	$28,193,631.5321	$46,875,762.82
2013	$33,574,834.1572	$80,450,596.98
2014		$80,450,596.98
Total	**$80,450,596.9823**	**$80,450,596.9823**

Figure 1.5 The quick measure accumulates sales over years, and it's produced by the "Running total" quick measure.

1.2.3 Analyzing a DAX Query

In this practice, you'll intercept the DAX query behind a report visual in order to analyze its execution time and to see the actual query statement. Power BI Desktop has a Performance Analyzer feature for this purpose.

Practice
Start by enabling Performance Analyzer.

1. In Power BI Desktop, click the View ribbon and check the Performance Analyzer setting. This will open the Performance Analyzer pane.

2. Click Start Recording in the Performance Analyzer pane. Once you start recording, any action that requires refreshing a visual, such as filtering or cross-highlighting, will populate the Performance Analyzer pane. You'll see the statistics of each visual logged in the load order with its corresponding load duration.

3. You can click the "Refresh visuals" link in Performance Analyzer to refresh all visuals on the page and capture all queries. However, once you are in a recording mode, every visual adds a new icon to help you refresh only that visual. To practice this, hover on the Table visual you authored in the last practice and click the "Refresh this visual" icon that will appear below the visual.

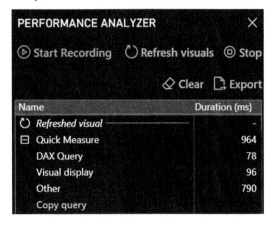

Figure 1.6 Use the Performance Analyzer statistics to capture the query duration.

Output
Next, let's examine the captured duration statistics (all numbers are in milliseconds).

- DAX query - The length of time to execute the query.
- Visual display - How long it took for the visual to render on the screen after the query is executed.
- Other – This is the time that the visual spent in other tasks, such as preparing queries, waiting for other visuals to complete, or doing some other background processing.

1. Click the "Copy query" link. Click Stop.

2. Open Notepad (or favorite text editor) and paste the query. You should see this code:

```
// DAX Query
EVALUATE
 TOPN (502,
  SUMMARIZECOLUMNS(
   ROLLUPADDISSUBTOTAL('DimDate'[CalendarYear], "IsGrandTotalRowTotal"),
   "SalesAmount_RT", 'FactResellerSales'[SalesAmount RT],
```

```
 "SumSalesAmount", CALCULATE(SUM('FactResellerSales'[SalesAmount]))
 ),
 [IsGrandTotalRowTotal], 0,
 'DimDate'[CalendarYear], 1  )
ORDER BY
 [IsGrandTotalRowTotal] DESC, 'DimDate'[CalendarYear]
```

Analysis

When the user interacts with a report, Power BI Desktop autogenerates DAX queries and sends them to the Analysis Services Tabular service that is behind every Power Desktop instance.

 TIP   Open the Windows Task Manager (Ctl+Shft+Esc), find Power BI Desktop in the Processes tab, and expand it. The Microsoft SQL Server Analysis Services process is the backend Analysis Services Tabular instance that hosts the Adventure Works model. Every time you open a new Power BI Desktop instance and load a file, Power BI spins a new Tabular process, so you could have several running in the background.

You can capture and analyze these queries, such as to find which query slows down the report. Compared to almost a second to refresh the visual, the query took only 78 milliseconds, so it doesn't warrant further performance optimization.

1.3   Summary

In this lesson, I introduced you to DAX and emphasized its role as a programming language in the Microsoft BI platform. You learned how to create basic calculated columns and measures, and how to capture DAX queries that Power BI generates when you interact with a report. The next lesson will provide a quick overview of the Adventure Works model that you'll be using throughout this book.

Lesson 2

Exploring the Model

As I explained in the previous lesson, you can use DAX to extend Power BI, Power Pivot, and Analysis Services models. Power BI Desktop is the Microsoft premium modeling tool for self-service BI. Packed with features, Power BI Desktop is a free tool that you can download and start using immediately to gain insights from your data.

Since you'll be using the Adventure Works sample model throughout this book, it would be worthwhile to get familiar with it. This lesson walks you through its structure and introduces fundamental data modeling concepts, including schemas and relationships.

2.1   Data Modeling Fundamentals

Power BI organizes data in tables, like how Excel allows you to organize data into Excel lists. Each table consists of columns, also called *fields*. Data can be imported (cached) in tables or left in the original data source. When data is left at the data source, Power BI has a special mechanism called DirectQuery to connect to the data source. When it does this, it converts DAX queries to native queries that the data source understands. Not all data sources support DirectQuery and DirectQuery doesn't support all DAX functions.

NOTE   DirectQuery has DAX limitations which are described in more detail in the "Using DirectQuery in Power BI" article at https://docs.microsoft.com/power-bi/desktop-directquery-about. The Adventure Works model has all its data imported so you don't need to worry about these limitations.

2.1.1   Understanding Schemas

If all the data is provided to you as just one table, then you could count yourself lucky and skip this section altogether. Chances are, however, that your model might import multiple tables from the same or different data sources. This requires learning some basic database and schema concepts. The term "schema" here is used to describe the table definitions and how tables relate to each other. I'll keep the discussion light on purpose to get you started with data modeling as fast as possible.

NOTE   Having all data in a single table might not require modeling, but it isn't a best practice. Suppose you initially wanted to analyze reseller sales and you've got a single dataset with columns such as Reseller, Sales Territory, and so on. Then you decide to extend the model with direct sales to consumers to consolidate reporting that spans now two business areas. Now you have a problem. Because you merged business dimensions into the reseller sales dataset, you won't be able to slice and dice the two datasets by the same lookup tables (Reseller, Sales Territory, Date, and others). In addition, a large table might strain your computer resources as it'll require more time to import and more memory to store the data. At the same time, a fully normalized schema, such as having SalesOrderHeader and SalesOrderDetails tables, is also not desirable because you'll end up with many tables and the model might become difficult to understand and navigate. When modeling your data, it's important to find a good balance between business requirements and normalization, and that balance is the star schema.

Understanding star schemas

For a lack of better terms, I'll use the dimensional modeling terminology to illustrate the star schema (for more information about star schemas, see http://en.wikipedia.org/wiki/Star_schema). **Figure 2.1** shows two schema types. The left diagram illustrates a star schema, where the Reseller-Sales table is in the center. This table stores the history of the Adventure Works reseller sales, and each row represents the most granular information about the sale transaction. This could be a line item in the sales order that includes the order quantity, sales amount, tax amount, discount, and other numeric fields.

Dimensional modeling refers to these tables as *fact tables*. As you can imagine, the ResellerSales table can be very long if it keeps several years of sales data. Don't be alarmed about the dataset size though. Thanks to the state-of-the art underlying storage technology, your Power BI data model can still import and store millions of rows!

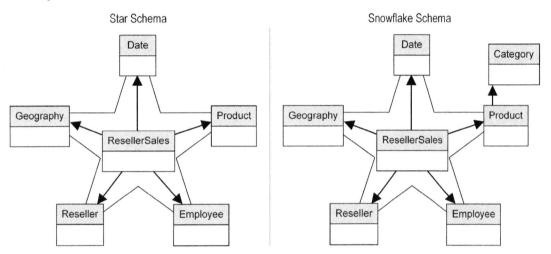

Figure 2.1 Power BI models support both star and snowflake schema types, but the star schema is recommended.

The ResellerSales table is related to other tables, called *dimension* or *lookup* tables. These tables provide contextual information to each row stored in the ResellerSales table. For example, the Date table might include date-related fields, such as Date, Quarter, and Year columns, to allow you to aggregate data at day, quarter, and year levels, respectively. The Product table might include ProductName, Color, Size fields, and so on.

The reason why your data model should have these fields in separate lookup tables, is that, for the most part, their content doesn't need a historical record. For example, if the product name changes, this probably would be an in-place change. By contrast, if you were to continue adding columns to the ResellerSales table, you might end up with performance and maintenance issues. If you need to make a change, you might have to update millions of rows of data as opposed to updating a single row. Similarly, if you were to add a new column to the Date table, such as Fiscal-Year, you'll have to update all the rows in the ResellerSales table.

Are you limited to only one fact table with Power BI? Absolutely not! For example, you can add an InternetSales fact table that stores direct sales to individuals. In the case of multiple fact tables, you should model the fact tables to share some common lookup tables so that you could match and consolidate data for cross-reporting purposes, such as to show reseller and Internet sales side by side and grouped by year and product. This is another reason to avoid a single monolithic dataset and to have logically related fields in separate tables (if you have this option). Don't worry if this isn't immediately clear. Designing a model that accurately represents requirements is difficult even for BI pros, but it gets easier with practice.

 NOTE Another common issue that I witness with novice users is creating a separate dataset for each report, e.g. one dataset for a report showing reseller sales and another dataset for a report showing direct sales. Like the "single dataset" issue I discussed above, this design will lead to data duplication and inability to produce consolidated reports that span multiple areas. Even worse would be to embed calculations in the dataset, such as calculating Profit or Year-to-Date in a SQL view that is used to source the data. Like the issue with defining calculations in a report, this approach will surely lead to redundant calculations or calculations that produce different results from one report to another.

Understanding snowflake schemas

A *snowflake* schema is where some lookup tables relate to other lookup tables but not directly to the fact table. Going back to **Figure 2.1**, you can see that product categories are kept in a Category table that relates to the Product table and not directly to the ResellerSales table. One strong motivation for snowflaking is that you might have another fact table, such as SalesQuota, that stores data not at a product level but at a category level. If you keep categories in their own Category table, this design would allow you to join the Category lookup table to the SalesQuota table, and you'll still be able to have a report that shows actual and budget data grouped by category (and any other shared dimension tables).

Power BI supports snowflake schemas just fine. However, if you have a choice, you should minimize snowflaking when it's not needed. This is because snowflaking increases the number of tables in the model, making it more difficult for other users to understand it. If you import data from a database with a normalized schema, you can minimize snowflaking by merging snowflaked tables. For example, you can use a SQL query that joins the Product and Category tables. However, if you import text files, you won't have that option because you can't use SQL. Instead, you can handle denormalization tasks in the Power Query, or by adding calculated columns that use DAX expressions, such as by adding a column to the Product table to look up the product category from the Category table. Then you can hide the Category table.

To recap this schema discussion, you can view the star schema as the opposite of its snowflake counterpart. While the snowflake schema embraces normalization as the preferred designed technique to reduce data duplication, the star schema favors denormalization or data entities and reducing the overall number of tables, although this process results in data duplication (a category is repeated for each product that has the same category). Denormalization (star schemas) and BI go hand in hand. That's because star schemas reduce the number of tables and required joins. This makes your model faster and more intuitive.

2.1.2 Exploring Schemas

Let's take a moment to explore the schema of the Adventure Works data model in Power BI Desktop. The Adventure Works model imports several tables from the sample AdventureWorksDW database which is designed as a data warehouse database and consists of several fact and dimension tables.

Practice

You can use the Model View tab to a see a graphical diagram showing how tables relate to each other at a glance.

1. In Power BI Desktop, click the Model View tab in the left navigation bar.

2. Notice that the "All tables" tab shows all tables in the model. However, as the number of tables grow, it becomes difficult to analyze the diagram, so I created three other layouts that show subsets of the schema.

 TIP A layout helps you analyze a subset of the model schema. You can create a new layout by adding a new tab in the Model View diagram. Then drag a table from the Fields pane. To add related tables, right-click the table you added in the Fields pane and click "Add related tables".

3. Click the Reseller Sales tab. Notice that the FactResellerSales table is surrounded by five dimension tables, forming a typical star schema.

4. In the Fields pane, right-click the DimProduct table and click "Add related tables". Power BI adds the DimProductSubcategory table because it's related to DimProduct.

5. In the Fields pane, right-click the DimProductSubcategory table and click "Add related tables". Power BI adds the DimProductCategory table because it's related to DimProductSubcategory.

6. (Optional) Explore the Internet Sales and Sales Quotas diagrams.

Analysis
The Adventure Works model imports 11 tables from the AdventureWorksDW SQL Server database. Most tables form star schemas, with a fact table surrounded by related dimension tables. There is some snowflaking, such as in the case of DimProduct, DimProductSubcategory, and DimProductCategory. I've decided to leave the original table names so you can quickly see which tables are fact tables (prefixed with "Fact") and dimension tables (prefixed with "Dim"). In real life, you should consider renaming tables and columns to make them more user friendly.

 TIP When it comes to naming conventions, I like to keep table and column names as short as possible so that they don't occupy too much space in report labels. I prefer camel casing, where the first letter of each word is capitalized. I also prefer to use a plural case for fact tables, such as ResellerSales, and a singular case for lookup (dimension) tables, such as Reseller. You don't have to follow this convention, but it's important to have a consistent naming convention and to stick to it. While I'm on this subject, Power BI supports identical column names across tables, such as SalesAmount in the ResellerSales table and SalesAmount in the InternetSales table. However, it might be confusing to have fields with the same names side by side in the same visual unless you rename them. Power BI supports renaming labels in the visual (just double-click the field name in the Visualizations pane). Or, you can rename them in the Fields pane by adding a prefix to have unique column names across tables, such as ResellerSalesAmount and InternetSalesAmount. Or, you can create DAX measures with unique names and then hide the original columns.

2.1.3 Exploring Fact Tables

Next, let's explore the data in some of the tables that you'll be using for subsequent practices.

Practice
You can use the Data View tab to browse the table data.

1. In Power BI Desktop, click the Data View tab in the left navigation bar.

2. In the Fields pane, click FactInternetSales to select it. This table stores sales to individual customers, such as when customers place orders on the Adventure Works website. Each row in the table represents a line item in the customer order. For example, if the customer ordered two items, the corresponding order will have two order lines which will be represented by two rows in FactInternetSales. The SalesOrderNumber column captures the order number and the SalesOrderLineNumber column stores the line sequence number.

Analysis

Notice that the first eight columns are suffixed with "Key". They relate to the corresponding dimension tables to give additional context to each row, such as what product was sold, when it was sold, which customer ordered it, and so on. Notice that there are a few numeric fields that are typical for a sales transaction, such as SalesAmount, OrderQuantity, TaxAmt, and DiscountAmount. The dimensional methodology refers to such fields as *facts*. They are extremely useful because they can be aggregated across the related dimensions, such as to summarize the sales amount by product to find the top 10 bestselling products.

Similarly, the FactResellerSales table represents sales from retail stores. It has a very similar schema as FactInternetSales but there are differences in the dimension keys. For example, the CustomerKey column is missing because are no individual customers placing orders. Instead, there is a ResellerKey column to designate the reseller that was associated with the sale. There is also an EmployeeKey column to associate a salesperson with the order.

Finally, the third fact table, FactSalesQuota, captures the quarterly sales quota that is assigned to each salesperson so that you can analyze actual versus budget sales.

2.1.4 Exploring Dimension Tables

A dimension (lookup) table gives context to facts stored in a fact table and let you analyze them in many ways, such as for analyzing sales by year, quarter, and month. Each field in a dimension table is a candidate for exploring facts in the related fact tables by this field.

Practice

Let's look at a few dimension tables:

1. Make sure that the Data View tab is selected in the left navigation bar.
2. Almost every model has a Date table because time analysis is so common. In the Fields pane, select the DimDate table.

Analysis

A dimension table typically has a column that uniquely identifies each row. In DimDate, this column is DateKey, but the Date column can serve this purpose too.

 NOTE The original column name in the AdventureWorksDW database was FullDateAlternateKey. However, because we'll use this column a lot in DAX formulas, I renamed it to Date. You can right-click DimDate and click Edit Query to open Power Query and see what transformations are made to a table, including renaming columns.

The rest of the columns are typical for date tables. Adventure Works has a fiscal calendar, which explains the FiscalSemester, FiscalQuarter, and FiscalYear columns. It also supports multiple languages and it has corresponding columns that store the language translations. For example, EnglishMonthName stores the name of the month in English. There is more to date tables that you need to know but I'll stop here for now.

The rest of the dimension tables follow the same pattern. For example, the CustomerKey column in DimCustomer uniquely identifies each customer. Such columns are called *surrogate* keys in dimensional modeling. The "alternate key" columns, such as CustomerAlternateKey, are called *business keys* and they typically correspond to identifiers in the source systems. For example, the first customer listed, Larry Gill, is probably identified as AW00011602 in the Adventure Works ERP system. However, there could be changes to Larry, such as when he moves to a new address. The source system might simply overwrite Larry's record and the data warehouse could follow this pattern (dimensional modeling refers to overwrites as Type 1 changes). Of course, such overwrites "lose" historical changes.

But other changes could be important for data analytics and need to be preserved in the data warehouse. Suppose you do analysis by cities and Larry moved from New York to Atlanta. If his address is overwritten, his whole sales history will be contributed to Atlanta which can inflate the historical Atlanta sales. If this is problematic, one option is to add a new row for Larry in DimCustomer that is associated now with his new geography. Dimensional modeling refers to this type of change as a Type 2 change. However, because CustomerAlternateKey is not unique anymore, a system-generated CustomerKey was introduced as a unique (surrogate) key.

2.2 Relationship Fundamentals

Once you have multiple tables, you need a way to relate them. If two tables aren't related, your model won't aggregate data correctly when you use both tables on a report. Because relationships are very important to Power BI data modeling and DAX, let's quickly cover their fundamentals.

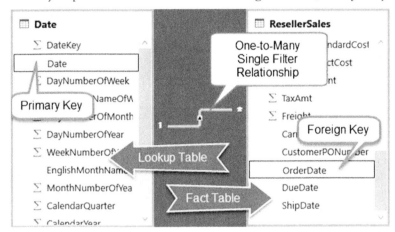

Figure 2.2 The Date column (primary key) in the Date table is related to the matching OrderDate column (foreign key) in the ResellerSales table.

2.2.1 Understanding Relationships

In order to relate two tables, there must be data commonalities between the two tables. This isn't much different than joins in relational databases, such as Microsoft Access or SQL Server. For example, you won't be able to analyze sales by product if there isn't a common column between the ResellerSales and Date tables that ties a date to a sale (see **Figure 2.2**).

Auto-detecting relationships
If the underlying data source has relationships (referential integrity constraints) defined, Power BI Desktop will detect and carry them to the model (this is controlled by the "Import relationships from data sources" setting in File ⇨ Options and setting ⇨ Options ⇨ Data Load under the Current File session). If not, Power BI is capable of auto-detecting relationships using internal rules (this is controlled by the "Autodetect new relationships after data is loaded" setting in the same section).

Of course, you can also create relationships manually. It's important to understand that your data model is layered on top of the original data. No model changes affect the original data source and its design. You only need rights to read from the data source so that you can import the data you need.

Understanding related columns

You'll typically create a relationship between a fact table and a dimension table. A relationship requires common columns in each table. Usually, the dimension table will have a column that uniquely identifies each row in a table. Such a column is called a *primary* key. For example, the Date column uniquely identifies each row in the Date table and no other row has the same value. An employee identifier or an e-mail address can be used as a primary key in an Employee table. To join Date to ResellerSales, in the ResellerSales table, you must have a matching column, which is called a *foreign key*. For example, the OrderDate column in the ResellerSales table is a foreign key.

A matching column means a column in the fact table that has matching values in the lookup table. The column names of the primary key and foreign key don't have to be the same (values are important, not names). For example, if the ResellerSales table has a sale recorded on January 1, 2015, there should be a row in the Date table with a date in the Date column of January 1, 2015. If there isn't, the data model won't show an error, but all the sales that don't have matching dates in the Data table would appear under an unknown (blank) value in a report that groups ResellerSales data by some column in the Date table. Typically, a fact table has several foreign keys, so it can be related to different lookup tables.

 NOTE Relationships from fact tables to the same lookup table don't have to use the same column. For example, ResellerSales can join Date on the Date column but InternetSales might join it on the DateKey column, for example in the case where there isn't a column of a Date data type in InternetSales. If a column uniquely identifies each row, the lookup table can have different "primary key" columns.

As I mentioned, you'll join a dimension (lookup) table to a fact table and the dimension table will have a primary (unique) key that you'll relate to the corresponding column in the fact table. But a primary key is not required. For example, you might have Invoices and Orders tables, where the Orders table has the invoice number, which may not be unique in the Invoices table (an invoice can have several lines). However, you can still join these two tables unless you run into some of the Power BI relationship limitations, such as that redundant relationship paths are not allowed. For example, A ⇨ C and A ⇨ B ⇨ C form redundant relationships between tables A and C.

About relationship cardinality

The relationship cardinality reflects the number of rows in one table that are associated with rows in the related table. Power BI uses the relationship carnality for data validation. Notice that in **Figure 2.2**, the number 1 is shown on the left side of the relationship towards the Date table and an asterisk (*) is shown next to the ResellerSales table. This denotes a one-to-many cardinality. To understand this better, consider that one row (one date) in the Date table can have zero, one, or many recorded sales in ResellerSales, and one product in the Product table corresponds to one or many sales in ResellerSales, and so on. The important word here is "many".

Although not a common cardinality, Power BI also supports a one-to-one relationship type. For example, you might have Employee and SalesPerson tables in a snowflake schema, where a salesperson is a type of an employee and each salesperson relates to a single employee. By specifying a one-to-one relationship between Employee and SalesPerson, you're telling Power BI to check the data cardinality and show an error if the one-to-many relationship is detected on data refresh. A one-to-one relationship also brings additional simplifications when working with DAX calculations, such as to let you interchangeably use the DAX RELATED and RELATEDTABLE functions.

Lastly, Power BI supports a many-to-many relationship cardinality but don't confuse it with the many-to-many relationship type that typically requires a bridge table and it's discussed in the "Many-to-many Relationships" lesson. The Orders-Invoices relationship that I just mentioned is an example of a many-to-many cardinality because the invoice number is not unique in the Invoices table.

About relationship cross filter direction

While the relationship cardinality is only useful to validate the expected association between rows in two tables, a more important characteristic is the filter direction. Also note that in **Figure 2.2**, there's an arrow indicator pointing toward the ResellerSales table. This indicates that this relationship has a single cross filtering direction between the Date and Reseller tables. In other words, the ResellerSales table can be analyzed using the Date table, but not the other way around.

For example, you can have a report that groups sales by any of the fields in the Date table. However, you can't aggregate dates, such as counting them, by a field in the ResellerSales table, which is probably meaningless anyway. That said, there are valid business requirements that can benefit from bidirectional relationships and we'll explore them later in this book.

 NOTE Why not have bidirectional relationships by default for maximum flexibility? Bidirectional relationships may also result in redundant paths which Power BI Desktop will detect and disallow. As a best practice, Power BI starts with a unidirectional model, but you can turn on bidirectional cross filtering only when needed.

Active and inactive relationships

A standing limitation in Power BI is that it only supports one active relationship between two tables. An active relationship is a relationship that Power BI follows to automatically aggregate the data between two tables when both tables are used in a report. Glancing back to **Figure 2.2**, the relationship ResellerSales[OrderDate] ⇨ Date[Date] is the only relationship between the two tables and it's active because it has a solid line. You can also double-click the relationship and examine the "Make this relationship active" flag. Consequently, when you create a report that slices InternetSales by Date, Power BI automatically aggregates sales by the order date associated with each sale.

What if you want to give the user an option to analyze sales by ship date or due date? Power BI will let you create these relationships, but it will make them inactive and they will have dotted lines. Power BI will also deactivate relationships when it discovers redundant relationships, such as attempting to relate tables A ⇨ B ⇨ C and A ⇨ C. Although Power BI doesn't have user interface to let the end user traverse inactive relationships, they are still useful because you can use DAX to navigate them programmatically.

That's all you need to know about relationships for now. Let's take a moment to explore the existing relationships in the Adventure Works model.

2.2.2 Exploring Relationships

As it stands, the Adventure Works model has 11 tables. Because the AdventureWorksDW SQL Server database has foreign keys defined, Power BI has detected them and created corresponding relationships.

Exploring the Reseller Sales diagram

Let's examine the Reseller Sales diagram in the Model View tab. Notice that the FactResellerSales table is related to five dimensions: DimReseller, DimDate, DimSalesTerritory, DimEmployee, and DimProduct. All the relationships are many-to-one from FactResellerSales to the corresponding dimensions. All the relationships are unidirectional which is indicated by the arrow pointing toward FactResellerSales. Consequently, you can aggregate FactResellerSales by any dimension.

The relationships between FactResellerSales and DimDate deserve more attention. Hover on the relationship that has a solid line (or double-click it to open its properties). This is an active FactResellerSales[OrderDateKey] ⇨ DimDate[Date] relationship. When you hover on it, Power BI shows the related columns. The other two relationships are inactive because they have dotted lines.

NOTE AdventureWorksDW uses a "smart" integer primary key for the Date table in the format YYYYMMDD. This is a common practice for data warehousing, but it's not required and probably redundant since FactResellerSales has date columns. For example, you can recreate the relationship between FactResellerSales[OrderDate] and DimDate[Date] columns and remove the OrderDateKey column.

There is another inactive relationship between DimSalesTerritory and DimEmployee. Power BI has deactivated it because there is already an active relationship between FactResellerSales and DimEmployee. If the user analyzes FactResellerSales by DimEmployee, should Power BI use the direct relationship or go through DimSalesTerritory? The second scenario could be useful if you want to analyze sales only by employees who are assigned to a sales territory. However, because as it stands Power BI can't prompt the user which relationship to use, Power BI has deactivated DimEmployee-[SalesTerritoryKey] ⇨ DimSalesTerritory[SalesTerritoryKey].

Finally, the snowflaked DimProduct, DimProductSubcategory, and DimProductCategory tables are related. Such relationships are sometimes called *cascading* relationships and Power BI supports them. For example, you can analyze FactResellerSales by DimProductCategory. When performing this analysis, Power BI will traverse the relationships among these three tables before it gets to FactResellerSales.

Exploring the Internet Sales diagram

The Internet Sales diagram is much simpler. FactInternetSales is related to four dimensions: DimProduct, DimDate, DimCustomer, and DimSalesTerritory. All relationships are unidirectional and many-to-one. Like FactResellerSales, FactInternetSales has one active relationship to DimDate; the other two are inactive.

Exploring the Sales Quota diagram

This layout is even simpler. FactSalesQuota relates to DimEmployee and DimDate with unidirectional, many-to-one relationships.

NOTE While analyzing the schema, note that the three fact tables share some dimensions. Dimensional modeling refers to such common dimensions as *conformed*. This is very powerful because it allows you to have measures from different fact tables sliced by shared dimensions in the same visual! For example, you can summarize FactResellerSales[SalesAmount] and FactInternetSales[SalesAmount] by any field in DimDate, DimProduct, and DimSalesTerritory side by side in one visual! Or, you can compare salesperson's actuals (FactResellerSales) versus budget (FactSalesQuota) by DimDate and DimEmployee.

Practice

Let's see what happens when you attempt to analyze data in one table by an unrelated table.

1. Add a Table visual (or refer to the Unrelated Tables report in the \Source\Intro\Adventure Works).

2. Bind it to DimEmployee[FirstName] and FactInternetSales[SalesAmount]. Compare your results with **Figure 2.3**.

FirstName	SalesAmount
A. Scott	$29,358,677.2207
Alan	$29,358,677.2207
Alejandro	$29,358,677.2207
Alex	$29,358,677.2207
Alice	$29,358,677.2207
Amy	$29,358,677.2207
Total	**$29,358,677.2207**

Figure 2.3 Analyzing by an unrelated table produces repeating values.

Analysis

The report repeats the grand total for each employee. This is the behavior you'll get if there's no relationship between the two tables. If Internet sales should aggregate by employee, you must somehow define a relationship to DimEmployee to resolve this issue.

2.3   Summary

One of the most prominent strengths of Power BI is that it supports flexible data models which could include multiple fact and dimension tables. In this lesson, you explored how the Adventure Works model has star and snowflake schemas, and how it uses relationships to relate tables. Having laid the necessary foundation, it's now time to learn a bit more about how Power BI stores and processes data.

Lesson 3

Understanding Storage

Our overview of data modeling fundamentals won't be complete until you learn how Power BI stores data in the model. It's the storage engine that gives your Power BI reports excellent performance even with millions of rows. It's important to have a least a high-level understanding of the storage engine to better understand how DAX formulas work. In addition, your model storage design might affect DAX performance.

This lesson introduces you to xVelocity (also known as VertiPaq) which powers the three implementations of semantic layers in the Microsoft BI platform: Power BI, Power Pivot and Analysis Services Tabular. It will also teach you how to analyze storage of your data model, such as to understand what columns take up the most memory.

3.1 Understanding the Storage Engine

When Microsoft started work on Power Pivot, they realized it needed a new type of storage that would be more suitable for data analytics. To provide the best storage performance, Microsoft implemented a proprietary in-memory store called VertiPaq, which was later rebranded as xVelocity.

3.1.1 Introducing xVelocity

xVelocity is an in-memory database, which means it loads data in the computer main memory, which is the fastest storage medium. So, while you save your Power BI Desktop file to disk for durable storage, all data in this file is unpacked and loaded in memory from where all reporting queries are answered.

Understanding columnar storage
As the original VertiPaq name suggests, the storage engine stores and compresses data vertically by columns to pack as much data as possible in order to minimize the storage footprint. Column-based storage fits BI like a glove because data is typically analyzed by columns. And, the lower the data cardinality (that's the more repeating values a column has), the higher its compression rate is. **Figure 3.1** shows a hypothetical table containing some sales data.

Examining the data, we see that across all rows the Date column has only two unique values, ProductName has seven, ProductSubcategory has five, ProductCategory two, and SalesAmount five. Consequently, the Product Category and Date columns will compress the most since they have the most repeating values, while the ProductName column won't compress as well. Since it's common to have columns with many repeating values in large datasets, expect a high data compression ratio (five times or higher). The efficient compression is the reason why you can pack and analyze millions of rows on the desktop without running out of memory.

Two distinct values	Seven distinct values	Five distinct values	Two distinct values	Five distinct values

Date	ProductName	Product Subcategory	ProductCategory	SalesAmount
1/1/2011	Hitch Rack - 4-Bike	Bike Racks	Accessories	44.88
1/1/2011	Bike Wash - Dissolver	Cleaners	Accessories	2.9733
1/1/2011	Mountain-400-W Silver, 38	Mountain Bikes	Bikes	419.7784
1/2/2011	Mountain-400-W Silver, 40	Mountain Bikes	Bikes	419.7784
1/2/2011	Road-250 Red, 44	Road Bikes	Bikes	1518.7864
1/2/2011	Road-250 Red, 48	Road Bikes	Bikes	1518.7864
1/2/2011	Sport-100 Helmet, Red	Helmets	Accessories	12.0278

Figure 3.1 xVelocity compresses columns with many repeating values well.

Processing queries

When Power BI receives a DAX query, its formula engine parses the query and creates an execution plan. This execution plan will likely include many queries for data retrieval that the formula engine sends in parallel to xVelocity. Think of xVelocity as a highly efficient memory scanner. For the most part, all it does is scan the column values loaded in the computer memory. For example, even if a DAX query asks for sales for a single product, xVelocity must go through the following steps:

1. Scan the entire ProductName and SalesAmount columns.

2. Cross-join the two columns to find sales for that product.

3. Aggregate SalesAmount depending on the requested aggregation type (SUM, AVG, or other).

Therefore, xVelocity performs very well when the query requests a few columns which is typical for data analytics, such as to summarize sales by product (only two columns involved). But it might not be that efficient as reports get more granular and the number of columns and data volumes increase, such as to produce a detailed report that shows the customer's first name, last name, email, phone number, and so on.

The more columns the report requests, the more columns xVelocity needs to scan and cross join. Although its memory storage goes a long way to crunch data efficiently, it has its limits. You might not see much performance degradation with the few thousand rows in the Adventure Works model, but with millions of rows it will be probably more efficient to produce such detail reports directly from a relational database, such as SQL Server or Oracle, that retrieves data by rows and not columns. Keep this in mind and choose the right tool for the reporting task at hand.

3.1.2 Understanding Column Data Types

A table column has a data type associated with it. When Power BI connects to the data source, it attempts to obtain the column data type from the data provider and then maps it to a data type it supports.

Understanding supported data types

Table 3.1 lists the xVelocity data types (Power Query has a few more types that don't have equivalents).

Table 3.1   This table shows the column data types supported by xVelocity.

Query Data Type	Storage Data Type	Description
Text	String	A Unicode character string with a max length of 268,435,456 characters
Decimal Number	Decimal Number	A 64 bit (eight-bytes) real number with decimal places
Fixed Decimal Number	Fixed Decimal Number	A decimal number with four decimal places of fixed precision useful for storing currencies.
Whole Number	Whole number	A 64-bit (eight-bytes) integer with no decimal places
Date/Time	Date/Time	Dates and times after March 1st, 1900
Date	Date	Just the date portion of a date
Time	Time	Just the time portion of a date
TRUE/FALSE	Boolean	True or False value
Binary	Binary data type	Blob, such as file content (supported in Query Editor but not in the data model)

Reviewing and changing the column data type

To review the column data type in Power BI Desktop, click the Data View tab, select the table column, and examine the "Data type" dropdown in the Modeling ribbon. You can use this dropdown to change the column data type. Changing the column data type changes how the data is physically stored in the model. For example, changing from Decimal Number to Whole Number will remove decimals. You can always change the data type back to Decimal Number and reimport the data to restore the precision.

You should review and change the column data type for the following reasons:

- Data aggregation – You can sum or average only numeric columns.
- Data validation – Suppose you're given a text file with a SalesAmount column that's supposed to store decimal data. What happens if an 'NA' value sneaks into one or more cells? The query will detect it and might change the column type to Text. You can examine the data type after import and detect such issues.

 TIP   Although you can perform limited validation in DAX, I recommend you address data quality issues ideally in the data source. When this is not an option, tackle them in Power Query because it has the capabilities to remove errors or replace values. Data should enter your model clean and DAX isn't the right tool to shape and transform the data.

3.2   Exploring Storage

When you browse the data in Power BI Desktop (Data View tab), there is nothing that indicates that data is stored in columns. In fact, you might be tricked into believing that data is stored in rows as in a relational database. In this practice, you'll use the VertiPaq Analyzer community tool to gain more understanding about how the data is stored in the Adventure Works model.

3.2.1   Getting Started with Vertipaq Analyzer

The VertiPaq Analyzer is implemented as an Excel Power Pivot model. It can collect storage statistics from the three Microsoft products that use xVelocity: Power BI, Power Pivot, and Analysis Services Tabular. The steps that follow are specific to analyzing storage of Power BI Desktop models.

Finding how to connect to the model

Recall from Lesson 1 that a background Analysis Services Tabular instance hosts your Power BI Desktop model. Unfortunately, each time you restart Power BI Desktop, it creates a new instance that listens on a different network port. As a first step, you need to determine that port and the easiest way to do so is to use DAX Studio.

1. Open Power BI Desktop and then open the Adventure Works.pbix file from the \Source\Practice folder.

2. Open DAX Studio. In the Connect window, choose the "PBI/SSDT Model" model option and select the Adventure Works model. Click Connect.

3. Once DAX Studio connects, look at the bottom status bar and obtain the server name and port. You should see something like *localhost:55892*. That's all you need for the connection string.

Collecting statistics

Next, configure and run the VertiPaq Analyzer.

1. Download the VertiPaq Analyzer from https://www.sqlbi.com/tools/vertipaq-analyzer/ and unzip it. For your convenience, I provided the Excel 2013 version in the \Source\Intro folder.

2. In the Excel Data ribbon, click Manage Data Model to open the Power Pivot model.

3. In the Power Pivot Home ribbon, click Existing Connections. Select the SSAS data source and click Edit.

4. In the "Specify a connection string" window, click the Build button.

5. In the "Data link properties" window, change the Data Source setting to localhost:<port> and replace <port> with the actual port number you got from DAX Studio.

6. Expand the "Enter the initial catalog to use" and select the model name which should be a globally unique identifier (guid), such as 7a622512-cf0c-4097-a41d-caa62bc88ba4.

7. Press "Test Connection" to test connectivity and if all is well, press OK. Your connection string should like something like this:

```
Provider=MSOLAP.8;Integrated Security=SSPI;Persist Security Info=False;Initial Catalog=7a622512-cf0c-4097-a41d-
caa62bc88ba4;Data Source=localhost:55892;Update Isolation Level=2
```

8. Click Save. Back to the "Existing Connections" window, click Refresh. Power BI will query specific Analysis Services data management views (DMV) and load some statistics into Power Pivot tables.

9. Verify that all tables are successfully refreshed in the status window and then click Close twice.

10. Finally, close the Power Pivot window to return to Excel.

3.2.2 Analyzing Storage Results

Although it captures much more information than this, I typically use the VertiPaq Analyzer to determine which tables and columns take the most storage.

Practice

The first tab (Tables) in the Excel spreadsheet contains useful summary information.

1. Click the Tables tab in the VertiPaq Analyzer Excel file.

2. Sort the "Columns Total Size" column in descending order both at table and column levels. Compare your results with **Figure 3.2**.

Row Labels	Cardinality	Table Size	Columns Total Size	Data Size	Dictionary Size	Columns H
⊟DimCustomer	18,484	4,402,413	4,388,317	402,584	3,222,477	
EmailAddress	18,484		910,045	36,976	725,149	
FullName	18,400		744,535	36,976	560,311	
CustomerAlternateKey	18,484		673,871	36,976	488,975	
AddressLine1	12,797		653,847	36,976	514,455	
BirthDate	6,139		404,240	36,976	318,112	
Phone	8,890		358,695	36,976	250,551	
CustomerKey	18,484		111,056	36,976	120	
DateFirstPurchase	1,124		85,600	29,576	46,984	
FirstName	670		61,694	24,648	31,638	
LastName	375		49,510	21,128	25,342	
GeographyKey	336		33,736	21,128	9,872	
⋯	43			9 568	17,628	

Figure 3.2 Use VertiPaq Analyzer to analyze the data model storage.

Analysis

The report shows that the table that takes the most storage is DimCustomer, which has 18,484 rows (see the Cardinality column). The Table Size column states that the entire table occupies 4,402,413 bytes (or around 4.5 Mb). Another good column to examine is "Database Size %" which shows the table or column storage size as a percentage of the model's overall size.

You can also see that EmailAddress takes the most space because it's a text column that has a lot of unique values. Internally, xVelocity stores all data types as integers but it needs to encode text values. If you don't need email address for analysis, you should remove it to save about seven percent storage.

If you scroll all the way down and examine the "Table Size" column again, you can see that the entire model takes about 18.5 Mb, of which 3 MB is just the data size (Data Size column) and 12 MB (Dictionary Size column) are for additional runtime structures called *dictionaries* that Power BI uses to decompress and look up data. The model data size should correspond roughly to the size of the Adventure Works.pbix file.

Finally, notice that there are many "LocalDateTable" tables shown in the table list that add more than six megabytes to the model size. Where do they come from? By default, Power BI generates a date table for every date column in every table it encounters. Power BI generates these tables so you don't have to add an explicit date table, but they can surely bloat your model. If you have a date table as the Adventure Works model does, you can turn off the hidden date tables by unchecking the "Auto Date/Time" setting in the File ⇨ Options and settings ⇨ Options, Data Load tab (under Current Settings). We'll revisit date tables in the "Working with Date Tables" lesson.

3.3   Summary

In this lesson, you learned how Power BI stores data. Power BI imports all the data into the xVelocity store: a highly efficient, in-memory columnar database. The lower the column cardinality, the higher the chance for that column to compress well and to take less storage. Currently, Power BI itself doesn't include storage statistics, but you can use the VertiPaq Analyzer community tool to analyze the model storage.

This lesson concludes the introductory part of this book. Let's dive in DAX and learn how to implement calculated columns.

PART 2

Calculated columns and tables

Y ou can use DAX to extend your model with custom columns and tables. In this part of the book, you'll learn how to do this. Previously, you learned the data modeling fundamentals and how Power BI stores data. Next, you'll learn how to extend your tables with basic and advanced calculated columns, including columns for looking up, aggregating, and filtering data.

You'll find how calculated columns are evaluated and how to change the evaluation context. And you'll discover how calculated tables can help you implement role-playing dimensions, date tables, and summarized tables. Along the way you'll get introduced to important DAX functions for relating and filtering data.

When going through the exercises, remember to use your version of the Adventure Works model, which you should have saved in the \Source\Practice folder. If you need to refer to the completed exercises and reports for this part of the book, you'll find them in the Adventure Works model in the \Source\Part2 folder included in the book source code.

Lesson 4

Understanding Custom Columns

In the first lesson, I explained that one of the DAX usage scenarios is to extend tables with calculated columns. You practiced creating a simple calculated column that concatenates the customer's first name and last name. This lesson examines calculated columns in more detail. You'll learn how they are evaluated and stored.

More importantly, you'll understand when to use and not to use calculated columns. You'll also learn about other approaches for creating custom columns. You'll find the DAX formulas for this lesson in \Source\Part2\Understanding Calculated Columns.dax.

4.1   Understanding Calculated Columns

A calculated column is a table column that uses a DAX formula for its values. This is conceptually like a formula-based column added to an Excel list, although DAX formulas reference columns instead of cells.

4.1.1   Understanding Calculated Column Storage

DAX newcomers are often confused about the difference between calculated columns and measures and where to use each. To understand calculated columns better, you need to understand how they are stored and evaluated.

How are calculated columns stored?
When a column contains a formula, the storage engine computes its value for each row and saves the results. To use a techie term, values of calculated columns get "materialized" or "persisted". The difference is that regular columns import their values from a data source, while calculated columns are a byproduct of DAX formulas and they are evaluated and saved after the regular columns are loaded. Because of this, the formula of a calculated column can reference regular columns and other calculated columns.

However, a calculated column can't reference any runtime conditions, such as to obtain the selected value from a report filter. Again, this is because the DAX formula is evaluated *after* the data is loaded but *before* report queries are executed. The DAX formula of a calculated column is evaluated once for each row in the table and from this point on its values don't change.

 NOTE   The storage engine might not compress calculated columns as much as regular columns because they don't participate in the sorting and re-ordering algorithm that optimizes the compression. So, if you have a large table with a calculated column that has many unique values, this column might have a larger memory footprint than a regular column. Use the Vertipaq Analyzer to analyze the column storage and compare it with the other implementation approaches you'll learn in this lesson that might result in less storage.

How are calculated columns updated?

If data is imported, Power BI has everything it needs to evaluate DAX formulas in calculated columns. If data is not imported, such as when a table uses DirectQuery to connect to a SQL Server database, calculated columns are evaluated on the fly, but not all DAX functions are supported (for example, time intelligence functions, such as TOTALYTD, are not supported). Even if the calculated column references other tables, Power BI has the data and it doesn't need to reload the table when the column is first created.

Suppose that the data in the underlying data source has changed. If data is imported, you need to refresh all or some of the tables in your model to synchronize them with changes in the data source. Power BI updates calculated columns, as well as relationships and hierarchies, on refresh. If the calculated column references only columns in the same table, it will be updated when the home table is refreshed. If the calculated column references other tables, it will be updated when each of the dependent tables is refreshed. In other words, a calculated column is always in sync with the data that is currently in the model. But you must refresh the data to update calculated columns. You can't refresh specific calculated columns. Power BI refreshes all calculated columns in a table when it discovers that dependent tables are updated.

4.1.2 Understanding Evaluation Context

Every DAX formula is calculated in a specific evaluation context. By "context", we'll mean restrictions that are implicitly and explicitly applied to the formula to operate on specific data, such as user-defined filters, relationships between tables, and explicit filters in formulas. DAX recognizes two context types: row context and filter context.

Introducing row context

Think of the row context as the "current row" in which the DAX formula is executed. There are two scenarios that result in a DAX formula evaluated in the row context:

- Evaluating a calculated column – The row context includes the values from the columns in the current row. Therefore, the FullName column you implemented in Lesson 1 returns the full name of the customer for each row in the table.

- Using an iterator function – Several DAX functions iterate over table rows, such as FILTER, SUMX, ADDCOLUMNS. When they iterate a row, they create a row context for that row.

Although the row context doesn't automatically propagate to related tables, you can use DAX functions, such as RELATED and RELATEDTABLE, to propagate it in order to select rows in other tables that are related to the current row, such as to look up the product cost from another table.

Introducing filter context

The filter context represents the subset of data in which a DAX formula operates. For example, the running total measure you implemented in Lesson 1 produces different results for each report "cell". It does so because Power BI evaluates it in the filter context of every cell. Going back to **Figure 1.5**, we see that the SalesAmountRT measure accumulates sales for all years up to and including the year corresponding to the current cell. In other words, the running total is evaluated as of a specific year. In this case, the "as of" year is whatever year corresponds to a given report cell, but it also could be obtained from a report filter or slicer.

Usually, every report cell has a different filter context that is inherited from the cell location. However, there are DAX filter functions, such as CALCULATE that can change the filter context, and other functions, such as ALL and ALLEXCEPT, that can ignore it. Irrespective if it's implicit (cell location and user filters) or explicit (overwritten by DAX functions), the filter context never affects the row context.

 NOTE The DAX documentation differentiates between "query context" (implicit filters) and "filter context" (explicit filters). To keep things simple, I'll refer to both types as filter context because they operate in the same way.

The filter context can be empty. For example, the FullName calculated column has an empty filter context. Because its formula is evaluated at design time, Power BI can't pass any report filters to a calculated column, so there is no implicit filter context. And there is no explicit filter context because the FullName formula doesn't modify the filter context. However, even calculated columns can use DAX functions, such as CALCULATE, that create or modify a filter context. Therefore, the calculated column's formula can have row and filter contexts, just like a measure can have both.

4.1.3 Considering Calculated Columns

No matter how comprehensive your data model is it can probably benefit from custom columns. Let's see when calculated columns could be useful and when you would consider other approaches.

When to use calculated columns
In a nutshell, consider a calculated column when you seek to extend a table with a custom column, and you prefer to use DAX. Here are a few good examples for using calculated columns:

- Aggregate data from another table, such as to calculate the customer overall sales rank.
- Look up a value from a related table if doing so in DAX is more efficient than other approaches (more on this in the next section).
- Create buckets for a range of values in a column, such as Customer Age (0-20, 21-30, and so on).

 TIP Although custom table columns could be created in different ways, sometimes you don't have a choice but to use DAX. Consider a calculated column when the expression can be evaluated more efficiently with a DAX formula.

Once the calculated column is in place, it can be used just like a regular column. For example, you can place the FullName column in the Table visual's Rows or Columns areas or use it in a report filter or slicer. You can add a calculated column to the visual's Values area and sum it up (if it's numeric) or use Count or Discount Count functions (if it's a text column). Make no mistake though. Although you can aggregate a calculated column, it's not a measure. When the calculated column is aggregated, Power BI creates an implicit measure on top of the calculated column, just like it does when a regular column is added to the Values area.

When not to use calculated columns
To start with, you can't use a calculated column when the expression depends on some runtime condition, such as report filters or identity of the interactive user. For example, you can't use a calculated column to produce year-to-date (YTD) sales as of a date specified by the user. When the formula depends on end user selection, you need a measure and not a calculated column. A DAX formula may work for both, but the results and computation are very different. The output from a calculated column is fixed at design time, while measures are dynamically calculated at runtime.

There are also cases where other implementation approaches could be preferable, such as when you need more complicated expressions that might benefit from custom SQL. This brings us to the next section that discusses alternative approaches for implementing custom columns.

4.2 Other Options for Implementing Custom Columns

Using DAX is not the only way to extend tables with custom columns. You can introduce custom columns outside the data model, such as by applying custom SQL (if you retrieve data from a relational database), or by using Power Query.

4.2.1 Evaluating Implementation Options

Table 4.1 compares three approaches for implementing custom columns, sorted by their proximity to the data model (more upstream options first). Ultimately, the implementation choice depends on your skillset and the task at hand.

Table 4.1   Comparing three common options for implementing custom columns.

Characteristics	SQL Expression Column	Power Query Custom Column	DAX Calculated Column
Language	SQL (custom query or SQL view)	M	DAX
Evaluation	Before the data is loaded in the model	As the data is loaded in the model	After data is loaded in the model
Require table refresh	Yes	Yes	No
Level of transformation	High	Low	Medium
Storage footprint	Regular compression	Regular compression	May not compress well

SQL expression columns
If you load data from a relational database, you can use a custom SQL query or SQL views to add expression-based columns. SQL has been evolving for decades, so you'd be hard pressed to face a data manipulation or shaping requirement that you can't meet with SQL. If you know SQL, not only can you apply the skills you already have, but you'll gain in performance and delegate data crunching to the relational database, which is what it's designed to do.

 REAL LIFE In my consulting practice, I always implement SQL views to "wrap" the tables in a relational database that I need to import in the data model. Sooner or later, a requirement pops up for an expression-based column, such as to derive a higher-level grouping from a list of values. Sometimes, these columns require more involved lookups and delegating this task to the relational database is usually the best option.

Power Query custom columns
Using Power Query could be a good choice for implementing basic custom columns, especially when you're new to DAX. Power Query has its own expression-based language called "M", but its user interface can often auto-generate the "M" code so you might be able to avoid learning yet another language. Consider Power Query especially for cleansing column values, such as to remove a currency symbol to make the column numeric. Power Query can also look up values from another table (in fact, it supports fuzzy lookups!), but you need to test how much the Power Query lookups add up to the table refresh time.

Calculated columns
Implementing a calculated column requires knowledge of DAX. The formula is evaluated at design time and it doesn't require reloading the data if it's already imported. Subsequent table refreshes automatically recalculate the column. I ranked the transformation capabilities as medium because it's not as powerful as SQL, although it has functions that are specifically designed for data analytics.

4.2.2 Performing Arithmetic Operations

Creating a custom column that performs some arithmetic operations for each row in a table is a common requirement. Although you can use SQL or Power Query to create such columns, let's implement another DAX calculated column to create a LineTotal column that calculates the total amount for each row in the FactResellerSales table by multiplying the order quantity, discount, and unit price.

Practice
While working on the formula, let's see what happens when the formula has a wrong column reference.

1. Besides the New Column ribbon button, another way to add a calculated column is to use the Fields pane but make sure that the Data View (or Report View) tab in the navigation page is selected. In the Fields pane, right-click the FactResellerSales table and then click "New column".

1. In the formula bar, enter the following formula and press Enter. Notice that I purposely omitted the table name from the column references to show you that calculated columns don't have to use fully-qualified column names. In addition, I've intentionally misspelled the OrderQty column reference to force an error.

LineTotal = [UnitPrice] * (1-[UnitPriceDiscountPct]) * [OrderQty]

Output
This expression multiplies UnitPrice times UnitPriceDiscountPrc times OrderQty. Notice that when you type in a recognized function in the formula bar and then enter a parenthesis "(", AutoComplete shows the function syntax. Notice that the formula bar shows this error:

"Column 'OrderQty' cannot be found or may be used in this expression".

In addition, the LineTotal column shows "#ERROR" in every cell. Because OrderQty doesn't exist, Power BI underlines with a red squiggly line in the formula bar.

1. In the formula bar, replace the OrderQty reference with OrderQuantity as follows:

LineTotal = [UnitPrice] * (1-[UnitPriceDiscountPct]) * **[OrderQuantity]**

2. Press Enter. Now, the column should work as expected.

3. (Optional) Create a report that summarizes LineTotal by a field in a related table, such as DimProduct[EnglishProductCategoryName] (or refer to the "Arithmetic Operations" visual on the "Understanding CC" page in \Source\Part2\Adventure Works.pbix.

EnglishProductCategoryName	LineTotal
Accessories	$571,298
Bikes	$66,302,382
Clothing	$1,777,841
Components	$11,799,077
Total	**$80,450,597**

Figure 4.1 The LineTotal calculated column aggregates just like a regular numeric column.

Analysis
Runtime formula errors are detected and shown in the formula bar. In case of a runtime error in a calculated column, all column values show #ERROR. Logical errors are not detected and it's up to you to test and fix them.

4.2.3 Using Power Query for Custom Columns

Before we continue our DAX tour, let's quickly demonstrate how you can implement a FullName custom column in Power Query that produces the same results as its DAX counterpart.

 NOTE This practice requires a connection to the AdventureWorksDW database because every change you make in Power Query necessitates a table refresh to apply the change to the model. If you want to follow along, read the instructions in the book front matter to install and configure this database. If this is too much trouble, you can choose to ignore this exercise because you won't need the custom column in the practices that follow.

Practice

Think of Power Query as a layer between the data source and your data model that you can use to define transformation steps for shaping and cleansing data. It's important to understand that Power Query contains only the definitions of these transformations described in the "M" language. Assuming that data is imported, the actual transformation steps happen when the table is refreshed.

1. Right-click the DimCustomer table and then click "Edit query". The Power Query window opens with the DimCustomer table selected.

2. Select the "Add Column" ribbon. You can use the Custom Column button to create a new column, but this requires some experience in "M". Instead, hold the Ctrl key and select the FirstName and LastName columns in the preview pane.

3. In the "Add Column" ribbon, expand the "Column From Examples" and then chose "From Selection". This tells Power Query to auto-generate the "M" code from an example you'll provide that involves the selected columns.

Output

Next, you'll type the result you expect.

1. In the new "Column1" column that appears to the right of the table columns, double-click the first cell and type the desired result. In our case, type *Jon Yang*, because that's the full name of the first customer (see **Figure 4.2**).

2. Press Enter. Notice that Power Query auto-fills the rest of the column values. In addition, Power Query shows you the "M" code behind the new column at the top of the window.

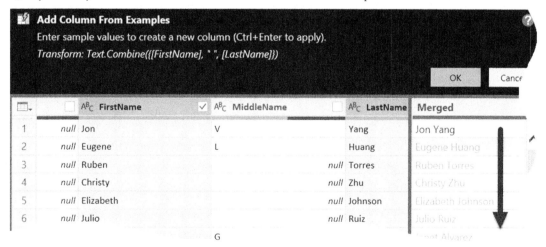

Figure 4.2 Power Query can autogenerate custom columns from an example you provide.

3. Double-click the column header of the new column (should be called Merged) and type "FullNamePQ" to differentiate the new column from the existing FullName calculated column (column names must be unique within a table). Click OK.

4. Click the Home ribbon and then click the Close & Apply button to refresh the DimCustomer table.

Analysis

Back to the Power BI Desktop window, expand DimCustomer in the Fields pane and notice that it now has the FullNamePQ column. Unlike the FullName calculated column, FullNamePQ doesn't have any icon. As far as the data model is concerned, FullNamePQ is just a regular column. The "M" formula was applied during table refresh but before the data was loaded into the data model. As you can see in the Data View tab, the FullName and FullNamePQ columns have the same values but their implementation is vastly different.

4.3   Summary

In this lesson, you learned about how calculated columns work and how their expressions are evaluated. I introduced you to a very important topic in DAX: the expression evaluation context, which consist of a row context and a filter context. The row context typically applies to calculated columns. The filter context is typically associated with DAX measures. You also learned about other approaches to implement custom columns and I provided guidance on which option to choose.

Lesson 5

Relating Data

If you are a heavy Excel user, you've probably used its omnipresent VLOOKUP function to look up values from another cell or to aggregate data in a range. This is a common task for data modeling too, although you use relationships and tables as opposed to cells and ranges. This lesson teaches you how to navigate tables whether physical relationships exist or not. You'll find the DAX formulas for this lesson in \Source\Part2\Relating Data.dax.

5.1   Navigating Existing Relationships

Recall from Lesson 2 that relationships are very important to Power BI data models. They promote self-service data exploration without requiring you to create queries that join tables. If a relationship exists between a dimension table and a fact table, you can slice and dice the fact data by any field in the dimension table. Calculated columns can benefit from existing relationships too to let you "look up" or aggregate values from a related table. DAX has two functions, RELATED and RELATEDTABLE, for navigating active relationships.

5.1.1   Navigating Many-to-One Relationships

Suppose you want to calculate the net profit for each row in the FactResellerSales table. For our purposes, you'll calculate the line net profit by subtracting the product cost from the line item total. As a first step, you need to look up the product cost in the DimProduct table. In other words, for each row (line item) in FactResellerSales table, you need the product identifier (ProductKey column), then follow the relationship to DimProduct, and look up the value in DimProduct[Standard-Cost]. This is a many-to-one relationship from the FactResellerSales table perspective (notice the * symbol in **Figure 5.1**)

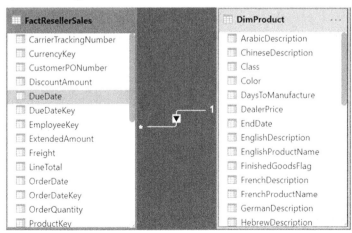

Figure 5.1 Looking up the product cost in DimProduct requires navigating the many-to-one relationship for each row in FactResellerSales.

35

Practice

When working on a complicated formula, consider breaking it up into multiple steps. Let's focus on looking up the StandardCost first.

1. Make sure the Data or Report View tab is selected in the navigation pane. In the Fields pane, right-click the FactResellerSales table and then click "New column".

2. In the formula bar, enter the following formula and press Enter:

NetProfit = RELATED(DimProduct[StandardCost])

Output

Power BI adds a new NetProfit column to DimProduct and populates it with standard cost for that product that is recorded in the DimProduct[StandardCost] column.

Analysis

This expression uses the RELATED function to look up the value of the StandardCost column in the Product table. Since a calculated column inherits the current row context, this expression is evaluated for each row. Unfortunately, Power BI doesn't automatically propagate the row context to related tables. Hence, you must use RELATED which is designed to follow a many-to-one relationship and to apply the row context. RELATED has the following definition:

Related(<column>)

For each row in FactResellerSales, Power BI constructs a row context consisting of all column values in that row, including the ProductKey value. Then, it navigates the FactResellerSales[ProductKey] ⇨ DimProduct[ProductKey] relationship, and retrieves the standard cost for that product from the DimProduct[StandardCost] column.

 NOTE RELATED requires a row context and an active relationship to the table where the column is located. If there is no active relationship, RELATED returns an error.

To recap, RELATED needs a row context and can be used only in two cases:

- A calculated column expression.
- In an extended "X" function, such as SUMX, that iterates over a table and creates a row context for each row.

Practice

Complete the NetProfit formula to calculate the line net profit:

1. Change the formula as follows;

NetProfit = [LineTotal] - (RELATED(DimProduct[StandardCost]) * FactResellerSales[OrderQuantity])

2. In the Fields list, select FactResellerSales[NetProfit]. In the Modeling ribbon (Formatting group), format the column values without decimal places.

3. (Optional) Test the NetProfit column, such as to aggregate it by DimDate[CalendarYear], or refer to the "RELATED Function" visual on the page "Relating Data" in \Source\Part2\Adventure Works.pbix, which is shown in **Figure 5.2**.

Analysis

While browsing the values in the NetProfit column in the Data View tab, notice that when the line item's product cost exceeds the line total, the result is a negative value. This is the expected result so don't be alarmed.

CalendarYear	NetProfit
2010	$17,033
2011	$29,420
2012	$915,899
2013	($491,870)
Total	**$470,483**

Figure 5.2 The NetProfit calculated column uses the RELATED function to look up the product standard cost.

Remember that a calculated column can be placed in any area of the report when it makes sense. In this case, NetProfit is a numeric column and you can place it in the visual's Values area to aggregate it. This doesn't make it a measure though. Instead, Power BI creates an implicit measure to summarize the calculated column.

5.1.2 Simplifying the Model Schema

You can use the RELATED function to simplify a snowflake schema by reducing the number of tables. For example, unless there is a good reason to keep these tables separate, you can consolidate DimProduct, DimProductSubcategory and DimProductCategory. While you can accomplish this with custom SQL or Power Query, let's use calculated columns.

 TIP Although this is a useful exercise for calculated columns, I recommend you use SQL or Power Query for data shaping. SQL and Power BI are better suited for transformation tasks, such as replacing empty values that don't have a match.

Practice
Denormalizing the product schema with DAX requires two new calculated columns:

1.Add these two columns to DimProduct so that this table has both product category and subcategory:

EnglishProductSubcategoryName = RELATED(DimProductSubcategory[EnglishProductSubcategoryName])
EnglishProductCategoryName = RELATED(DimProductCategory[EnglishProductCategoryName])

2.(Optional) Hide the DimProductSubcategory and DimProductSubcategory tables. To hide a table, right-click the table in the Fields pane (make sure that the Data View tab or Model View tab are selected) and click "Hide in report view".

Output
The DimProduct table now has the product subcategory and category as calculated columns that derive their values from the related tables. As a result, you managed to collapse three tables into one and thus you simplified the model schema. Notice that the new columns have empty values when there is no match.

Analysis
You can use the RELATED function to navigate many-to-one cascading relationships and look up values from tables that are not directly related to the home table. Think of RELATED as a SQL left join between two tables. In the case where there is no match, it returns an empty value.

5.1.3 Navigating One-to-Many Relationships

Another DAX function, RELATEDTABLE, lets you navigate a relationship in either direction. This is useful when the formula needs to follow a one-to-many relationship, that is from the dimension table to the fact table. It has the following definition:

RELATEDTABLE(<tableName>)

Like RELATED, RELATEDTABLE propagates the row context. Because it returns a table with a subset of rows that match the current row context, you typically need to aggregate the results if you want to use this function in a calculated column.

 NOTE Although less common, Power BI also supports relationships with a many-to-many data cardinality (not to be confused with many-to-many relationships discussed in the lesson "Many-to-many relationships"), such as between two fact tables or between tables in different storage modes (imported and DirectQuery). You can also use RELATEDTABLE to navigate such relationships. For more information about relationships with a many-to-many cardinality, refer to the article "Relationships with a many-many cardinality in Power BI Desktop" at https://docs.microsoft.com/power-bi/desktop-many-to-many-relationships.

Practice

Suppose you need a calculated column in the DimProduct table that summarizes the reseller sales from FactResellerSales for each product: In your first attempt, add the following calculated column to DimProduct:

ResellerSales = SUM(FactResellerSales[SalesAmount])

Outcome

The DimProduct[ResellerSales] calculated column returns a repeating value that represents the overall sales across the entire FactResellerSales.

Analysis

The formula doesn't propagate the row context of the "current product".

Practice

Change the formula of the calculated column as follows:

ResellerSales = SUMX(RELATEDTABLE(FactResellerSales), FactResellerSales[SalesAmount])

Outcome

Now the calculated column returns the expected results. Notice that some products, such as accessories, show no sales because they are never sold.

1. (Optional) Test the ResellerSales column, such as to aggregate it by DimProduct[EnglishProductCategoryName], or refer to the "RELATEDTABLE" visual on the report page "Relating Data" in \Source\Part2\Adventure Works.pbix, which is shown in **Figure 5.3**.

EnglishProductCategoryName	ResellerSales
Accessories	$571,298
Bikes	$66,302,382
Clothing	$1,777,841
Components	$11,799,077
Total	**$80,450,597**

Figure 5.3 The ResellerSales calculated column uses the RELATEDTABLE function to aggregate related sales.

Analysis
The RELATEDTABLE function transitions the row context from DimProduct to FactResellerSales in order to filter the sales transactions for each product. Because it returns a table of matching rows, the SUMX extended function is used to iterate row by row over the returned table and summarize FactResellerSales[SalesAmount]. You can use COUNTROWS(RELATEDTABLE(FactResellerSales)) to see how many rows are matched.

Behind the scenes, RELATEDTABLE is a shortcut to the DAX CALCULATETABLE function. This formula produces the same result.

ResellerSales = SUMX(CALCULATETABLE(FactResellerSales), FactResellerSales[SalesAmount])

5.2   Navigating Virtual and Inactive Relationships

Active relationships are easy to work with and you should always create and use relationships when possible as they'll give you the best performance when joining tables. But what if two tables can't be related or they have an inactive relationship? Fortunately, DAX has functions to help you.

5.2.1   Looking up Values

You can use the LOOKUPVALUE function to look up a single value from another table. The LOOKUPVALUE function has the following definition:

LOOKUPVALUE(<result_columnName>, <search_columnName>, <search_value>[, <search_columnName>, <search_value>]...[, <alternateResult>])

LOOKUPVALUE searches and returns the value in a column that meets one or more conditions. The search conditions must result in a single value or multiple (but identical) values to avoid an error. If no match is found, the function returns a blank value which you can substitute with another value specified in the alternateResult argument.

Practice
The DimEmployee table has a SalesTerritoryKey column that associates a salesperson with a sales territory in the DimSalesTerritory table. Suppose you want to look up the assigned country and add it as a column to DimEmployee. Add a SalesTerritoryCountry calculated column to DimEmployee with this formula:

SalesTerritoryCountry = LOOKUPVALUE(DimSalesTerritory[SalesTerritoryCountry],
    DimSalesTerritory[SalesTerritoryKey], DimEmployee[SalesTerritoryKey])

Output
Most employees are not salespeople and they don't have an associated sales territory. In this case, the SalesTerritoryCountry calculated column shows 'NA' because that's the corresponding country for SalesTerritoryKey of 11. Otherwise, the column shows the associated country.

LastName	SalesTerritoryCountry
Anderson	NA
Ansman-Wolfe	United States
Arifin	NA
Bacon	NA
Baker	NA
Barbariol	NA

Figure 5.4 The SalesTerritoryCountry uses LOOKUPVALUE to look up the country associated with a salesperson.

Analysis

The first argument (DimSalesTerritory[SalesTerritoryCountry]) is the value you want to retrieve. The second argument (DimSalesTerritory[SalesTerritoryKey]) is the column to search. The third argument is the search value. It must be a scalar expression that returns a single value whose type matches the column to be searched and cannot refer to any column in the searched table.

5.2.2 Navigating Inactive Relationships

Strictly speaking, the Adventure Works model has an inactive relationship between the DimEmployee and DimSalesTerritory tables. However, Power BI makes it difficult to use this relationship in calculated columns. For the sake of completeness, I'll provide the formula, but I recommend you use LOOKUPVALUE instead to avoid added complexity.

Practice

Unfortunately, RELATED and RELATEDTABLE can't navigate inactive relationships. The only way to navigate an inactive relationship is to use the USERELATIONSHIP function, which has the following definition:

USERELATIONSHIP(<columnName1>,<columnName2>)

The two columns must be from two different tables related with an inactive relationship. The first column should be on the many side of the relationship (foreign key), but Power BI will swap the columns if you change the order, so you don't have to remember this rule. The final formula is:

```
SalesTerritoryCountry = CALCULATE(
        CALCULATE(VALUES(DimSalesTerritory[SalesTerritoryCountry]), DimEmployee),
        USERELATIONSHIP(DimEmployee[SalesTerritoryKey], DimSalesTerritory[SalesTerritoryKey]))
```

Analysis

The outermost CALCULATE function transitions the row context to a filter context and uses USERELATIONSHIP as a second argument. The VALUES function returns the distinct values in a column, which in this case is the list of countries in the DimSalesTerritory[SalesTerritoryCountry] column. However, if you know that VALUES would return just one value, you can use it in a formula when a single value is expected.

So that only the associated country is returned, the formula uses a second CALCULATE function which filters only the countries (the outcome will be just one country) that intersects with the DimEmployee table over the inactive relationship. So, there are two context transitions:

1. From the row context of the current employee to the filter context over the inactive relationship.

2. A second context transition caused by the nested CALCULATE.

5.3   Summary

Calculated columns must often retrieve values from other tables. Use the RELATED and RELATEDTABLE functions to look up values from tables related with an active physical relationship. Use LOOKUPVALUE to lookup a single value when a physical relationship doesn't exist.

Lesson 6

Aggregating Data

One of the most common tasks in data analytics is aggregating data, such as to summarize the sales for each product or rank customers based on their overall sales. In this lesson you'll learn how to aggregate data in calculated columns. It also revisits the evaluation context in which a formula is evaluated, and how the context is propagated to related tables. You'll find the DAX formulas for this lesson in \Source\Part2\Aggregating Data.dax.

6.1   Aggregating Columns

DAX supports various aggregation functions and **Table 6.1** shows the ones that you'd probably use the most. You can use these functions in both calculated columns (the subject of this lesson) and measures.

Table 6.1   This table shows the most common aggregation functions in DAX.

Aggregation Function	Description	Extended Function
AVERAGE*	Returns the average (arithmetic mean) of all the numbers in a column	AVERAGEX
COUNT*	Counts the number of values in a column that contain numbers	COUNTX
DISTINCTCOUNT	Counts the number of distinct values in a column	
MAX*	Returns the largest numeric value in a column, or between two scalar expressions	MAXX
MEDIAN*	Returns the median of numbers in a column	MEDIANX
MIN*	Returns the smallest numeric value in a column, or between two scalar expressions	MINX
RANX.EQ*	Returns the ranking of a number in a list of numbers	RANKX
SUM*	Adds all the numbers in a column	SUMX

6.1.1   Understanding Aggregation Functions

DAX "borrows" many aggregation functions from Excel, but instead of taking cells or ranges, the DAX counterparts reference table columns. For example, SUM(FactResellerSales[SalesAmount]) summarizes the SalesAmount column in the FactResellerSales table.

 NOTE   Remember that when used in calculated columns, none of these functions transition the row context into a filter context and they will return nonsensical results. You need a function that transitions the context, such as RELATED, RELATEDTABLE, CALCULATE or CALCULATETABLE.

Some of these functions, such as the ones I marked with an asterisk (*) next to the function name, operate on numeric values. For example, COUNT expects a column that contains numbers, dates, or text that can be converted to a number. However, COUNT also has an "A" counterpart (COUNTA), which counts values of any data type that aren't empty. Likewise, MIN finds the smallest value in a column that contains numbers or dates, whereas MINA can operate on text values.

Practice

Let's add a calculated column to the DimCustomer table that shows how many times a customer bought something. Because each row in FactInternetSales represents an order line item, you'll overstate the result if you count rows. Instead, you'll use the DISTINCTCOUNT function to count the SalesOrderNumber column. In your first attempt, add a #Sales calculated column to DimCustomer with the following formula:

#Sales = DISTINCTCOUNT(FactInternetSales[SalesOrderNumber])

Outcome

The formula doesn't produce the expected results. Like the DimProduct[ResellerSales] column in the previous lesson, #Sales returns a repeating number representing the distinct count of SalesOrderNumber across the entire FactInternetSales table. There are 27,659 sales orders but that's across all customers.

Analysis

None of the aggregation functions transition the row context to the related tables. Unfortunately, DISTINCTCOUNT doesn't have an extended function, such as DISTINCTCOUNTX, that would allow us to use RELATEDTABLE or CALCULATETABLE, as you did in the previous lesson with SUMX. This brings us to the CALCULATE function.

6.1.2 Introducing the CALCULATE Function

CALCULATE is a very important and versatile function, especially for measures. In fact, this function is so important, that it will take a few lessons to cover it in enough detail. Let's start with its definition:

CALCULATE (<Expression> [, <Filter> [, <Filter> [, ...]]])

Understanding evaluation

When used in a calculated column, CALCULATE goes through the following steps to create the context in which the expression is evaluated:

1. Evaluates the existing row context. For example, if a calculated column has a formula that uses CALCULATE, a row context will be created for each iterated row.

2. Discards the original row context because CALCULATE requires a filter context.

3. Performs the context transition. For example, when used in a calculated column, CALCULATE creates a filter context formed by each value of the table columns in the row that it's being iterated.

4. Evaluates the filter arguments and overwrites the context if it encounters one of the following functions: USERELATIONSHIP, CROSSFILTER, ALL, ALLEXCEPT, ALLSELECTED, and ALLNOBLANKROW.

5. Applies the other filter arguments.

Practice

Change the #Sales formula as follows:

#Sales = **CALCULATE**(DISTINCTCOUNT(FactInternetSales[SalesOrderNumber]))

Outcome

The formula works now. For example, #Sales returns 1 for the first customer (Latasha Suarez). To test, browse FactInternetSales in the Data View tab, and filter the CustomerKey column to 11471 (the key value for Latasha). As an optional exercise, create a visual with DimCustomer[FullName] and #Sales, as shown in **Figure 6.1**.

FullName	#Sales
Aaron Allen	1
Aaron Baker	1
Aaron Campbell	1
Aaron Collins	2
Aaron Diaz	2
Aaron Evans	1

Figure 6.1 The #Sales calculated column counts distinct orders in the FactInternetSales table.

Analysis

CALCULATE creates a new filter context from all the column values for the row being iterated. DISTINCTCOUNT is evaluated in that context so it returns the number of orders for each customer.

6.2   Understanding Extended Functions

Besides the aggregation functions that take only a column as an argument, DAX has extended versions. Going back to **Table 6.1**, you can see that several aggregation functions have extended versions suffixed with "X", such as SUMX.

6.2.1   Understanding Extended Syntax

For example, the SUMX function, which you used in the previous lesson, has this syntax:

SUMX (<Table>, <Expression>)

The extended versions are iterators, meaning that they calculate the expression for each row in the table passed as the first argument.

 NOTE As it turns out, the regular aggregation functions are just wrappers on top of the extended functions. For example, SUM(table[column]) is internally translated to SUMX(table, SUM([column])).

The extended functions are particularly powerful in measures because their evaluation context propagates to the table passed as the first argument. For example, if you have a Matrix visual with years in the column labels, and product in the row labels, and then you use a measure with the formula SUMX(FactResellerSales, [UnitPrice] * [OrderQuantity]), then each report cell will show the aggregated sales belonging to the corresponding year and product by calculating the expression for each sales transaction and then rolling up the result. Let's understand how this works in more detail.

6.2.2 Understanding Iteration

Consider the following formula:

SUMX(FactInternetSales, [UnitPrice] * [OrderQuantity])

As an iterator, SUMX iterates each row in FactInternetSales and calculates the expression [UnitPrice] * [OrderQuantity]. Then it sums up the result in the filter context of each report cell. If the formula uses AVERAGEX, it would compute the average over the expression calculated for each row. Some of the extended functions take additional arguments. For example, RANKX, which you'll use in the next practice, has this syntax:

RANKX(<table>, <expression>[, <value>[, <order>[, <ties>]]])

The ties argument can be either Skip (default value) or Dense. When set to Dense, the function doesn't skip numbers for tied ranks.

Practice

Suppose you want to rank each customer based on the customer's overall sales. The RANKX function can help you implement this requirement. As a first attempt, add a SalesRank calculated column to DimCustomer as follows:

SalesRank = RANKX(DimCustomer, SUM(FactInternetSales[SalesAmount]),,,Dense)

Outcome

Unfortunately, the formula returns the same value (1) for each customer. To fix this issue, use one of the following formulas:

SalesRank = RANKX(DimCustomer, SUMX(**RELATEDTABLE**(FactInternetSales), [SalesAmount]),,,Dense)
SalesRank = RANKX(DimCustomer, **CALCULATE**(SUM(FactInternetSales[SalesAmount])),,,Dense)

As an optional step, create a visual that shows DimCustomer[FullName], DimCustomer[SalesRank], and FactInternetSales[SalesAmount] (see **Figure 6.2**).

FullName	SalesRank	SalesAmount
Nichole Nara	1	$13,295
Kaitlyn Henderson	2	$13,294
Margaret He	3	$13,269
Randall Dominguez	4	$13,266
Adriana Gonzalez	5	$13,243
Rosa Hu	6	$13,216

Figure 6.2 The SalesRank calculated column ranks each customer based on the customer overall sales.

Analysis

As RANKX iterates over each row in DimCustomer, it evaluates the expression passed in the second argument, which in this case is SUM(FactInternetSales[SalesAmount]). As an iterator function, RANKX doesn't propagate by default the row context to the expression. This causes the formula to evaluate the rank over the same sales amount for each customer.

To fix this issue, the first formula uses RELATEDTABLE to transition the row context to a filter context. Because RELATEDTABLE returns a table, you need to use a function that takes a table as an argument. The function for summing values is SUMX. The second formula uses CALCULATE to transition the context. It uses SUM in the second argument. Alternatively, you can use SUMX:

SalesRank = RANKX(DimCustomer, CALCULATE(SUMX(FactInternetSales, FactInternetSales[SalesAmount])),,,Dense)

6.3　Summary

DAX supports various aggregation functions which have their roots in Excel. Most aggregation functions take a table column as their only argument. However, DAX provides extended versions (with "X" suffix) that are more versatile. Remember that for these functions to work in calculated columns you must somehow transition the row context into a filter context, such by using the RELATED or RELATEDTABLE functions, or by using CALCULATE.

Lesson 7

Filtering Data

DAX formulas often need to apply filters to narrow the context in which the formula operates. This lesson teaches you different ways to filter data with the CALCULATE and FILTER functions, and how to remove filters to expand the evaluation context. You'll find the DAX formulas for this lesson in \Source\Part2\Filtering Data.dax.

7.1   Adding Filters

DAX has various functions related to filtering data, including functions to apply and remove filters, and functions to detect the filter selection (detecting the filter context is useful for measures only). **Table 7.1** shows the most common filter functions to apply filters.

Table 7.1   **This table shows the most common functions for applying filter conditions.**

Filter Function	Description
CALCULATE	Evaluates a scalar expression in a context that is modified by specified filter conditions that can either add or remove filters
CALCULATETABLE	Like CALCULATE but evaluates a table expression
EARLIER (avoid)	Returns the current value of the specified column in an outer evaluation pass of the mentioned column. Use variables instead
FILTER	Returns a table by applying a filter expression

7.1.1   Using the Filter Function

The FILTER function is one of the most used (and abused) DAX functions. It has the following syntax:

FILTER (<Table>, <FilterExpression>)

The FILTER function is an iterator. It scans each row in the table passed as the first argument and check if it meets the condition specified in the filter expression. The FilterExpression argument must be a valid DAX Boolean expression that can include multiple conditions using the logical operators AND (&&) and OR (||), such as:

FactInternetSales[OrderDate] <=DATE(2012, 12, 31)
FactInternetSales[OrderDate] <=DATE(2012, 12, 31) || FactInternetSales[ShipDate] = BLANK()
FactInternetSales[OrderDate] >=DATE(2011, 1,1) && FactInternetSales[OrderDate] <=DATE(2012, 12, 31)

Practice
Let's adds a new calculated column to DimCustomer that returns the customer's sales for the year 2013. In your first attempt, you might come up with the following formula:

```
2013Sales = CALCULATE(SUM(FactInternetSales[SalesAmount]),
                FILTER(FactInternetSales,
                FactInternetSales[OrderDate] >= DATE(2013, 1, 1)
                && FactInternetSales[OrderDate] <= DATE(2013, 12, 31)))
```

 NOTE What if you want the formula to be evaluated as of a date specified by the user, such as by using a report filter or slicer? Remember that calculated columns can't access runtime conditions, so to meet this requirement you need a measure and not a calculated column. To emphasize this, the example uses fixed dates.

Output
The 2013Sales column doesn't work as expected. Specifically, it shows the same value across all customers. This value corresponds to the sum of SalesAmount for year 2013 across the entire table.

Analysis
As you learned before, the CALCULATE function transitions the row context to a filter context, causing the SUM function to evaluate for each customer. However, as a row iterator, the FILTER function creates a new filter context that includes the entire FactInternetSales table causing the repeated values. Change the formula as follows:

```
2013Sales = CALCULATE(SUM(FactInternetSales[SalesAmount]),
                FILTER(RELATEDTABLE(FactInternetSales),
                FactInternetSales[OrderDate]>=DATE(2013, 1, 1) &&
                FactInternetSales[OrderDate]<=DATE(2013, 12, 31)) )
```

Now the formula works as expected. RELATEDTABLE propagates the row context to FactInternetSales causing the FILTER function to filter only sales for the iterated row in DimCustomer. Another way to accomplish the same result and make the formula more efficient is to use the ALL function:

```
2013Sales = CALCULATE(SUM(FactInternetSales[SalesAmount]),
                FILTER(ALL(FactInternetSales[OrderDate]),
                FactInternetSales[OrderDate]>=DATE(2013, 1, 1) &&
                FactInternetSales[OrderDate]<=DATE(2013, 12, 31)) )
```

The ALL function removes the filter from the OrderDate column. The reason why this is more efficient is that the FILTER function will now iterate only through the OrderDate values (1,124 versus 60,398 rows in FactInternetSales). To optimize things even further in this case, use the YEAR function (returns the year from a date) to replace the two filter conditions with one:

```
2013Sales = CALCULATE(SUM(FactInternetSales[SalesAmount]),
                FILTER(ALL(FactInternetSales[OrderDate]),
                YEAR(FactInternetSales[OrderDate]) = 2013) )
```

Practice
Assuming ShipDate can be empty, change the formula to include sales where ShipDate is empty.

```
2013Sales = CALCULATE(SUM(FactInternetSales[SalesAmount]),
                FILTER(ALL(FactInternetSales[OrderDate], FactInternetSales[ShipDate]),
                YEAR(FactInternetSales[OrderDate])=2013 || FactInternetSales[ShipDate] = BLANK()) )
```

Analysis
The OR (||) operator is used in the FILTER function to filter where the sales year is 2013 or ShipDate is blank. In DAX, checking for empty (NULL) values is accomplished by checking for blank values (like Excel). Or, you can use the ISBLANK() function which returns TRUE if the value is blank:

```
2013Sales = CALCULATE(SUM(FactInternetSales[SalesAmount]),
```

```
FILTER(ALL(FactInternetSales[OrderDate], FactInternetSales[ShipDate]),
    YEAR(FactInternetSales[OrderDate])=2013 || ISBLANK(FactInternetSales[ShipDate]))) )
```

In the case where there are only two AND (or OR) conditions, you can use the AND and OR functions, as follows:

```
2013Sales = CALCULATE(SUM(FactInternetSales[SalesAmount]),
    FILTER(ALL(FactInternetSales[OrderDate], FactInternetSales[ShipDate]),
    OR(YEAR(FactInternetSales[OrderDate])=2013, ISBLANK(FactInternetSales[ShipDate]))))
```

Note the special use of the ALL function to return the unique combinations between OrderDate and ShipDate. This reduces the number of rows that the storage engine needs to scan.

> **TIP** When you need to filter on a few columns, you could make the formula more efficient by using ALL(column1, column2,..) to get the unique combinations among the columns. Use DAX Studio to check the count of rows from the following query: EVALUATE ALL(FactInternetSales[OrderDate], FactInternetSales[ShipDate])
> If you get substantially less rows than the total row count in the fact table, it's more efficient to use ALL. However, as the number of filtered columns increase, you'll get closer and closer to the cardinality of the entire table and RELATED or RELATEDTABLE might be a better choice as it makes the syntax shorter for calculated columns.

Practice

Change the 2013Sales formula to return sales only for the Accessories product category. This will require joining FactInternetSales and DimProduct.

```
2013Sales = CALCULATE(SUM(FactInternetSales[SalesAmount]),
    FILTER(RELATEDTABLE(FactInternetSales),
    (YEAR(FactInternetSales[OrderDate])=2013 || ISBLANK(FactInternetSales[ShipDate]))
    && RELATED(DimProduct[EnglishProductCategoryName]) = "Accessories"))
```

Create a report that shows side by side DimCustomer[FullName] and 2013Sales (see **Figure 7.1**).

FullName	2013Sales
Aaron Adams	$63.97
Aaron Bryant	$74.98
Aaron Butler	$14.98
Aaron Campbell	$34.99
Aaron Carter	$39.98
Aaron Chen	$39.98
Aaron Coleman	$61.96
Aaron Collins	$34.99

Figure 7.1 The 2013Sales calculated column shows the customer's sales for year 2013 and Accessories product category.

Analysis

This formula uses the RELATED function to navigate the relationship between FactInternetSales and DimProduct to filter where the DimProduct[EnglishProductCategoryName] column is "Accessories". Notice that the formula uses the AND (&&) logical operator.

7.1.2   Using the CALCULATE Function

As explained in the previous lesson the CALCULATE function takes filter arguments.

```
CALCULATE ( <Expression> [, <Filter> [, <Filter> [, ... ] ] ] )
```

Therefore, in many cases you can use CALCULATE instead of FILTER for a shorter syntax and better performance.

Understanding filter arguments

CALCULATE evaluates the expression passed as the first argument in a context modified by the filter arguments. The filter argument can be one of these three types:

- Filter elimination – DAX functions, such as ALL and ALLEXCEPT, can remove filters.
- Filter restoration – The DAX function ALLSELECTED can ignore innermost filters but restore outer filters.
- Table expression – Similar to using the FILTER function, you can use a filter to narrow the context of the expression evaluation.

Each filter argument acts as an AND condition. For example, if you have two filter arguments, the filtered results must match both. Each argument can apply multiple filtering criteria, but they must use the same column.

Practice

Like the first practice in this lesson, create a new 2013SalesC column that returns 2013 sales for each customer using the CALCULATE function:

2013SalesC = CALCULATE(SUM(FactInternetSales[SalesAmount]), YEAR(FactInternetSales[OrderDate])=2013)

Analysis

The formula returns the same results as its FILTER counterpart, but it doesn't need the RELATED function to transition the row context. It may seem faster because it's more compact, but internally the formula engine will replace it with this formula:

2013SalesC = CALCULATE(SUM(FactInternetSales[SalesAmount]),
          FILTER(ALL(FactInternetSales[OrderDate]),
          YEAR(FactInternetSales[OrderDate])=2013))

Just like the FILTER version, the formula will scan the FactInternetSales[OrderDate] column, so it will be executed 1,124 times (the unique values in FactInternetSales[OrderDate]).

Practice

Change the 2013SalesC formula to include sales where OrderDate is empty. Then, replace Order-Date with ShipDate to include sales where ShipDate is empty.

2013SalesC = CALCULATE(SUM(FactInternetSales[SalesAmount]),
          YEAR(FactInternetSales[OrderDate])=2013 **|| FactInternetSales[OrderDate]=BLANK()**)

2013SalesC = CALCULATE(SUM(FactInternetSales[SalesAmount]),
          YEAR(FactInternetSales[OrderDate])=2013 **|| FactInternetSales[ShipDate]=BLANK()**)

Analysis

Notice that while the first formula works, the second fails with the error "The expression contains multiple columns, but only a single column can be used in a True/False expression that is used as a table filter expression". The reason for this error is that unlike the FILTER function, a filter argument in CALCULATE must reference the same column.

 NOTE A single filter condition involving two or more columns doesn't work with CALCULATE. For OR filters, use the FILTER function instead. For a better performance, consider FILTER (ALL(column1, column2), <conditions>).

Practice

Extend the 2013SalesC calculated column to include only sales where product category is accessories.

2013SalesC = CALCULATE(SUM(FactInternetSales[SalesAmount]),
        FILTER(ALL(FactInternetSales[OrderDate], FactInternetSales[ShipDate]),
          YEAR(FactInternetSales[OrderDate])=2013 || ISBLANK(FactInternetSales[ShipDate])),
        DimProduct[EnglishProductCategoryName] = "Accessories")

Analysis

Recall that CALULATE can take multiple filter arguments that act as AND filters. While you can include all filter conditions in a single FILTER function, you might get a better performance if you use separate AND filters if you need to filter on multiple columns. This formula uses the FILTER function for the OR filter as before. Because the product category filter is an AND filter (filter on the dates *and* category), the formula passes it as another filter argument.

Why is this faster? If you use the FILTER function for all conditions, the formula will scan all the rows in FactInternetSales. By breaking it into two filters, the formula will scan 1,124 rows (the FILTER function with the OR condition), and 158 rows (the number of unique values in the FactInternetSales[ProductKey] column).

 TIP When you need multiple AND filters on different columns, test performance with a single FILTER function and multiple filters in CALCULATE. The chances are that multiple filters will perform better with larger tables.

Practice

Change the 2013SalesC formula to return sales for product categories Accessories or Sales.

2013SalesC = CALCULATE(SUM(FactInternetSales[SalesAmount]),
    FILTER(ALL(FactInternetSales[OrderDate], FactInternetSales[ShipDate]),
    YEAR(FactInternetSales[OrderDate])=2013
    || ISBLANK(FactInternetSales[ShipDate])),
    DimProduct[EnglishProductCategoryName] **IN {"Accessories", "Bikes"}**)

Analysis

To keep the syntax shorter, use the IN operator to filter on multiple values. Notice that the IN operator requires curly braces to surround the values. Text values need to be surrounded with quotes.

7.2 Removing Filters

Sometimes, your formula may require removing filters. This is especially useful for measures, such as to calculate "percent of total" measures, but you might need to remove filters in calculated columns too.

7.2.1 Understanding the "ALL" Functions

Table 7.2 shows the most common DAX functions to remove existing filters.

Table 7.2   These three functions are commonly used to remove filters.

Filter Function	Description
ALL	Ignores all filters and returns all rows in table or column.

Filter Function	Description
ALLEXCEPT	Ignores all filters and returns all rows in table or column except specified columns that retain their filters.
ALLSELECTED	Removes context filters from columns and rows in the current query, while retaining all other context filters or explicit filters.

Understanding the ALL function
The ALL function has the following definition:

ALL([<table> | <column>[, <column>[, <column>[,...]]]])

It takes either a table (as a single argument) or one or more columns. When a table is used as an argument, it ignores all filters and returns all rows in the table. When used with columns, it removes their filters but retains filters on other columns in the table. In the previous practices in this lesson, you used the ALL function to remove active filters from OrderDate and ShipDate columns.

Understanding the ALLEXCEPT function
This function has the following syntax:

ALLEXCEPT (TableName, <ColumnName> [, <ColumnName> [, ...]])

ALLEXCEPT removes active filters from the table passed as the first argument but retains active filters on the columns specified as subsequent arguments. It's useful when you want to avoid specifying many columns in the ALL function. For example, these two formulas produce the same results over a table with three columns.

ALL(table, column1, column2)
ALLEXCEPT(table, column3)

Understanding the ALLSELECTED function
The syntax of ALLSELECTED is:

ALLSELECTED([<tableName> | <columnName>])

This function takes either a table or a column as a single argument. ALLSELECTED is typically used for measures to produce visual totals.

7.2.2 Applying and Removing Filters

Let's practice what we've learned by creating a formula that finds duplicate values in a table column. This could be useful to determine which value(s) prevents a column to serve as a primary key in a dimension table that you want to join to a fact table. The ProductAlternateKey column in DimProduct represents the business key that is used in the source system to identify a product. Because some historical changes, such as changing the product price, are significant, the modeler has decided to treat these changes as Type 2 changes. When a change is detected in these columns, a new row is added to the table for that product. The Status column is set to "Current" to the latest "version" of the row. Therefore, ProductAlternateKey may contain duplicate values.

Practice
In your first attempt, you can come up with the following formula for the RowCount calculated column:

RowCount = COUNTROWS(FILTER(DimProduct, DimProduct[ProductAlternateKey] = DimProduct[ProductAlternateKey]))

Outcome

This formula doesn't work and returns the same number (606) in every row in DimProduct. That's because the FILTER function iterates over all rows in DimProduct and each row meets the condition (a column value always equals itself). Knowing about filter transition, your second attempt could be to surround the entire formula with CALCULATE only to find that now the RowCount calculated column returns 1 in each row. As a consolation prize, you managed to propagate the row context to DimProduct so that only the "current" product is filtered. One way to produce the correct results is a two-step approach:

1. Remember the value of the ProductAlternateKey column for the current product.
2. Find other rows that have the same value.

Practice

Change the formula as follows:

```
RowCount = COUNTROWS(FILTER(DimProduct,
DimProduct[ProductAlternateKey] = EARLIER(DimProduct[ProductAlternateKey])))
```

This formula works as you can see by expanding the dropdown in the header of the ProductAlternateKey column. Most rows have RowCount=1 but there are duplicate rows where the count is 2 and 3. The EARLIER function retrieves the outer context for the current row (before the FILTER function iterates the row). Think of this as the first pass in the two-step evaluation. However, the EARLIER function should be avoided because of its complexity and unexpected side effects. Instead, use a variable that accomplishes the same result.

```
RowCount = VAR CurrentProduct = DimProduct[ProductAlternateKey]
          RETURN
          COUNTROWS(FILTER(DimProduct, DimProduct[ProductAlternateKey] = CurrentProduct ) )
```

Analysis

I'll discuss variables in more detail in the second part of the book. For now, think of a variable as a constant that is evaluated once for each row in the row context (once for each product being iterated). Like EARLIER, the CurrentProduct variable returns the value of ProductAlternateKey in that row context.

Practice

Yet, another way to accomplish the same result is to use the ALLEXCEPT function.

```
RowCount = CALCULATE (COUNTROWS(), ALLEXCEPT(DimProduct, DimProduct[ProductAlternateKey]))
```

Create a report, such as the one shown in **Figure 7.2**, that shows DimProduct[ProductKey], DimProduct[EnglishProductName], and RowCount, to test the RowCount calculated column.

ProductKey	EnglishProductName	RowCount
212	Sport-100 Helmet, Red	3
213	Sport-100 Helmet, Red	3
214	Sport-100 Helmet, Red	3
215	Sport-100 Helmet, Black	3
216	Sport-100 Helmet, Black	3
217	Sport-100 Helmet, Black	3
220	Sport-100 Helmet, Blue	3

Figure 7.2 The RowCount calculated column shows the count of rows with the same ProductAlternateKey.

Analysis

The ALLEXCEPT function removes the filter context for all columns except ProductAlternateKey. COUNTROWS without an argument instructs the function to count rows in the current table, which is the same as COUNTROWS(DimProduct). COUNTROWS is executed for each product but it retains the filter context (current product). The net result is counting rows in the table where ProductAlternateKey equals the key of the current row.

7.3   Summary

Filtering is an important concept in DAX. DAX has an assortment of functions for adding or removing filters. I recommend you rely most on the CALCULATE function because it has the simplest syntax and it might give you the best performance. For more complicated filter conditions, use the FILTER function. Use the ALL, ALLEXCEPT, and ALLSELECTED functions to remove filters when needed.

Lesson 8

Grouping and Binning Values

Calculated columns are especially useful for grouping and binning data, such as to analyze customer sales by age buckets. This lesson starts by showing you the Power BI built-in capabilities for grouping and binning. Then it shows you how to apply your own DAX formulas when you need more control. You'll find the DAX formulas for this lesson in \Source\Part2\Grouping and Binning.dax.

8.1 Applying Grouping and Binning

Dynamic grouping allows you to create your own groups, such as to group countries with negligible sales in the "Others" category. In addition to grouping categories together, you can also create bins (also referred to as buckets or bands) from numerical and time fields, such as to segment customers by revenue or to create aging buckets.

8.1.1 Implementing Groups

Consider the two charts shown in **Figure 8.1**. The chart on the left displays sales by country. Because European countries have lower sales, you might want to group them together in the European Countries group, as shown on the right.

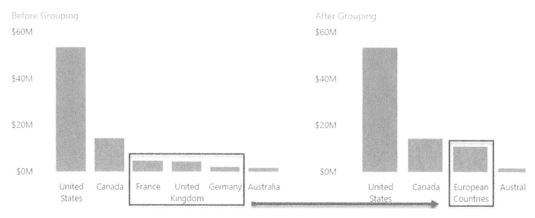

Figure 8.1   The second chart groups European countries together.

Creating a group
Follow these steps to implement the group:

1. Create a Stacked Column Chart with DimSalesTerritory[SalesTerritoryCountry] in the Axis area and FactResellerSales[SalesAmount] in the Values area.

2. Hold the Ctrl key and click each of the data categories you want to group. Currently, only charts support this way of selecting group members. To group elements in tables or matrices, expand the drop-down next to the field in the Visualizations pane (or click the ellipses button in the Field list), and click New Group.

3. Right-click any of the selected countries and click Group from the context menu. Power BI Desktop adds a new SalesTerritoryCountry (group) field to the DimSalesTerritory table. This field represents the custom group and it's prefixed with a double-square icon. Power BI Desktop adds the field to the chart's Legend area.

4. In the Fields pane, click the ellipsis (…) button next to SalesTerritoryCountry (group). Click Rename and change the field name to *European Countries*.

Editing a group

To make changes to an existing group:

1. Click the ellipsis (…) button next to the European Countries field and then click Edit Groups.

2. In the Groups window (see **Figure 8.2**), you can change the group name and see the grouped and ungrouped members. If the "Include Other group" checkbox is checked (default setting), the rest of the data categories (Canada and United States) will be grouped into an "Other" group.

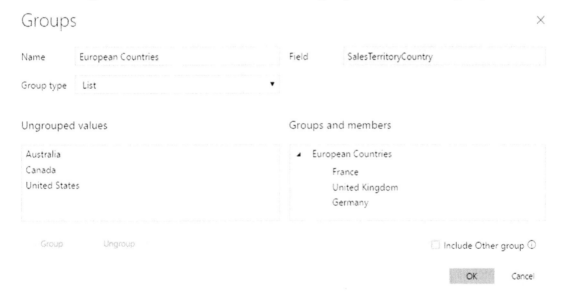

Figure 8.2 Use the Groups window to view the grouped values and make changes.

3. Uncheck the "Include Other group" checkbox so that Canada and United States show as separate data categories. Click OK.

4. Back to the report, remove SalesTerritoryCountry from the Axis area. Add the European Countries field to the Axis area. Compare your report with the right chart shown in **Figure 8.1**.

> **TIP** Although Power BI Desktop doesn't currently support lassoing categories as a faster way of selecting many items, you can use the Groups window to select and add values to the group. Instead of clicking elements on the chart, right-click the corresponding field in the Fields pane and then click New Group to open the Groups window. Select the values in the "Ungrouped values" (hold the Shift key for extended selection) and then click the Group button to create a new group.

8.1.2 Implementing Bins

Besides grouping categories, Power BI Desktop is also capable of discretizing numeric values or dates in equally sized ranges called *bins*.

Understanding binning

Suppose you want to group customers in different bins based on the customer's overall sales, such as $0-$99, $100-$200, and so on (see the chart's X-axis in **Figure 8.3**). This report counts distinct values of CustomerAlternateKey field (the business key of the DimCustomer table). This requires navigating the FactInternetSales[CustomerKey] ⇨ DimCustomer[CustomerKey] relationship because the SalesAmount field in the FactInternetSales table will become the "dimension" while the measure (Count of Customers) comes from the Customer table.

Figure 8.3 This report counts customers in bin sizes of $100 based on their overall sales.

Creating the bins

Follow these steps to create the report:

1. In the Model View, if the FactInternetSales[CustomerKey] ⇨ DimCustomer[CustomerKey] relationship has a single arrow (cross filter direction is Single), double-click it to open the Edit Relationship window and change the "Cross filter direction" drop-down to Both. Consequently, you can filter data in DimCustomer by fields in FactInternetSales. Click OK.

2. Switch to the Report View tab (or Data View tab). In the Fields pane, click the ellipsis (…) button next to the SalesAmount field in the FactInternetSales table and then click New Group.

3. In the Groups window, change the bin size to 100 (you're grouping customers in bins of $100). Give the group a descriptive name, such as *SalesAmount (bins),* and then click OK.

4. Add a Stacked Column Chart visualization. Add the "SalesAmount (bins)" field that you've just created to the Axis area of the Visualizations pane (you'll be grouping the chart data points by the new field).

5. Add the DimCustomer[CustomerAlternateKey] field to the Value area. Expand the drop-down next to the CustomerAlternateKey field in the Value area and switch the aggregation to Count (Distinct). Compare your results with **Figure 8.3**.

8.2   Creating Custom Groups

Power BI implements grouping and binning as calculated columns, but it hides the column formula to avoid breaking the user interface if you change the formula. However, it could be interesting to see the actual formula so you can learn from it but there is no easy way to script a Power BI Desktop file.

 TIP   You can try the approach that I outlined in my "Upgrading Power BI Desktop Models to Tabular" blog at https://prologika.com/upgrading-power-bi-desktop-models-to-tabular/ to script a Power BI Desktop file. Even easier, if you publish the Power BI Desktop file to a Power BI Premium workspace, you can directly connect SQL Server Management Studio (SSMS) to it and script the published dataset.

8.2.1   Analyzing Power BI Groups and Bins

Power BI generated two calculated columns: FactInternetSales[SalesAmount (bins)] and DimSalesTerritory[European Countries]. Let's examine the formulas which I obtained by using SSMS to script the Adventure Works model that I had published to powerbi.com.

Analyzing the binning formula
Let's start with the FactInternetSales[SalesAmount (bins)] formula as it's easier to understand:

```
IF(ISBLANK('FactInternetSales'[SalesAmount]), BLANK(), INT('FactInternetSales'[SalesAmount] / 100) * 100)
```

This formula uses the IF statement to check if SalesAmount for the current customer is empty (blank) by using the ISBLANK function. If this is the case, the BLANK function returns an empty value. Otherwise, it divides SalesAmount by 100 to get rid of the last two digits since the bin size you specified was 100. Then, it uses the INT function to convert the result to an integer value and removes the decimal places. Finally, it multiplies the result by 100. So, if the sales amount is 4,234.34, it will be assigned to the bin with a left boundary of 4,200.

Analyzing the grouping formula
And here is the formula behind the European Countries group:

```
SWITCH(TRUE,
    ISBLANK('DimSalesTerritory'[SalesTerritoryCountry]), "(Blank)",
    'DimSalesTerritory'[SalesTerritoryCountry] IN {"France", "United Kingdom","Germany"}, "European Countries",
    'DimSalesTerritory'[SalesTerritoryCountry])
```

To avoid multiple nested IF functions, this expression uses the SWITCH function, which has this syntax:

```
SWITCH(<expression>, <value>, <result>[, <value>, <result>]...[, <else>])
```

Like the SELECT CASE statement in SQL, the SWITCH function takes an expression as a first argument and compares it to the values passed as additional arguments. If a match is found, SWITCH returns the result corresponding to the matched value. Because the values are produced by formulas, Power BI uses a handy trick to pass TRUE as the expression argument, thus causing all conditions to be evaluated. The first condition checks if the country is blank and assigns it to a "(Blank)" group if that's the case. Otherwise, if the country is one of the European countries, it returns "European Countries". If none of these conditions are met, the original country name is returned.

8.2.2 Implementing Custom Groups

Power BI grouping and binning are convenient features, but they lack in flexibility. For example, you can't configure specific boundaries. Now that you've seen how Power BI generates groups and bins, let's use this knowledge to create your own groups. As an example, you'll bucket the Adventure Works customers in age groups, such as "0-20", "21-40", "41-60", and "61 and above".

Practice
The DimCustomer table doesn't have an Age column. Start by creating an Age calculated column using this formula:

Age = DATEDIFF(DimCustomer[BirthDate], TODAY(), YEAR)

This formula uses the DATEDIFF function, which computes the difference between two dates using the interval you specify as the third argument. Like Excel, the TODAY function returns the system date without time. If you need the system time, you can use the NOW function.

Now that we have the Age column, create a new "Age (groups)" calculated column with this formula:

```
Age (groups) = SWITCH (TRUE,
           [Age]<=20, "0-20",
           [Age]>20 && [Age]<=40, "21-40",
           [Age]>40 && [Age]<=60, "41-60",
           [Age]>60, "61 and above",
           "Other" )
```

Output
The new formula assigns every customer to an age group depending on the customer's age. To test the calculated column, create a chart report that has FactInternetSales[SalesAmount] in the Value area and "Age (groups)" in the Axis area (see **Figure 8.4**). Observe that most sales are contributed by customers in the 41-60 age group.

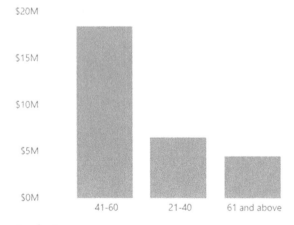

Figure 8.4 This report groups sales by the age groups.

Analysis
Like the formula generated by Power BI, the "Age (groups)" formula uses the SWITCH function to check which group the customer's age falls in. If none of the conditions are met, the customer is assigned to the "Other" group.

As an optional practice, use a similar approach to create a Tier calculated column that assigns each customer to a tier based on the DimCustomer[SalesRank] calculated column you implemented before.

8.3 Summary

Calculated columns are one option for implementing custom groups and bins (the other options are Power Query or custom SQL). Consider custom groups to meet more advanced requirements than auto-generated Power BI groups and bins can provide.

Lesson 9

Implementing Calculated Tables

Besides calculated columns, Power BI supports calculated tables. This lesson starts by explaining what a calculated table is and when to consider it. Then, it walks you through a few examples for implementing calculated tables to handle role-playing dimensions, generate date tables, and improve performance. You'll find the DAX formulas for this lesson in \Source\Part2\Calculated Tables.dax.

9.1   Understanding Calculated Tables

If you have used Power BI Desktop for a while, you've probably noticed that it's a versatile tool and there are usually different options to accomplish a given task. For example, I've already explained that you have at least three options to implement a custom column: calculated column, Power Query, and custom SQL. Custom tables are no exception.

9.1.1   What Is a Calculated Table?

Like a calculated column, a calculated table is a custom table that's based on a DAX formula. The DAX formula must return a table, such as by using FILTER, SUMMARIZECOLUMNS, CALCULATETABLE, or other DAX table-producing functions. You create a calculated table by using the New Table button in the Power BI Desktop Modeling ribbon.

 TIP   Don't confuse the New Table button in the Modeling ribbon with the Enter Data button in the Home ribbon. The latter is for creating Power Query tables by entering explicit values, such as in the case when you need a reference table and you prefer to enter the column values manually. Once the "Enter Data" table is imported, it becomes just like a regular table. By contrast, calculated tables are produced with DAX formulas and you can't enter the data directly. And they don't have a query behind them.

Understanding storage
In its simplest syntax, you introduce a calculated table by just referencing an existing table without any modifications, such as in this example that creates a DimShipDate calculated table by referencing the DimDate table:

DimShipDate = DimDate

You may think that DAX creates just a shortcut to DimDate without duplicating the DimDate data. However, behind the scenes, Power BI copies the data into a new DimShipDate table. Specifically, it copies all the columns and their values. It then compresses the data. Once the formula is evaluated and the table is created, you can see it in the Fields pane. You can browse its data in the Data View tab and even add calculated columns to it. The following restrictions apply to calculated tables:

- You can't remove columns from calculated tables in the Fields pane. You need to change the DAX formula to exclude columns.

- A calculated table doesn't have a query. You need to change the DAX formula, such as to filter some rows.

- A calculated table can't be explicitly refreshed.

- The data in the calculated table can't depend on runtime conditions, such as user selection in filters or slicers. Like calculated columns, the reason for this is that calculated tables are evaluated and stored before the report is run.

Refreshing calculated tables
Like calculated columns, Power BI automatically refreshes calculated tables according to their dependencies to other tables. For example, the DimShipDate table will be automatically updated when you refresh the DimDate table. So, a calculated table is always up to date with the imported data in the model and there is nothing you need to do to synchronize it.

Unlike calculated columns, which may not compress so well, calculated tables compress their columns like native columns. Specifically, when Power BI refreshes a calculated table, it iterates over the rows from the table returned by the DAX formula just like it does when it refreshes a regular table (when it iterates over the rows coming from the data source).

9.1.2 Considering Calculated Tables

Calculated tables can help in certain scenarios but don't overuse them. Keep in mind these considerations when you're evaluating calculated tables.

When to use calculated tables
A common scenario for using a calculated table is producing additional date tables. I've previously said that Power BI supports only one active relationship between two tables. But if you want to let users analyze sales by Ship Date or Due Date? One option is to clone DimDate. Dimensional methodology refers to such dimension tables as *role-playing dimensions* because the same dimension table plays multiple roles. You can duplicate tables in DAX, SQL or Power Query. Like calculated columns, the choice depends on several factors, such as your skillset and the level of transformations required.

 TIP Speaking of date tables, you can use a calculated table and DAX functions, such as CALENDAR and CALENDARAUTO, to quickly generate a date table if you don't have one in your data warehouse database or Excel. The practice in this lesson demonstrates these two functions.

Another reason to use calculated tables is to simplify or speed up DAX calculations. For example, you might have a large Customer table and you want to produce a report that shows the count of customers who subscribed to your company's services by month. Instead of querying the Customer table directly, you can add a calculated table that summarizes the results.

Lastly, when testing complex DAX formulas, it might be easier to store the intermediate results in a calculated table and see whether the formulas work as expected.

When not to use calculated tables
To start with, calculated tables are not a replacement for complex data transformations. For example, if you need multiple steps to shape the data, it might be better to do this in Power Query or SQL. More involved data preparation tasks might even require external data transformation processes developed by a BI pro.

Like calculated columns, calculated tables add up to the overall refresh time of your data model. And so will transformations in Power Query. You need to test the refresh time with different implementation options for implementing custom tables.

Moving down the list, calculated tables are evaluated and saved before reports run. Therefore, their DAX formulas can't evaluate runtime conditions, such as selected values in filters or slicers. Only DAX measures can evaluate such conditions.

9.2　Working with Calculated Tables

Now that you know about calculated tables, let's go through a few exercises to practice common scenarios that could benefit from them.

9.2.1　Implementing Role-playing Dimensions

Suppose you want to analyze sales by the order ship date. Recall that both FactInternetSales and FactResellerSales join DimDate on the OrderDateKey. Since now you need to join the tables on another column, you have two options to support this requirement:

- Create measures that navigate inactive relationships – You can create measures, such as ShipSalesAmount and ShipOrderQuantity that use the USERELATIONSHIP function to travel the inactive relationship on ShipDate. This might be a preferable approach when you want to use the existing date table exactly as it is. On the downside, it requires additional measures. The practice in this lesson demonstrates how to use USERELATIONSHIP.

- Add a DimShipDate table – You can duplicate DimDate and rename it to *ShipDate*. You can implement this with a DAX calculated table, Power Query, or custom SQL.

Practice
Let's add a new DimShipDate table as a DAX calculated table.

1. In the Modeling ribbon, click New Table.

2. In the formula bar enter the following formula and press Enter:

DimShipDate = DimDate

3. Power BI adds a new DimShipDate table to the Fields pane.

4. Create a new inactive relationship FactInternetSales[ShipDate] ⇨ DimShipDate[Date] (or FactInternetSales[ShipDateKey] ⇨ DimShipDate[DateKey])

Output
Create a new report for analyzing FactInternetSales[SalesAmount] by DimShipDate[CalendarYear].

CalendarYear	SalesAmount
2011	$6,978,821
2012	$5,801,073
2013	$16,281,620
2014	$297,163
Total	**$29,358,677**

Figure 9.1 This report shows sales grouped by the CalendarYear column in the DimShipDate calculated table.

Analysis
The DimShipDate table behaves just like any other table. You can extend the table by adding hierarchies or calculated columns. You can also hide columns you don't need.

Practice

As a progression from the previous practice, change the DimShipDate formula to return only ship dates that exist in the FactInternetSales[ShipDate] column. This requires a more involved formula:

```
DimShipDate = FILTER(
              ADDCOLUMNS(
                  CALCULATETABLE( DimDate ,
                      USERELATIONSHIP(FactInternetSales[ShipDateKey], DimDate[DateKey])),
                  "RowCount", CALCULATE(COUNTROWS(FactInternetSales)))
              , NOT ISBLANK([RowCount]))
```

Output

Observe that the DimShipDate table now has only 1,124 rows compared to 3,652 rows in DimDate. The rest of the dates don't exist in FactInternetSales.

Analysis

To understand complicated formulas, it might make sense to work your way from the innermost formula outward. The CALCULATETABLE function uses the USERELATIONSHIP function to navigate the FactInternetSales[ShipDateKey] ⇨ DimDate[DateKey] inactive relationship.

Then the ADDCOLUMNS function is used to add (project) a new column (RowCount) to Dim-Date that returns count of rows in FactInternetSales that are related to the iterated row in DimDate. The RowCount column is a temporary expression-based column that only exists within the formula. As you know by now, when the formula uses an iterator function, such as ADDCOLUMNS, it needs CALCULATE to propagate the row context. Finally, the FILTER function removes rows where RowCount is blank.

 NOTE Removing rows from a date table may result in gaps that will make it an invalid date table. Consequently, time calculations and quick measures for time intelligence won't work. A date table can't have gaps, as I explain in more detail in the "Working with Date Tables" lesson.

9.2.2 Generating Date Tables

You can use a simple DAX formula to quickly generate a date table if you don't have one in your data warehouse database. DAX has two functions for this purpose:

```
CALENDAR (<StartDate>, <EndDate>)
CALENDARAUTO ([FiscalYearEndMonth])
```

CALENDAR returns a calculated table with a single "Date" column containing a consecutive range of dates between the StartDate and EndDate you specify as arguments. CALENDARAUTO scans all tables in the model to find the earliest and latest dates by evaluating all date columns that are not calculated columns or included in calculated tables. Then, it calls the CALENDAR function passing these two dates as arguments.

CALENDARAUTO takes an optional FiscalYearEndMonth argument to let you specify the last month of your fiscal year. For example, if the earliest discovered StartDate is March 15, 2010 and EndDate is April 27, 2019, CALENDARAUTO(6) returns a date range between March 15, 2010 and June 30, 2020, so you have enough dates until the end of the fiscal year.

 TIP A designated date table in a corporate data warehouse or being available as a shared Power BI dataset managed by a data steward is a best practice. Such a table allows you to incorporate features that are very hard to implement with Power Query or DAX, such as manufacturing calendars, holiday flags, non-working days, and others.

Practice

Suppose your company doesn't have a data warehouse and you're looking for a quick way to generate a date table in your model. You want your date table to automatically add rows as new dates appear in the tables, but you want to avoid spurious dates that are outside a reasonable range (starting in 2010 and ending in one year from the system date) and that are probably introduced by data quality issues. Let's assume that your company's fiscal year ends in June. Create a new DimMyDate calculated table with this formula:

DimMyDate = FILTER(CALENDARAUTO(6), YEAR([Date])>=2010 && YEAR([Date]) <= YEAR(TODAY()+1))

As an optional step, add calculated columns for Year and Month that use the DAX functions YEAR and MONTH respectively.

Output

The DimMyDate table in the Adventure Works model has a single column (Date) that contains a consecutive range of dates between January 1, 2010 and June 30, 2010.

Analysis

Without the FILTER function, CALENDARAUTO(6) returns dates starting in 1915, but the FILTER function limits the range starting in year 2010 and ending in one year from the system date. However, because the maximum date across all tables is in year 2015, the end date of the calculated table is June 30, 2015.

9.2.3 Creating Summarized Tables

The DateFirstPurchase column in the DimCustomer records the date when the customer bought something for the first time. Let's create a summary table that shows the count of new customers by month.

Practice

To simplify the formula for the calculate table, start by adding a calculated column to DimCustomer.

1. Add a MonthJoined calculated column to DimCustomer with this formula:

MonthJoined = EOMONTH(DimCustomer[DateFirstPurchase], 0)

The EOMONTH function returns the month's end date from the DateFirstPurchase column without offsetting the date (the second argument is 0).

2. In the Modeling ribbon, click "New Table" and enter this formula in the formula bar:

CustomerBase = SUMMARIZECOLUMNS(DimCustomer[MonthJoined], "CustomerCount", COUNTROWS(DimCustomer))

MonthJoined	CustomerCount
5/31/13	1141
7/31/13	1052
1/31/12	252
10/31/13	1134
8/31/13	1074
'30/1⁻	⁻154

Figure 9.2 The CustomerBase calculated table summarizes the count of customers by month based on the date of first purchase.

Output

The CustomerBase calculated table stores the count of customers by month (see **Figure 9.2**).

Analysis

The DAX SUMMARIZECOLUMNS function allows you to group tables (like the GROUP BY clause in SQL). The formula uses SUMMARIZECOLUMNS to group DimCustomer by the MonthJoined column. Like ADDCOLUMNS, SUMMARIZECOLUMNS lets you add temporary measures by specifying the measure name and formula. In this case, the formula adds a new measure named "CustomerCount" that counts rows. Because SUMMARIZECOLUMNS is not an iterator, CALCULATE is not required but the formula will produce the same results if you include it.

9.3   Summary

A DAX calculated table is an expression-based table that you can use like any other regular table. You specify a formula that returns a table and Power BI takes care of recalculating the table when dependent tables are refreshed. You can use calculated tables to implement role-playing dimensions, date tables, and summary tables.

Measures

A data model is rarely complete without important business metrics. Power BI promotes rapid personal business intelligence (BI) for essential data exploration and analysis. Chances are, however, that in real life you might need to go beyond just simple aggregations, such as counting and summing. Business needs might require you to extend your model with metrics that go beyond summing and counting fields. This is where DAX measures come in. They give you the needed programmatic power to travel the "last mile" and unlock the full potential of Power BI.

This part of the book teaches you how to implement measures. After introducing you to measures, it shows you how to create basic measures. Then, it moves to more advanced concepts, such as restricting and ignoring the filter context, as well as grouping and filtering data.

You'll find the completed exercises and reports for this part of the book in the Adventure Works model that is included in the \Source\Part3 folder.

Lesson 10

Understanding Measures

Besides calculated columns, you can use DAX to define measures. Unlike calculated columns, which might be avoided by using other implementation approaches, measures typically can't be replicated in any other way – they need to be written in DAX. DAX measures are very useful because they typically aggregate data, such as to summarize a SalesAmount column or to calculate a distinct count of customers with sales.

This lesson will help you understand how DAX measures work and what types of measures are supported by Power BI. I'll revisit the filter context because it's very important for measures. You'll also learn how measures compare to calculated columns and when to use each. You'll find the DAX formulas for this lesson in \Source\Part3\Understanding Measures.dax.

10.1 Understanding DAX Measures

I'll define a DAX measure as a runtime calculation that uses a DAX formula. The most important word in this definition is "runtime", which means that Power BI executes the measure formula when the report runs. Unlike calculated columns, measures never store their formula results. And this makes measures much more flexible than calculated columns.

10.1.1 Revisiting Filter Context

Recall that every DAX expression is evaluated in a specific context which consists of a row context and a filter context. The row context is typically associated with calculated columns because their formulas are evaluated for each iterated row in the home table. On the other hand, the filter context is the default context for measures but DAX iterator functions, such as FILTER or SUMX, introduce a row context.

Visualizing filter context
DAX measures are evaluated *at runtime* for each report *cell* as opposed to calculated columns which are evaluated once for each table row. Moreover, measures are evaluated in the filter context of each cell, as shown in **Figure 10.1**.

Figure 10.1 Measures are evaluated for each cell, and they operate in the cell filter context.

This report summarizes the SalesAmount measure by countries on rows and by years on columns. The report is further filtered to show only sales for the Bikes product category. The filter context of the highlighted cell is the Germany value of the DimSalesTerritory[SalesTerritoryCountry] field (on rows), the 2008 value of the DimDate[CalendarYear] field (on columns), and the Bikes value of the DimProduct[ProductCategory] field (used as a filter).

Although measures are associated with a table, they don't show in the Data View's data preview pane as calculated columns do. Instead, they're only accessible in the Fields pane. When used on reports, measures are typically added to the Value area of the Visualizations pane.

Relating filter context to SQL WHERE

If you're familiar with the SQL language, you can think of the DAX filter context as a SQL WHERE clause that limits the scope of the query. Going back to the report shown in **Figure 10.1**, when Power BI calculates the expression for that cell, it scopes the formula accordingly, such as to sum the sales amount from the rows in the FactResellerSales table where the SalesTerritoryCountry value is Germany, the CalendarYear value is 2008, and the ProductCategory value is Bikes.

NOTE Remember that every DAX measure is evaluated in both row and filter contexts. Simple measure formulas might not have row context but measures that use iterators do. For example, as SUMX(<table>, <expression>) iterates through the rows in the table passed as the first argument, it propagates the row context to the expression passed as the second argument.

10.1.2 Understanding Measure Types

Although Power BI hides the formula, every time you drop a field in the Values area of a visual, Power BI creates an implicit measure. You can also create explicit measures by entering your own DAX formulas.

Understanding measure types

Power BI Desktop supports two types of measures:

- Implicit measures – To get you started as quickly as possible with data analysis, Microsoft felt that you shouldn't have to write formulas for basic aggregations. Any field added to the Value area of the Visualizations pane is treated as an implicit measure and is automatically aggregated based on the column data type. For example, numeric fields are summed while text fields are counted.

- Explicit measures – You'll create explicit measures when you need an aggregation behavior that goes beyond the standard aggregation functions. For example, you might need a year-to-date (YTD) calculation. Explicit measures are measures that have a custom DAX formula you specify.

When to use measures

In general, measures are most frequently used to aggregate data. Explicit measures are typically used when you need a custom aggregation, such as time calculations, aggregates over aggregates, variances, and weighted averages. Suppose you want to calculate year-to-date (YTD) of reseller sales. As a first attempt, you might decide to add a SalesAmountYTD calculated column to the Fact-ResellerSales table. But now you have an issue because each row in this table represents an order line item. It's meaningless to calculate YTD for each line item.

As a second attempt, you could create a summary table in the database that stores YTD sales at a specific grain, such as product, end of month, reseller, and so on. While this might be a good approach for report performance, it presents issues. What if you need to lower the grain to include other dimensions? What if your requirements change and now YTD needs to be calculated as of any date? A better approach would be to use an explicit measure that's evaluated dynamically as users slice and dice the data. And don't worry too much about performance. Thanks to the memory-resident nature of the storage engine, most DAX calculations are instantaneous!

 NOTE The performance of DAX measures depends on several factors, including the complexity of the formula, your knowledge of DAX (and how efficient the formulas are), the amount of data, and even the hardware of your computer. While most measures, such as time calculations and basic filtered aggregations, should perform very well, more involved calculations, such as aggregates over aggregates or the number of open orders as of any reporting date, will probably be more expensive.

Comparing calculated columns and measures

Beginner DAX practitioners often confuse calculated columns and measures. They start with a calculated column (because it's easier to work with since you see the results), find that it doesn't produce expected results, then copy the formula into a measure, and get disappointed that it still doesn't work. Although calculated columns and measures use DAX, their behavior and purpose are completely different. **Table 10.1** should help you understand these differences.

Table 10.1 Comparing calculated columns and measures.

	Calculated Column	Measure
Evaluation	Design time (before reports are run)	Run time (when reports run)
Typical context	Row context (and sometimes filter context)	Filter context (and row context with iterators, such as SUMX)
Storage	Formula results are stored	No storage
Performance impact	Increase refresh time (for imported data)	Increase report execution time
Alternative implementation	Possibly Power Query or custom SQL (unless DAX formulas are required)	Usually no alternatives
Typical usage	Row-based expressions, lookups	Custom aggregation, such as YTD, QTD, weighted averages

The most important difference is that Power BI automatically evaluates calculated columns when data is refreshed (assuming that data is imported) but *before* reports run. Therefore, formulas in calculated columns can't access runtime conditions, such as the identity of the user who runs the report or filters that are set by the interactive user. If this is what you're after, you need a measure and not a calculated column.

From a performance standpoint, the performance of a calculated column is no different than any other column, but calculated columns may increase the table refresh time assuming that data is imported. By contrast, measures always impact the report execution time because they don't have storage and their formulas are evaluated at runtime.

Because measures are dynamic, you can change their home table (the table in which the measure appears in the Fields pane) at any time. Just click the measure in the Fields pane to select it. Then, in the ribbon's Modeling tab, use the Home Table dropdown (Properties group) to change the table. Switching the measure home table doesn't affect the measure. By contrast, a calculated column is always bound to the table where the calculated column is defined.

10.2 Quiz: Calculated Column or Measure?

Now that you know about measures and how they compare to calculated columns, let's go through a few brainstorming exercises to see if we could implement a calculated column with a measure and vice versa.

10.2.1 Evaluating Calculated Columns as Measures

You have quite a few calculated columns implemented already. You'll go through a few of them and check if they could be converted to measures.

Concatenating fields
In Lesson 1, you implemented a DimCustomer[FullName] calculated column to concatenate Dim-Customer[FirstName] and DimCustomer[LastName]. Could you implement it as a measure? The answer is that although you could, you probably shouldn't. Technically, we can implement it as a measure whose most basic formula would be:

FullName (m) = SELECTEDVALUE(DimCustomer[FirstName]) & " " & SELECTEDVALUE(DimCustomer[LastName])

The SELECTEDVALUE function returns the value of a column when it's filtered down to only a single row. Remember that measures are dynamic, and their formula output depends on the actual report. What happens if we have a report that has the FirstName and LastName columns? The measure will return the expected result, except that the report will show all customers. For example, if a Table visual has FirstName, LastName, FullName, and SalesAmount, the report will show all customers irrespective if they have sales or not.

 TIP By default, all Power BI visuals remove rows and columns that don't have data. To change this behavior, expand the dropdown next to the field in whatever area of the Visualizations pane it's located, and select "Show items with no data".

But what if the report doesn't include FirstName and LastName columns at all? Then, the measure will return nothing. In this case, you don't want the measure output to depend on the data used in the report. So, in this case, a measure is probably not a good choice.

Relating fields
You implemented FactResellerSales[NetProfit] as a calculated column with the following formula:

NetProfit = [LineTotal] - (RELATED(DimProduct[StandardCost]) * FactResellerSales[OrderQuantity])

The tricky part was looking up the product cost from DimProduct for every row in FactReseller-Sales. This calculated column can be converted as a measure. If the product cost is not available in FactResellerSales, you can use the following formula:

NetProfit (m) = SUMX(FactResellerSales, [LineTotal] - (RELATED(DimProduct[StandardCost]) *
FactResellerSales[OrderQuantity]))

This works because SUMX is an iterator function. For every cell in the report, the formula finds the qualifying rows in FactResellerSales, iterates each row and looks up the product cost using the RELATED function. You'll incur a runtime hit for navigating the FactResellerSales[ProductKey] ⇨ DimProduct[ProductKey]. This may add up if the DimProduct table has millions of products, but it will save storage cost for the calculated column and reduce refresh time.

If the product cost is already available in FactResellerSales, then the measure formula becomes simpler and more efficient because you don't need to navigate relationships. As it turns out, there is a column TotalProductCost in FactResellerSales which you can use for this purpose:

NetProfit (m) = SUMX(FactResellerSales, [LineTotal] – FactResellerSales[TotalProductCost])

 TIP Sometimes, the choice between a calculated column and a measure is a tradeoff between convenience and performance. Often, the best approach is the middle road. Look up and save specific columns, such as ProductCost, in the fact table, even if this results in redundant data (product cost is now in both DimProduct and FactResellerSales). Then, save storage and reduce refresh times by using measures instead of calculated columns for every formula that involves product cost. Remember that denormalization is preferred for data analytics even if it results in duplicated data.

Grouping and binning

In the previous part of the book, you implemented calculated columns for grouping and binning, such as DimCustomer[Age (groups)]. Like concatenating fields, such requirements are more suitable for custom columns (either calculated or derived in Power Query or custom SQL).

 TIP Consider calculated columns when you need to add text-based custom columns to a table, such as to create custom groups and bins.

10.2.2 Evaluating Measures as Calculated Columns

Let's turn the tables now and see if measures can be replaced with calculated columns and if this comes with any benefits. You don't have many measures implemented yet, but you already know the cardinal rule when this can't happen. If the measure formula depends on runtime conditions, it must stay a measure.

Measures that depend on filters

In Lesson 1, you created a [SalesAmount RT] measure for producing a running total as of a given calendar year, which had this formula:

```
SalesAmount RT = CALCULATE(
    SUM('FactResellerSales'[SalesAmount]),
    FILTER(
        ALLSELECTED('DimDate'[CalendarYear]),
        ISONORAFTER('DimDate'[CalendarYear], MAX('DimDate'[CalendarYear]), DESC)))
```

Like SELECTEDVALUE, the MAX function returns the last year in the filter context. So, if the user selects years 2010 and 2011 in a report slicer, MAX('DimDate'[CalendarYear]) will return 2011. The important part is "as of". The measure formula summarizes sales at runtime across all dates that are less than or equal to the last date in the "current" year. Because calculated columns are evaluated before reports run, they can't reference selected values. Specifically, the MAX function in a calculated column will return the last year across the *entire* DimDate table, and the formula won't work as expected.

When measures can be calculated columns

In general, measures might work as calculated columns if their formula uses columns from just one fact table and they don't depend on runtime conditions. I've already discussed that NetProfit can be implemented as both a measure and a calculated column. And, I already recommended that in such cases, I'd gravitate toward measures to reduce the number of calculated columns and storage and decrease the model refresh time. However, if the measure performance is inadequate, it might benefit from "materializing" the entire formula or a part of it as columns. You need to test because every model and calculation are different.

10.3 Summary

This lesson should help you understand DAX measures and how they are evaluated. Unlike calculated columns, which might be avoided by using other implementation approaches, measures typically can't be replicated in other ways – they need to be written in DAX and implemented as measures (not calculated columns).

Lesson 11

Creating Basic Measures

Let's face it – DAX can be overwhelming for novice users. Wouldn't it be nice to avoid writing formulas? Of course, it would. Power BI supports different techniques to help you implement basic measures without requiring too much knowledge in DAX. In this lesson you'll learn how to work with implicit measures and quick measures, and how to implement a percent of total measures. You'll find the DAX formulas for this lesson in \Source\Part3\Basic Measures.dax.

11.1 Implementing Implicit Measures

To recap quickly what you already know, measures are typically used to aggregate values. Unlike calculated columns whose expressions are evaluated at design time for each row in the table, measures are evaluated at runtime for each cell in the report. DAX applies the filter context, such as row, column, and filter selections, when it evaluates the formula.

11.1.1 Understanding Implicit and Explicit Measures

Recall from the previous lesson that DAX supports implicit and explicit measures. An implicit measure is a regular column that's added to the Value area of the Visualizations pane. An explicit measure has a custom DAX formula.

Comparing measure types
Table 11.1 summarizes the differences between implicit and explicit measures.

Table 11.1 Comparing implicit and explicit measures.

Criterion	Implicit Measures	Explicit Measures
Design	Automatically generated	Manually created or by using Quick Measures
Accessibility	Use the Visualization pane to change the aggregation function	Use the formula bar to change the formula
DAX support	Standard aggregation functions only	Any valid DAX expression that works for measures

Implicit measures are automatically generated by Power BI Desktop when you add a field to the Value area of the Visualizations pane. By contrast, to create an explicit measure, you click the New Measure button in the Modeling ribbon (or right-click a table in the Fields pane, and then click "New measure"). Then, like calculated columns, you write the measure formula in the formula bar. Once the implicit measure is created, you can use the Visualizations pane to change its aggregation function. By contrast, explicit measures become a part of the model, and their formula must be changed in the formula bar (it can't be changed on the report).

Understanding limitations of implicit measures

Implicit measures are specific to Power BI only. Other clients, such as Excel, Power BI Report Builder or third-party, don't support implicit measures. For example, when you use the Analyze in Excel feature to connect Excel to Power BI, the Excel PivotTable Fields pane shows only explicit measures. You can't drag and drop table fields to the pivot's Values area.

 TIP If you plan to support other reporting tools, such as Excel or Tableau, create explicit measures even for basic aggregations, such as Sales = SUM(FactInternetSales[SalesAmount]). Otherwise, the user won't be able to create reports as these tools probably won't support implicit measures.

Implicit measures can only use standard aggregation functions: Sum, Count, Min, Max, Average, Distinct Count, Standard Deviation, Variance, and Median. However, explicit measures can use any DAX formula, such as to define a custom aggregation behavior like year-to-date.

11.1.2 Working with Implicit Measures

In this exercise, you'll work with implicit measures. This will help you understand how implicit measures aggregate and how you can control their default aggregation behavior.

Changing the default aggregation behavior

When you add a column to the Value area, Power BI Desktop automatically creates an implicit measure and aggregates it based on the column data type. For numeric columns Power BI Desktop uses the DAX SUM aggregation function. If the column data type is Text, Power BI Desktop uses COUNT. Sometimes, you might need to overwrite the default aggregation behavior. For example, the CalendarYear column in the DimDate table is a numeric column, but it doesn't make sense to sum it up on reports.

1. Make sure that the Data View tab (or Report View tab) is active. In the Fields pane, click the CalendarYear column in the DimDate table. This selects the CalendarYear column.

2. In the ribbon's Modeling tab, expand the Default Summarization drop-down and change it to "Do Not Summarize". As a result, the next time you use CalendarYear on a report, it won't get summarized by default.

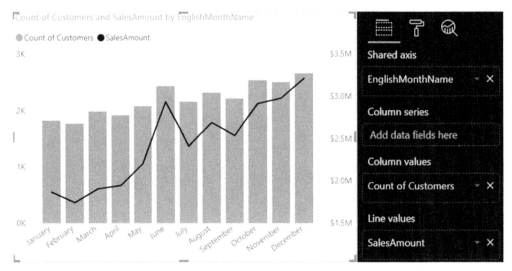

Figure 11.1 This combo chart shows the correlation between count of customers and sales.

Practice

Suppose you're trying to determine if there's any seasonality impact to your business. Are some months slower than others? If sales decrease, do fewer customers purchase products? To answer these questions, you'll create the report shown in **Figure 11.1**. Using the Line and Clustered Column Chart visualization, this report shows the count of customers as a column chart and the sales as a line chart that's plotted on the secondary axis. You'll analyze these two measures by month.

Let's start with visualizing the count of customers who have purchased products by month. Traditionally, you'd add some customer identifier to the fact table, and you'd use a Distinct Count aggregation function to only count unique customers. But the FactInternetSales table doesn't have the customer business key. The business key (CustomerAlternateKey) is in DimCustomer. Can you count on the CustomerAlternateKey column in the Customer table?

> **NOTE** Why not count on the CustomerKey column in FactInternetSales? This will work if the Customer table handles Type 1 changes only. A Type 1 change results in an in-place change. When a change to a customer is detected, the row is simply overwritten. However, chances are that business requirements necessitate Type 2 changes as well, where a new row is created when an important change occurs, such as when the customer changes addresses. Therefore, counting on CustomerKey (called a surrogate key in dimensional modeling) is often a bad idea because it might lead to overstated results. Instead, you'd want to do a distinct count on a customer identifier that is not system generated, such as the customer's account number.

1. Switch to the Report View. From the Fields pane, drag the CustomerAlternateKey column from the DimCustomer table, and then drop it in an empty area in the report canvas.

2. Power BI Desktop defaults to a table visualization that shows all customer identifiers. Switch the visualization type to "Line and Clustered Column Chart".

3. In the Visualizations pane, drag CustomerAlternateKey from the Shared Axis area to the Column Values area. Double-click the field and rename the implicit measure to *Count of Customers*.

4. Expand the drop-down in the "Count of Customers" field. Note that it uses the Count aggregation function, as shown in **Figure 11.2**.

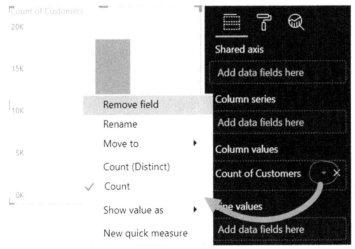

Figure 11.2 Text-based implicit measures use the Count function by default.

5. A product can be sold more than once within a given time period. If you simply count on the business key, you might get an inflated count. Instead, you want to count customers uniquely. Expand the drop-down next to the "Count of Customers" field in the "Column values" area and change the aggregation function from Count to Count (Distinct).

6. (Optional) Use the ribbon's Modeling tab to change the CustomerAlternateKey default summarization to Count (Distinct) so you don't have to overwrite the aggregation behavior every time this field is used on a report.

7. With the new visualization selected, check the DimDate[EnglishMonthName] field in the Fields pane to add it to the Shared Axis area of the Visualizations pane.

8. If months sort alphabetically on the chart, select the DimDate[EnglishMonthName] field in the Fields pane. In the Modeling ribbon, expand the "Sort By Column" dropdown and select MonthNumberOfYear. This sorts the DimDate[EnglishMonthName] field by the ordinal number of the month. If the chart sorting order doesn't change, remove DimDate[EnglishMonthName] from the chart and add it again.

Configuring bidirectional filtering

At this point, the chart might be incorrect. Specifically, the count of customers might not change across months. The issue is that the aggregation happens over the FactInternetSales fact table via the DimDate ⇦ FactInternetSales ⇨ DimCustomer path (notice that the relationship direction changes). Furthermore, the cardinality of the DimDate and DimCustomer tables is Many-to-Many (there could be many customers who purchased something on the same date, and a repeating customer could buy multiple times).

1. Switch to the Model View tab. Double-click the FactInternetSales ⇨ DimCustomer relationship. In the Advanced Options properties of the relationship, change the cross-filter direction to Both.

2. Switch to the Report View tab. Note that now the results vary by month.

3. Drag the FactInternetSales[SalesAmount] field to the Line Values area of the Visualizations pane. Note that because SalesAmount is numeric, Power BI Desktop defaults to the SUM aggregation function.

Analysis

Basic reports may not need explicit measures if the Power BI standard aggregation functions are enough. The Count of Customers measure counts distinct customers. Analyzing the report, you can conclude that seasonality affects sales. Specifically, the customer base decreases during the summer. And as the number of customers decreases, so do sales.

11.1.3 Creating Basic Explicit Measures

As I mentioned previously when comparing implicit and explicit measures, consider creating explicit measures to "wrap" basic calculations, such as to summarize or count. This approach makes your model more useful because users can use a reporting tool of their choice to create reports.

Practice

Let's create the Count of Customers explicit measure.

1. In the Report (or Data) tab, click the FactInternetSales table to select it in the Fields pane.

2. In the Modeling ribbon, click New Measure. Alternatively, right-click the FactInternetSales table in the Fields pane and then click "New measure". I prefer the latter approach because it's a sure way to specify the measure's home table. Otherwise, you have to remember to first select the table in the Fields pane before pressing the New Measure ribbon button.

3. Enter the following formula in the formula bar and press Enter:

```
Count of Customers = DISTINCTCOUNT(DimCustomer[CustomerAlternateKey])
```

4. Suppose you want the Count of Customers measure to show up under the DimCustomer table in the Fields pane. Click "Count of Customers" in the Fields pane to select it. In the Modeling ribbon, expand the Home Table dropdown and select DimCustomer.

5. (Optional) Rename the measure to *CustomerCount*. Notice that renaming measures (and columns) doesn't break existing reports thanks to the Power BI "smart" rename feature.

 REAL LIFE I recommended in Lesson 1 you come up with a naming convention and stick to it. What if you want your explicit measures to have the same name as the base columns, such as SalesAmount? Unfortunately, the measure name must be unique. I typically rename the base numeric columns, such as SalesAmountBase, hide them, and then implement wrapper explicit measures.

Output
Add the CustomerCount explicit measure to the Values area of the chart report and notice that it produces the same result as it's implicit measure counterpart. As an optional step, publish the Adventure Works.pbix file to the Power BI Service (powerbi.com). Use the "Analyze in Excel" feature (https://docs.microsoft.com/power-bi/service-analyze-in-excel) to create an Excel pivot table connected to the published model.

Analysis
The measure's home table is just a metadata operation and changing it doesn't break existing reports. Excel recognizes DAX explicit measures, allowing you to create Excel pivot reports. Excel doesn't support Power BI implicit measures (you can't just drag a field in the Values area of the pivot report).

11.2 Working with Built-in Measures

As you've started to realize, DAX is a very powerful programming language. The only issue is that there is a learning curve involved. At the same time, there are frequently used measures that shouldn't require extensive knowledge of DAX. This is where "show value as" and quick measures could help.

11.2.1 Implementing "Show value as" Measures

A common requirement is to show the measure value as a percent of the total. Fortunately, there is a quick and easy way to meet this requirement because Power BI includes a feature called "Show value as".

Practice
Let's create a report that shows the percent of total sales that each country contributes:

1. Add a Matrix visual with DimSalesTerritory[SalesTerritoryCountry] and FactResellerSales-[SalesAmount] fields in the Values area. Add DimDate[CalendarYear] to the Columns area.

2. Add the FactResellerSales[SalesAmount] field one more time to the Values area.

3. In the Values area of the Visualizations pane, expand the dropdown next to the second SalesAmount field and choose "Show value as". Select "Percent of column total". Compare your results with **Figure 11.3**. Notice that the "%CT SalesAmount" now shows the contribution of each country to the column total.

4. (Optional) In the Visualizations pane (Fields tab), double-click the "%CT Sales Amount" field and rename it to *% of Total Sales*.

CalendarYear	2005		2006	
SalesTerritoryCountry	SalesAmount	%CT SalesAmount	SalesAmount	
United States	$6,552,075.85	81.24%	$17,622,549.51	
Canada	$1,513,359.46	18.76%	$4,822,999.20	
France			$857,123.18	
United Kingdom			$841,757.76	
Germany				
Australia				
Total	$8,065,435.31	100.00%	$24,144,429.65	

(Values panel: SalesAmount — No calculation / Percent of grand total / Show value as / Percent of column total / New quick measure / Percent of row total)

Figure 11.3 The %CT SalesAmount field shows each value as a percent of the column total.

Analysis

"Show value as" changes an existing measure in place to show its output as a percentage of a column, row, or grand total. It doesn't create a new measure. Power BI implements this feature internally so don't try to find or change the DAX formula. If you require more control, I'll walk you through implementing an explicit measure in the " Changing Filter Context" lesson that does the same thing but with a DAX formula you write.

11.2.2 Working with Quick Measures

Before further honing in on your DAX skills, let's look at another feature that may help you avoid, or at least, help you learn DAX. Quick measures are prepackaged DAX formulas for common analytical requirements, such as time calculations, aggregates, and totals. Unlike "show value as", quick measures are implemented as DAX explicit measures, so you can see and change the quick measure formula.

Practice

In the first lesson, you used a running total quick measure. Let's practice another quick measure to produce a year-to-date (YTD) sales report (see **Figure 11.4**).

CalendarYear	EnglishMonthName	SalesAmount	SalesAmount (qm) YTD
2010	December	$489,329	$489,329
2011	January	$1,538,408	$1,538,408
2011	February		$1,538,408
2011	March	$2,010,618	$3,549,026
2011	April		$3,549,026
2011	May	$4,027,080	$7,576,107
2011	June		$7,576,107
2011	July	$713,117	$8,289,223
2011	August	$3,356,069	$11,645,293
2011	September	$882,900	$12,528,193

Figure 11.4 The SalesAmount (qm) YTD measure accumulates sales over years and it's produced by the "Year-to-date total" quick measure.

1. Because the quick measure formula will use the DimDate table, as a prerequisite you need to mark this table as a date table. In the "Working with Date Tables" lesson, I'll explain in more detail why this change is necessary. In the Fields pane, right-click DimDate and click "Mark as date table". In the "Mark as date table" window, expand the dropdown and select the Date column. Click OK.

2. Create a new Table visualization that has DimDate[CalendarYear], DimDate[EnglishMonthName], and FactResellerSales[SalesAmount] fields in the Values area.

3. Right-click the FactResellerSales table in the Fields pane and then click "New quick measure". Alternatively, you expand the dropdown next to SalesAmount in the Fields pane (or visual's Values area) and then click "New Quick Measure".

4. In the "Quick measures" window (see **Figure 11.5**), expand the Calculation drop-down. Observe that Power BI supports various quick measures. Select "Year-to-date total" under the Time Intelligence section.

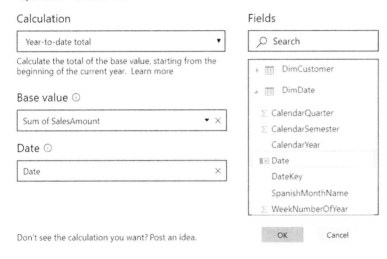

Figure 11.5 Power BI supports various quick measures to meet common analytical requirements.

5. Drag the SalesAmount field from the FactResellerSales table to the "Base value" area.

6. Drag the Date field from the DimDate table to the Date area. Click OK.

7. Power BI adds a new "SalesAmount YTD" field to the FactResellerSales table in the Fields pane.

8. In the Fields pane, rename the "SalesAmount YTD" field to *SalesAmount (qm) YTD*.

9. Add the "SalesAmount (qm) YTD" field to the report.

Analysis
Notice the field accumulates sales within each year as it should. Click the "SalesAmount (qm) YTD" field in the Fields pane. Notice that the formula bar shows this formula:

```
SalesAmount (qm) YTD =
IF(
    ISFILTERED('DimDate'[Date]),
    ERROR("Time intelligence quick measures can only be grouped or filtered by the Power BI-provided date hierarchy
        or primary date column."),
    TOTALYTD(SUM('FactResellerSales'[SalesAmount]), 'DimDate'[Date])
)
```

This formula checks if the DimDate[Date] field is directly or indirectly filtered in the report by using the ISFILTERED function. If this is the case, the formula uses the TOTALYTD function to calculate YTD sales. Unlike "show value as", once you create the quick measure, it becomes just like any explicit DAX measure. You can rename it or use it on your reports. However, you can't go back to the "Quick measures" dialog. To customize the measure, you must make changes directly to the formula, so you still need to know some DAX.

11.3 Summary

Power BI comes with features that can help you avoid writing DAX for basic calculations. You can aggregate any field on a report by using any of the standard aggregation functions, such as sum or average. The "Show value as" feature lets you implement "percent of total" measures. And you can create quick measures for some common calculations, such as YTD.

Lesson 12

Determining Filter Context

Power BI evaluates measures in the filter context of each report cell. No matter how you slice and dice the report, measures produce the correct results, and you don't have to worry about the internals. Sometimes, however, you many need to evaluate the filter context, such as to change the measure aggregation depending on the user selection. This lesson teaches you how to do just this. You'll find the DAX formulas for this lesson in \Source\Part3\Determining Filter Context.dax.

12.1 Understanding Filter Functions

DAX includes several functions to help you obtain filters applied to the filter context in which a measure operates. They include functions to help you determine if a column is filtered or cross-filtered, and functions to obtain the selected values.

12.1.1 Understanding Filtering and Cross-filtering

The first three functions (ISFILTERED, ISCROSSFILTERED, and ISINSCOPE) help you determine if a column is directly or indirectly filtered.

Determining direct filters
A table column is filtered directly when the column is explicitly filtered. A column could be directly filtered when it participates in a report filter or slicer, or when it appears in a visual. ISFILTERED returns TRUE if any direct filters are applied on a specific column or any column in a table.

ISFILTERED (<TableNameOrColumnName>)

Determining cross filtering
A column is cross filtered when there is no direct filter on the column itself but on other columns in the same table or in a related table. You can use the ISCROSSFILTERED function to check if a column or table is cross-filtered and this function has the same definition as ISFILTERED.

Determining hierarchy scope
Finally, the ISINSCOPE (<ColumnName>) function returns TRUE if the column is filtered directly and if it's a grouping column for the current row in the report. I'll clarify this with the report in the next section.

12.1.2 Understanding Applied Filters

Suppose you want to apply different calculations at different levels of a typical date hierarchy, consisting of Year, Quarter, and Month levels. As a first step, you need to understand what hierarchy level is filtered. By "hierarchy", I mean fields that represent logical 1:M relationships (a year has many quarters, a quarter has many months), and not necessarily a Power BI hierarchy that you can implement in the Fields pane.

Practice
Start by creating three measures to test how the three functions affect the filters on the DimDate-[EnglishMonthName] column. If you reference the \Source\Part3\Adventure Works, you'll find these measures in the Filters folder under the DimDate table in the Fields pane.

TIP You can organize the model metadata by placing fields in display folders. To do so, go to the Model View tab, select the field in the Fields pane, and enter the display folder name in the "Display folder" property in the field's Properties pane.

Add the following measures to the DimDate table:

```
Month (Filtered) = ISFILTERED(DimDate[EnglishMonthName])
Month (Cross-filtered) = ISCROSSFILTERED(DimDate[EnglishMonthName])
Month (IsInScope) = ISINSCOPE(DimDate[EnglishMonthName])
```

Outcome
Let's create a report to see the effect of the three measures.

1. Create a Matrix report with DimDate[CalendarYear], DimDate[CalendarQuarter], and DimDate-[EnglishMonthName] fields in the Rows area, and the three measures in the Values area.

2. Expand the year and quarter levels (see **Figure 12.1**).

CalendarYear	Month (Filtered)	Month (Cross-filtered)	Month (IsInScope)
2005	**False**	**True**	**False**
1	**False**	**True**	**False**
January	True	True	True
February	True	True	True
March	True	True	True
2	**False**	**True**	**False**
April	True	True	True
May	True	True	True
Total	**False**	**True**	**False**

Figure 12.1 This report demonstrates how you can determine direct and indirect filters applied to a column.

3. Drop a slicer visual on the report and bind it to DimDate[EnglishMonthName].

4. Select and deselect a month in the slicer and observe the changes in the visual's Total line.

Analysis
Month (Filtered) returns True only when the EnglishMonthName is explicitly filtered. This can happen when the current report cell is on a report row that has the month, or when a slicer or filter applies a filter to this column. Month (Cross-filtered) returns True when any column from the Dim-Date table is on the report or explicitly filtered. However, ISCROSSFILTERED would return False if the report includes columns from other tables.

Month (IsInScope) returns identical results as Month (filtered) if no direct filter is applied to EnglishMonthName. However, when this column is filtered by the slicer, ISFILTERED returns True in the Total line, while ISINSCOPE returns False in the Total line. Therefore, ISINSCOPE is useful when you need to overwrite the measure formula for the report totals. Using ISFILTERED to check for report totals is not reliable as it changes depending on the user-specified filters, so you should use ISINSCOPE instead.

12.2 Getting Selected Values

Now that you know how to determine the filter context, the next step will be to obtain the selected values. For example, this could be useful to determine the report date that the user has selected in a report slicer, or to determine the start and end range of the user selection. DAX offers several ways to get the selected values and has introduced even more functions to simplify this task. Next, we'll review the most popular functions to obtain a single selected value and range limits (in the case of selecting multiple values).

12.2.1 Working Single-Value Filters

If you expect a single value from the filter context, you can use the functions SELECTEDVALUE or VALUES.

Checking for a single value
You can use the HASONEVALUE function to determine if a column has been filtered down to a single value as a result of direct or indirect filters (another function HASONEFILTER checks only for direct filters). HASONEVALUE is typically used with the IF statement. For example, the following measure checks if the FactInternetSales[SalesOrderNumber] column is filtered down to a single value, and if this is the case, it constructs a link that includes the order number.

```
IF (HASONEVALUE(FactInternetSales[SalesOrderNumber]), "http://prologika.com?OrderNumber=" &
VALUES (FactInternetSales[SalesOrderNumber] ))
```

Getting the value
The formula uses the VALUES function. Recall that when the column is filtered down to one value, VALUES returns that single value; otherwise you'll get an error. To simplify checking for single values, DAX has another function called SELECTEDVALUE.

```
SELECTEDVALUE ( <ColumnName> [, <AlternateResult>] )
```

This function is a shortcut to:

```
IF(HASONEVALUE(<ColumnName >), VALUES(<ColumnName >), <AltnernateResult>)
```

You might think you can shorten the above formula by using SELECTEDVALUE:

```
SELECTEDVALUE(FactInternetSales[SalesOrderNumber])
```

However, this formula will return an empty value when the customer hasn't ordered anything, causing the formula to produce a link with no order number for every customer on the report. So, you'd probably still need to check if you have a filter selection before you do something with it, so the formula with the IF statement is a better option.

12.2.2 Working with Multi-value Filters

What if the user has filtered multiple values or selected a date period and you want to get the first or last date? When numeric values are filtered, you can use the MIN function to get the first selected value and the MAX function to get the last selected. The following measure (BOP stands for "beginning of period") returns the first filtered date:

```
BOP = MIN (DimDate[Date])
```

In the case of filtering dates, you can also use the FIRSTDATE and LASTDATE functions. The following measure achieves the same result:

BOP = FIRSTDATE (DimDate[Date])

For non-numeric values, you can use the FIRSTNONBLANK and LASTNONBLANK functions. For example, the following measure returns the last filtered product category.

SelectedCategory = LASTNONBLANK(DimProduct[EnglishProductCategoryName], TRUE)

12.3   Working with Filter Selection

Let's put what you've learned in practice and create measures that react to filters applied by the end user running the report. In the first exercise, you'll create a link that navigates the user to a web page and passes the "current" order number. The second exercise teaches you how to overwrite the measure aggregation across a hierarchy.

12.3.1 Creating Links

Consider the report shown in **Figure 12.**. This report displays customer's sales and allows the user to click a link to navigate the user to another system, such as to see the order details.

FullName	OrderDate	SalesOrderNumber	SalesAmount	OrderLink
Jared Peterson	1/30/2013	SO51980	$54	http://prologika.com?OrderNumber=SO51980
Jared Peterson	3/18/2013	SO54610	$54	http://prologika.com?OrderNumber=SO54610
Jared Peterson	5/6/2013	SO57567	$9	http://prologika.com?OrderNumber=SO57567
Jared Peterson	5/7/2013	SO57609	$70	http://prologika.com?OrderNumber=SO57609
Jared Peterson	7/11/2013	SO61928	$54	http://prologika.com?OrderNumber=SO61928
Jared Peterson	8/11/2013	SO64009	$78	http://prologika.com?OrderNumber=SO64009
Jared Peterson	9/15/2013	SO66375	$74	http://prologika.com?OrderNumber=SO66375
Jared Peterson	11/21/2013	SO71220	$9	http://prologika.com?OrderNumber=SO71220
Jared Peterson	1/24/2014	SO74977	$59	http://prologika.com?OrderNumber=SO74977
Jared Peterson	1/27/2014	SO75069	$59	http://prologika.com?OrderNumber=SO75069

Figure 12.2 The interactive user can click a link that navigates to another web page and passes the order number.

Practice
Start by creating a measure to construct the link.

1. Add the OrderLink measure to FactInternetSales with the following formula:

OrderLink = IF (HASONEVALUE(FactInternetSales[SalesOrderNumber]),
"http://prologika.com?OrderNumber=" & VALUES (FactInternetSales[SalesOrderNumber]))

2. Add a Table visual and add DimCustomer[FullName], FactInternetSales[OrderDate] (if it shows the date hierarchy, expand the dropdown to OrderDate in Values area and select OrderDate to ignore the hierarchy), FactInternetSales[SalesOrderNumber], FactInternetSales[SalesAmount], and the OrderLink measure.

3. In the Fields pane, click the OrderLink field to select it. In the Modeling ribbon, expand the Data Category drop-down and select Web URL. The link is now clickable, but it might not be desirable to show the URL.

4. (Optional) With the Table visual selected, select the Format tab in the Visualizations pane, expand the Values area, and then turn on the "URL icon" slider. This replaces the link with an icon.

Analysis

HASONEVALUE returns True for every row in the report because the visual includes the SalesOrderNumber field. But the filtered field doesn't have to be in the visual or directly filtered in a report filter or slicer. If the filter context can narrow down the field to one value, HASONEVALUE will return True and the link will still work. As an optional step, remove the SalesOrderNumber field from the visual. The OrderLink field will now show empty values for customers who submitted multiple orders on the same date.

12.3.2 Implementing Aggregates Over Aggregates

You face a difficult requirement. Management has requested a complicated aggregation for counting customers. At a level lower than calendar year, such as quarter, month, and date, the measure must return the distinct count of customers. However, at the year level, it must return the average of the customer count at the quarter level. This scenario is commonly referred to as "aggregate over aggregate".

Practice
Change the CustomerCount measure formula as follows:

```
CustomerCount = IF (
    ISFILTERED ( DimDate[Date] ) || ISFILTERED ( DimDate[EnglishMonthName] ) || ISFILTERED ( DimDate[CalendarQuarter]
),
    DISTINCTCOUNT ( DimCustomer[CustomerAlternateKey] ),
    AVERAGEX (
      ADDCOLUMNS (
        SUMMARIZE ( DimDate, DimDate[CalendarQuarter] ),
        "CustomerDCount", CALCULATE ( DISTINCTCOUNT ( DimCustomer[CustomerAlternateKey] ) )
      ),
      [CustomerDCount]   ))
```

Output
Create a report to test the measure:

1. Add a Matrix visual. Add DimDate[CalendarYear] and DimDate[CalendarQuarter] to the Rows area, and CustomerCount to the Values area.

2. Right-click any year on the report and click Expand ➪ All. Compare your results with **Figure 12.3**.

CalendarYear	CustomerCount
2011	554
1	438
2	561
3	566
4	651
2012	816

Figure 12.3 The CustomerCount measure computes a simple average over the year's quarters.

Analysis
The formula checks if the filter context is at a date, month, or quarter level. If that's the case, the measure returns the distinct count as the original measure. Otherwise, the formula uses the AVERAGEX function. Notice that you must check for lower hierarchy levels first because ISFILTERED returns TRUE at any level. The first argument is the summarized DimDate table at the CalendarQuarter level. Then, the formula uses ADDCOLUMNS to add the CustomerDCount column that computes the customer distinct count but at the quarter level.

The net effect is that for each year, SUMMARIZE produces a table with four rows (one for each quarter) and two columns: CalendarQuarter and AverageOfCustomers. Then, AVERAGEX computes a simple average over the projected column "CustomerDCount". Because ADDCOLUMNS is an iterator, CustomerDCount needs CALCULATE to transition the row context into a filter context.

 NOTE The formula can use just SUMMARIZE to add CustomerDCount without requiring ADDCOLUMNS and CALCULATE. However, using ADDCOLUMNS is better from a performance standpoint. I discuss aggregation functions (SUMMARIZE, SUMMARIZECOLUMNS, and ADDCOLUMNS) in more detail in the "Grouping Data" lesson.

12.4 Summary

When you implement measures you often need to evaluate the filter context. Use the DAX functions ISFILTERED, ISCROSSFILTERED, and ISINSCOPE to determine if a column is filtered directly or indirectly. Use HASONEVALUE, SELECTEDVALUE, and VALUES when the column is filtered down to a single value.

Lesson 13

Working with Variables

We'll take a short break from measure formulas to introduce DAX variables. Variables can help you simplify your DAX formulas, make them more efficient, and get around some annoying DAX limitations. This lesson starts by explaining how variables work and then walks you through exercises to practice variables. You'll find the DAX formulas for this lesson in \Source\Part3\Working with Variables.dax.

13.1 Understanding Variables

Like variables in programming languages, a DAX variable stores the result of a formula to reuse it later. Unlike programming languages, however, once a DAX variable is calculated, its value doesn't change. So, think of a DAX variable more as a constant than a storage location that can be changed at any time. Although this sounds somewhat limiting, DAX variables are very useful.

13.1.1 Defining Variables

You define a DAX variable inside the formula of a measure or a calculated column. You use the special VAR keyword for the variable declaration.

VAR <name> = <expression>

Understanding syntax
The name of the variable can't have delimiters, such as single quotes or square brackets, which also means that it can't have spaces. The variable expression can be any valid DAX expression that returns a scalar value or a table. You can define multiple variables in a formula. Consider this measure formula that calculates the year-over-year percentage variance:

```
YoY% =
    VAR Sales = SUM ( FactResellerSales[SalesAmount] )
    VAR SalesLastYear = CALCULATE ( SUM ( FactResellerSales[SalesAmount] ),
                    SAMEPERIODLASTYEAR ( DimDate[Date] ) )
    RETURN
    IF ( NOT ISBLANK(Sales) && NOT ISBLANK(SalesLastYear), DIVIDE ( Sales - SalesLastYear, Sales ) )
```

This formula defines two variables:

- Sales – This variable computes the current sales for the selected period. For example, the report shows sales by year, the Sales variable returns the sales for each year.

- SalesLastYear – This variable calculates the sum of sales for the same period in the previous year.

When the formula includes variables, it must also include a RETURN statement, which is followed by a formula that returns the result from the measure or calculated column (calculated columns can also use variables). In this case, the expression uses the IF operator to check if both variables return non-blank values and to perform a safe divide using the DIVIDE function (to avoid a division by zero if the current year's sales are zero). When the report is run, DAX will substitute the variables in the measure formula with their calculated values.

 NOTE As it stands, DAX doesn't support global variables, such as a variable that is declared once and reused in multiple DAX expressions and calculated columns. Therefore, although this may lead to redundant variable declarations, you must declare the same variable in every formula you plan to use it.

Understanding the variable evaluation context

Variables are evaluated where they are declared (not in the formula that uses them), and their evaluation context can't be overwritten. To make the formula simpler, you might attempt to rewrite it as follows:

```
YoY% =
    VAR Sales = SUM ( FactResellerSales[SalesAmount] )
    VAR SalesLastYear = CALCULATE ( Sales, SAMEPERIODLASTYEAR ( DimDate[Date] ) )
    RETURN
    IF ( NOT ISBLANK(Sales) && NOT ISBLANK(SalesLastYear), DIVIDE ( Sales - SalesLastYear, Sales ) )
```

The idea here is to reuse the Sales variable when computing the last year's sales in the SalesLastYear variable. Unfortunately, the formula always returns zero. This is because Power BI has already computed the value of the Sales variable at the point of its declaration and its context can't be further overwritten. That's why it's useful to think of variables as constants. You can't treat them as measures and use CALCULATE to overwrite their evaluation context.

13.1.2 Why Use Variables?

You can implement measures and calculated columns without variables. However, you should evaluate your formulas and use variables when it makes sense. Let's go through the potential benefits.

Simplifying syntax

As you can see from the YoY% formula, variables can help you simplify the formula syntax and make it more intuitive. If you don't use variables, you must repeat expressions:

```
YoY% = IF ( NOT ISBLANK(SUM ( FactResellerSales[SalesAmount] )) &&
    NOT ISBLANK(CALCULATE ( SUM ( FactResellerSales[SalesAmount] ), SAMEPERIODLASTYEAR ( DimDate[Date] ) )),
    DIVIDE ( SUM ( FactResellerSales[SalesAmount] ) - CALCULATE ( SUM ( FactResellerSales[SalesAmount] )
        , SAMEPERIODLASTYEAR ( DimDate[Date] ) ), SUM ( FactResellerSales[SalesAmount] )) )
```

This code is difficult to read. Granted, instead of variables, you can refactor this year's sales and last year's sales as separate measures. This would be a good approach if these measures are useful on their own. But using variables can also improve performance, which brings us to the next benefit.

Improving performance

As I mentioned, variables are evaluated once. When the query optimizer encounters a variable, it optimizes the query plan because it knows that it must evaluate the variable only once in a given evaluation context. This results in a faster execution plan when the same expression appears multiple times in a formula.

Working around DAX limitations

DAX has its own share of idiosyncrasies that can humble both novice and experienced users. Consider a common example where a measure attempts to return sales for the last date in the Date table (the last date filtered in a filter or a slicer). What makes this common is that many real-life calculations require measures that are calculated as of the user-specified date ("as of" date).

```
Sales=CALCULATE(SUM(FactResellerSales[SalesAmount]), MAX(DimDate[CalendarYear]) )
```

As simple and logically correct the measure is, it fails with the error "A function 'MAX' has been used in a True/False expression that is used as a table filter expression. This is not allowed." This is what the documentation states about this error:

"The filter expression, MAX('DimDate'[CalendarYear]) attempts to return the largest numeric value in the CalendarYear column. However, in context of the measure expression, it cannot be passed as a table filter expression to the CALCULATE function, causing an error."

This is an example where documentation has left some ground for improvement. First, the MAX function doesn't return a table but a scalar value. Second, the CALCULATE function can take filters. The actual issue is that DAX surrounds the MAX formula with a hidden CALCULATE and it's ambiguous in what context the maximum date should be evaluated.

To be consistent with the way filters propagate, it should be in the filter context outside of CALCULATE, but in the row context of the as-of date, which becomes a filter context with the MAX formula. But this is not what you would expect, so DAX fails safely with the error. The workaround suggested by the documentation is to filter the DimDate table and pass it as a table filter to calculate. This requires ignoring the filter context on the DimDate table, only to overwrite it later with the "as of" date.

```
Sales=CALCULATE( SUM(FactResellerSales[SalesAmount]),
FILTER( ALL( DimDate[CalendarYear]), [CalendarYear] = MAX(DimDate[CalendarYear]) ) )
```

A better solution is to use a variable. This example uses an EOP (End of Period) variable to return the last date:

```
Sales=
VAR EOP = MAX(DimDate[CalendarYear])
RETURN
CALCULATE(SUM(FactResellerSales[SalesAmount]), [CalendarYear] = EOP )
```

Because the EOP variable is evaluated where it's declared, there is no hidden context and the formula works. Unfortunately, DAX doesn't support global variables, so you need to include this variable in every measure that references the end of the period.

13.2 Practicing Variables

Now that you know about variable fundamentals, let's practice different usage scenarios where variables could be helpful. The next exercises demonstrate how variables can help you simplify formulas, improve performance, and work around DAX complexities and limitations.

13.2.1 Calculating Variances

In this exercise, you'll implement YoY% calculation without and with variables to calculate the percent variance of FactResellerSales[SalesAmount].

Practice
Add the following two measures to FactResellerSales:

```
SalesAmount YoY% (slow) =
IF (
    NOT ISBLANK ( SUM ( FactResellerSales[SalesAmount] ) )
        && NOT ISBLANK (
            CALCULATE (
                SUM ( FactResellerSales[SalesAmount] ),
                SAMEPERIODLASTYEAR ( DimDate[Date] )
            )
        ),
    DIVIDE (
        SUM ( FactResellerSales[SalesAmount] )
            - CALCULATE (
                SUM ( FactResellerSales[SalesAmount] ),
                SAMEPERIODLASTYEAR ( DimDate[Date] )
            ),
        SUM ( FactResellerSales[SalesAmount] )
    )
)

SalesAmount YoY% =
VAR Sales =
    SUM ( FactResellerSales[SalesAmount] )
VAR SalesLastYear =
    CALCULATE (
        SUM ( FactResellerSales[SalesAmount] ),
        SAMEPERIODLASTYEAR ( DimDate[Date] )
    )
RETURN
    IF (
        NOT ISBLANK ( Sales ) && NOT ISBLANK ( SalesLastYear ),
        DIVIDE ( Sales - SalesLastYear, Sales )
    )
```

Output

To test the measures, add a Table visual with DimDate[CalendarYear] and the two measures, as shown in **Figure 13.1**.

CalendarYear	SalesAmount YoY% (slow)	SalesAmount YoY%
2011	97.31%	97.31%
2012	35.47%	35.47%
2013	16.03%	16.03%

Figure 13.1 Both measures produce the same results.

Analysis

Both measures produce the same results. However, [SalesAmount YoY%] is easier to read. Moreover, it's faster. Using the techniques discussed in the "Queries" part of this book to analyze the query performance with DAX Studio (you can also use the Power BI Desktop Performance Analyzer, which I demonstrated in the first lesson), I obtained two sets of statistics (see **Figure 13.2**).

[SalesAmount YoY%] (statistics shown in the right half) is almost twice as fast as its non-variable counterpart. Specifically, it generates only seven queries to the storage engine (versus 13) and its overall execution time is 42 ms (versus 64). Although in this case the difference is milliseconds (the Adventure Works model has only a few thousand rows across all tables), it should be more pronounced with more involved calculations and larger data volumes.

Total	SE CPU		Total	SE CPU
64 ms	16 ms		42 ms	0 ms
	x1.0			x0.0

▓ FE	▓ SE		▓ FE	▓ SE
48 ms	16 ms		34 ms	8 ms
75.0%	25.0%		81.0%	19.0%

SE Queries	SE Cache		SE Queries	SE Cache
13	3		7	1
	23.1%			14.3%

Figure 13.2 Performance statistics shows that variables reduce the query execution time almost in half.

13.2.2 Implementing Filter Expressions

In the lesson "Filtering Data", you saw how a variable can be used as a substitute for using the EARLIER function in a calculated column. Let's now see how variables can help you work around some of the DAX limitations. Next, you'll implement a measure that returns the inception to date (ITD) sales. The SalesAmount ITD measure returns sales from the earliest date with data until the end date of the current period.

Practice
Attempt to add the following measure to FactResellerSales:

```
SalesAmount ITD =
CALCULATE (
    SUM ( FactResellerSales[SalesAmount] ),
    FactResellerSales[OrderDate] <= MAX ( DimDate[Date] ),
    ALL ( DimDate )
)
```

This measure doesn't work. Specifically, when you press Enter to commit the formula, Power BI Desktop shows the error "A function 'MAX' has been used in a True/False expression that is used as a table filter expression. This is not allowed." Change the formula as follows to fix it:

```
SalesAmount ITD =
VAR EOP = MAX ( DimDate[Date] )
RETURN
CALCULATE (
    SUM ( FactResellerSales[SalesAmount] ),
    FactResellerSales[OrderDate] <= EOP,
    ALL ( DimDate ))
```

Output
As an optional step, add the SalesAmount ITD measure to the report you produced in the previous exercise (see **Figure 13.3**).

Analysis
The formula uses a variable EOP that returns the end of the period selected on the report. This avoids the error. The ALL (DimDate) filter removes the current filter as a result of the FactResellerSales[OrderDateKey] ⇨ DimDate[Date] relationship.

CalendarYear	SalesAmount YoY% (slow)	SalesAmount YoY%	SalesAmount ITD
2010			$489,329
2011	97.31%	97.31%	$18,682,131
2012	35.47%	35.47%	$46,875,763
2013	16.03%	16.03%	$80,450,597
2014			$80,450,597
Total	**0.00%**	**0.00%**	**$80,450,597**

Figure 13.3 The SalesAmount ITD measure sums sales from the earliest date until the end of the period.

13.3 Summary

DAX variables help you simplify the formula syntax, improve performance, and work around issues with the evaluation context. Consider variables whenever they could be beneficial, such as to avoid repeating expressions in a formula.

Lesson 14

Changing Filter Context

In the "Filtering Data" lesson, you learned how you can manipulate the filter context when implementing calculated columns. This lesson builds upon this knowledge, but it focuses on the measure specifics. First, I'll show you how to reduce the filter context by applying filters and navigating inactive relationships. Then, I'll show you how to ignore existing filters. You'll find the DAX formulas for this lesson in \Source\Part3\Changing Filter Context.dax.

14.1 Overwriting the Filter Context

To briefly revisit what has been covered already, measures operate in a specific filter context, which is affected by the cell location on the report and additional filters applied to the measure. You must use the CALCULATE function to overwrite or ignore the filter context. If there is a mother of all DAX functions for measures, CALCULATE will be it. You won't go far with measures if you don't know CALCULATE.

14.1.1 Revisiting CALCULATE for Measures

Recall from Lesson "Aggregating Data" that CALCULATE has this definition:

CALCULATE (<Expression> [, <Filter> [, <Filter> [, ...]]])

Besides the expression passed to the first argument, CALCULATE takes one or more filter arguments and they can filter columns or tables. Each filter is treated as an AND condition. The order of the filter arguments doesn't matter.

> **NOTE** While the order of the arguments doesn't matter, their internal evaluation is a different story. Remember that filters from ALL, ALLEXCEPT, ALLSELECTED, and USERELATIONSHIP have a higher precedence than other filter arguments. In other words, regular filter arguments can't overwrite the effect of these functions because they expand the filter context.

You can apply multiple (AND or OR) filter conditions to the same column. To filter different columns, you must provide multiple filter arguments, typically one for each column you need to filter (which might give you a better performance anyway). More complicated filter conditions, such as OR conditions involving different columns, require the FILTER function. I also showed you in the previous lesson that when the filter argument references an aggregation function, such as MAX, you can avoid the error by using a variable.

Practice
Add a measure "Revenue by Top Tier Customers" to FactInternetSales that returns the sum of FactInternetSales[SalesAmount] for customers where the value of the DimCustomer[SalesRank] column is less than or equal to 100.

Profit by Top Tier Customers = CALCULATE(SUM(FactInternetSales[SalesAmount]), DimCustomer[SalesRank] <= 100)

Output

Add a Table visual and bind it to DimCustomer[FulName] and the new measure. Sort by "Profit by Top Tier Customers" in descending order and compare your results with **Figure 14.1**.

FullName	Profit by Top Tier Customers
Nichole Nara	$13,295
Kaitlyn Henderson	$13,294
Margaret He	$13,269
Randall Dominguez	$13,266
Adriana Gonzalez	$13,243
Rosa Hu	$13,216
Brandi Gill	$13,196
⁴ She	⁻ 173

Figure 14.1 This report shows top-ranked customers and their overall sales.

Analysis

Because the measure needs to filter on a column, the formula uses CALCULATE with a filter argument. Since the formula doesn't require an iterator function, such as SUMX or FILTER, it doesn't use RELATED. In fact, using RELATED will give you an error "The column DimCustomer[Sales-Rank] either doesn't exist or doesn't have a relationship to any table available in the current context".

You can specify a more advanced filtering condition on the *same* column. For example, the following formula filters customers with a sales rank between 80 and 100.

Profit by Top Tier Customers = CALCULATE(SUM(FactInternetSales[SalesAmount]),
DimCustomer[SalesRank] >= 80 && DimCustomer[SalesRank] <= 100)

Practice

Change the "Profit by Top Tier Customers" to return only customers in Germany or France. All three of these formulas meet this requirement:

Profit by Top Tier Customers = CALCULATE(SUM(FactInternetSales[SalesAmount]), DimCustomer[SalesRank]<=100,
DimSalesTerritory[SalesTerritoryCountry] = "France" || DimSalesTerritory[SalesTerritoryCountry] = "Germany")

Profit by Top Tier Customers = CALCULATE(SUM(FactInternetSales[SalesAmount]), DimCustomer[SalesRank]<=100,
OR (DimSalesTerritory[SalesTerritoryCountry] = "France", DimSalesTerritory[SalesTerritoryCountry] = "Germany"))

Profit by Top Tier Customers = CALCULATE(SUM(FactInternetSales[SalesAmount]), DimCustomer[SalesRank]<=100,
DimSalesTerritory[SalesTerritoryCountry] IN {"France", "Germany"})

Analysis

Because now you need to filter on a different column, you must pass another filter argument to CALCULATE. The following formula produces an error "This expression contains multiple columns, but only a single column can be used in a True/False expression that is used as a table filter expression" because it attempts to filter on two columns in the same filter argument.

Profit by Top Tier Customers = CALCULATE(SUM(FactInternetSales[SalesAmount]),
DimCustomer[SalesRank]<=100 **&&** DimSalesTerritory[SalesTerritoryCountry] IN {"France", "Germany"})

You can also use the FILTER function to filter on multiple columns in a single filter expression, but the syntax gets more complicated and probably less efficient than using CALCULATE with multiple filter arguments.

```
Profit by Top Tier Customers = CALCULATE(SUM(FactInternetSales[SalesAmount]),
FILTER(
    FactInternetSales, RELATED(DimCustomer[SalesRank])<=100 &&
    RELATED(DimSalesTerritory[SalesTerritoryCountry]) IN {"France", "Germany"})
    )
```

 TIP As a best practice, use CALCULATE with multiple filter arguments to filter on multiple columns when AND (&&) filter conditions are needed. You'll get a shorter syntax and probably better performance.

14.1.2 Navigating Inactive Relationships

Power BI relationships are the foundation of ad-hoc analysis because users don't have to create custom queries to join tables. But existing Power BI limitations don't allow relationships everywhere in the model, forcing you to inactivate some relationships. These relationships are still useful because the CALCULATE filter arguments can navigate inactive relationships programmatically using the USERELATIONSHIP function.

Practice
Add a ShipSalesAmount measure that calculates the sum of FactInternetSales[SalesAmount] using the FactInternetSales[ShipDateKey] ⇨ DimDate[DateKey] inactive relationship.

```
ShipSalesAmount = CALCULATE(SUM(FactInternetSales[SalesAmount]),
            USERELATIONSHIP(FactInternetSales[ShipDateKey], DimDate[DateKey]))
```

Output
Create a Table report with DimDate[CalendarYear], FactInternetSales[SalesAmount], and FactInternetSales[ShipSalesAmount], as shown in **Figure 14.2**.

CalendarYear	SalesAmount	ShipSalesAmount
2010	$43,421	
2011	$7,075,526	$6,978,821
2012	$5,842,485	$5,801,073
2013	$16,351,550	$16,281,620
2014	$45,695	$297,163
Total	**$29,358,677**	**$29,358,677**

Figure 14.2 This report compares sales by order date and ship date.

Analysis
USERELATIONSHIP forces the measure to navigate the FactInternetSales[ShipDateKey] ⇨ DimDate[DateKey] inactive relationship instead of the default FactInternetSales[OrderDateKey] ⇨ DimDate[DateKey] active relationship. In other words, the ShipSalesAmount measure analyzes sales by the date the order was shipped. The equivalent SQL statement would be:

```
select CalendarYear, SUM(SalesAmount)
from FactInternetSales fis
left join DimDate d on fis.ShipDateKey = d.DateKey
group by d.CalendarYear
```

14.2 Removing Filters

I've previously introduced you to DAX functions for ignoring the filter context in calculated columns (ALL, ALLEXCEPT, ALLSELECTED). You can also use these functions as filter arguments to CALCULATE to implement measures. This allows you to implement measures that require a modified filter context, such as a measure for implementing percent of total.

14.2.1 Implementing Percent of Total

In the lesson "Creating Basic Measures", I showed you how to use the Power BI "Show value as" built-in feature to quickly create a percent of total measures. However, the issue was that you can't access and modify its formula. Next, I'll show you how to implement a similar explicit measure in case you need more control over the formula.

Practice
Follow these steps to add a PercentOfTotal measure to DimSalesTerritory:

1. Make sure that the Data View (or Report View) is selected. In the Fields pane, right-click the DimSalesTerritory table and click "New measure".

2. In the Formula field, enter the following formula and press Enter:
```
PercentOfTotal = DIVIDE (SUM(FactResellerSales[SalesAmount]),
                 CALCULATE (SUM(FactResellerSales[SalesAmount]), ALL(DimSalesTerritory)))
```

3. In the Fields pane, select the DimSalesTerritory[PercentOfTotal] measure. In the Formatting section of the ribbon's Modeling tab, change the Format property to Percentage with two decimal places.

Output
Add a Matrix visual with DimSalesTerritory[SalesTerritoryCountry] on rows, DimDate[Calendar-Year] on columns, and the FactResellerSales[SalesAmount] and DimSalesTerritory[PercentOfTotal] measures in the Values area (see **Figure 14.3**).

CalendarYear	2010		2011	
SalesTerritoryCountry ▲	SalesAmount	PercentOfTotal	SalesAmount	PercentOfTotal
Australia				
Canada	$115,361	23.58%	$3,602,561	19.80%
France			$97,496	0.54%
Germany				
United Kingdom			$80,687	0.44%
United States	$373,968	76.42%	$14,412,059	79.22%
Total	**$489,329**	**100.00%**	**$18,192,803**	**100.00%**

Figure 14.3 The custom PercentOfTotal measure shows the contribution of the country sales to the overall sales.

Analysis
To avoid division by zero, the expression uses the DIVIDE function, which performs a safe divide and returns a blank value when the denominator is zero. The nominator formula calculates the sales for the "current" country (determined by the cell filter context). For example, the measure in the cell next to Canada will return the Canada sales.

The denominator uses the CALCULATE function to overwrite the filter context. The formula passes ALL(DimSalesTerritory) as a second argument in the CALCULATE function to force the evaluation of SUM(FactResellerSales[SalesAmount]) across all countries (and across all values of any other column in DimSalesTerritory).

14.2.2 Counting Pending Orders

Let's implement a measure that counts pending orders. The order is pending (unfulfilled) when it's placed but not yet shipped as of the report date. In other words, the measure needs to count orders where the report date is between the order date and ship date.

Practice
Add the PendingOrdersCount measure to FactInternetSales with the following formula:

```
PendingOrdersCount =
    VAR EOP = MAX ( DimDate[Date] )
    RETURN
      CALCULATE (
        DISTINCTCOUNT ( FactInternetSales[SalesOrderNumber] ),
        FactInternetSales[ShipDate] >= EOP,
        FactInternetSales[OrderDate] <= EOP
        , ALL(DimDate)
      )
```

Output
Create a Matrix report with DimDate[CalendarYear], DimDate[EnglishMonthName], and Dim-Date[Date] in the Rows area and the PendingOrdersCount measure in Values (see **Figure 14.4**).

CalendarYear	PendingOrdersCount
⊟ **2010**	**14**
⊟ **December**	**14**
12/29/2010	5
12/30/2010	9
12/31/2010	14
⊟ **2011**	**59**

Figure 14.4 The PendingOrdersCount measure count orders where the report date is between OrderDate and ShipDate.

Analysis
The EOP (end of period) variable returns the last date in the current time period. For example, for year 2010 EOP returns December 31, 2010. However, if you expand to January 2010, EOP returns January 31, 2010. Then the formula calculates the distinct count of the SalesOrderNumber column using the DISTINCTCOUNT function, where EOP is between the order date and ship date.

The ALL function ignores the filter context by the FactInternetSales[OrderDateKey] ⇨ Dim-Date[Date] active relationship. If you don't ignore it, the report will produce the same results at the month level, but it will understate the pending order count at the date level. That's because only orders whose order date falls in the current period will be evaluated. However, you might have an order that was placed outside the current date period but not shipped yet. Hence, it's important to ignore the active relationship to DimDate.

14.2.3 Nesting Measures

Lastly, I want to finish this lesson with a best practice when it comes to measures that overwrite filters. It's common to have measures that depend on other measures but overwrite their context. For example, the insurance industry typically requires measures such as Count of Claims, Count of Open Claims, Count of Closed Claims, and so on. To reduce maintenance effort, you should chain measures together where new measures piggyback on existing measures.

Practice

In the lesson "Creating Basic Measures", you implemented a CustomerCount measure that counted customers who placed orders on the Adventure Works website. This measure had a rather complicated formula that applied different aggregations across different levels of the date hierarchy. Suppose you need another measure that counts customers who are professionals (their occupation is Professionals). Instead of repeating the entire formula, you can use the following formula:

CustomerCount (pros) = CALCULATE([CustomerCount], DimCustomer[EnglishOccupation] = "Professionals")

DAX supports an alternative and shorter syntax when the first argument of CALCULATE is an existing measure:

[measure] (filter, filter)

Using this syntax, you can rewrite the formula as follows:

CustomerCount (pros) = [CustomerCount] (DimCustomer[EnglishOccupation] = "Professionals")

Analysis

Avoid duplicating formulas. Instead, build upon existing measures by adding or removing filters. If you follow this best practice, you can change the formula in one place, and all dependent measures will inherit the changes. For example, if the requirements change and all measures that count customers need to count now active customers, you can change only the base CustomerCount measure.

14.3 Summary

CALCULATE is the bedrock of measure formulas. CALCULATE is a very versatile function but it can be overwhelming to understand. This lesson demonstrated how you can use CALCULATE to narrow or expand the filter context.

Lesson 15

Grouping Data

Sometimes, you might face a requirement that calls for grouping data. For example, in the lesson "Determining Filter Context" you've implemented an aggregate-over-aggregate measure that produces different results across levels in a date hierarchy. This lesson goes into more detail of how to group data before you can calculate metrics on the aggregated results. It also teaches you how to add expression-based columns when using the grouping functions. You'll find the DAX formulas for this lesson in \Source\Part3\Grouping Data.dax.

15.1 Understanding Grouping Functions

CALCULATE (with possibly FILTER) should help you tackle most of your measure requirements. Grouping data is typically required to implement aggregate-over-aggregate measures, such as a measure that aggregates at a month level in one way but in a different way at a year level. As a relatively new language, DAX has had its fair share of growing pains and this is no more evident than in its grouping functions. I'll quickly go through these functions and provide recommendations about their usage. **Table 15.1** compares at a glance the three grouping functions that I'll discuss and lists their main characteristics.

Table 15.1 DAX supports various grouping functions.

Function	Notes	Pros	Cons
ADDCOLUMNS/ SUMMARIZE	Returns a summary table with optional extended columns. Retains column values with no data.	Less restrictions	Avoid extended columns in SUMMARIZE (use ADDCOLUMNS)
GROUPBY	Creates a summary of the input table grouped by the specified columns. Excludes column values with no data.	Can aggregate over extended columns	Requires an extended "X" function for extended columns
SUMMARIZE COLUMNS	Creates a summary table for the requested totals over a set of groups. Excludes column values with no data.	Best performance	Doesn't always work in modified filter context

15.1.1 Understanding SUMMARIZE

SUMMARIZE is the DAX earliest function for grouping data. As its name suggests, SUMMARIZE summarizes (groups) a table by one or more columns. It can add optional measures to extend the return table.

Understanding SUMMARIZE syntax
SUMMARIZE has the following definition:

SUMMARIZE(<table>, <groupBy_columnName>[, <groupBy_columnName>]...[, <name>, <expression>]...)

The first argument must be a table or an expression that returns a table, such as FILTER. Next, you must specify at least one column from the table or a related table that you want to group by. For example, the CustomerCount measure used SUMMARIZE to group the DimDate table by the CalendarQuarter column.

```
SUMMARIZE ( DimDate, DimDate[CalendarQuarter] )
```

The result is a table with a single column (CalendarQuarter) containing the unique values in CalendarQuarter. SUMMARIZE acts as a SQL left join and retains columns with no data. The same result could be achieved with VALUES(DimDate[CalendarQuarter]) with the small difference that SUMMARIZE doesn't sort the grouped column values in any way while VALUES returns them sorted (as they will appear on a report).

```
EVALUATE
ADDCOLUMNS (
   VALUES ( DimDate[CalendarQuarter] ),
   "CustomerDCount", CALCULATE ( DISTINCTCOUNT ( DimCustomer[CustomerAlternateKey] ) )
)
```

Understanding extended columns

SUMMARIZE can also add one or more expression-based columns by using the name-expression syntax. These columns are sometimes referred to as *extended* columns. They are typically custom measures whose formulas aggregate data (like SQL GROUP BY clause with aggregates, such as SUM). For example, you can add a CustomerDCount column that counts distinct customers for each quarter.

```
SUMMARIZE ( DimDate,
DimDate[CalendarQuarter] ),
"CustomerDCount",  DISTINCTCOUNT ( DimCustomer[CustomerAlternateKey] )
```

The equivalent SQL query would be:

```
select d.CalendarQuarter, COUNT (distinct CustomerAlternateKey)
from DimDate d left join FactInternetSales fis on fis.OrderDateKey = d.DateKey
left join DimCustomer c on fis.CustomerKey = c.CustomerKey
group by d.CalendarQuarter
```

Understanding ADDCOLUMNS

The problem with extended columns and SUMMARIZE is that they don't perform well, and Microsoft can't "fix" it without potential side effects. For best performance, add extended columns with ADDCOLUMNS that wraps SUMMARIZE instead of adding them in SUMMARIZE:

```
ADDCOLUMNS (
    SUMMARIZE ( DimDate, DimDate[CalendarQuarter] ),
    "CustomerDCount", CALCULATE ( DISTINCTCOUNT ( DimCustomer[CustomerAlternateKey] ) )
)
```

Note that because ADDCOLUMNS is an iterator, you must include CALCULATE (not required for extended columns in SUMMARIZE) when the extended column uses an aggregate function.

15.1.2 Understanding Other Grouping Functions

To simplify grouping and improve performance, Microsoft introduced two other functions that are worth mentioning: GROUPBY and SUMMARIZECOLUMNS.

Understanding GROUPBY

The GROUPBY function has the same syntax as SUMMARIZE but it requires an "X" aggregate function, such as SUMX or AVERAGEX, for the formula in the extended column.

```
GROUPBY( FactInternetSales,
    DimDate[CalendarQuarter],
    "SumSales", SUMX( CURRENTGROUP(), FactInternetSales[SalesAmount])
    )
```

Unlike SUMMARIZE, GROUPBY removes column values with no data, so it acts as a SQL inner join. In addition, it sorts the results in the way the column values are sorted in the model. Instead of specifying a table as a first argument to the "X" function, you use a special CURRENTGROUP() construct. Evaluate the performance of GROUPBY and ADDCOLUMNS/SUMMARIZE and choose the one that performs better when extended columns use "X" functions. This could be an issue if you want to use DISTINCTCOUNT which doesn't have an "X" counterpart.

 NOTE GROUPBY could be especially useful with nested groups where an outer group aggregates an extended column in an inner group. ADDCOLUMNS/SUMMARIZE doesn't support this.

Understanding SUMMARIZECOLUMNS

To make it easier for Power BI to group data in DAX report queries, DAX added a SUMMARIZECOLUMNS function, which has this syntax:

```
SUMMARIZECOLUMNS( <groupBy_columnName> [, < groupBy_columnName >]..., [<filterTable>]...[, <name>,
<expression>]...)
```

Like SUMMARIZE and GROUPBY, SUMMARIZECOLUMNS takes one or more columns group by. By contrast, it also takes filter tables which are especially useful for DAX queries. For example, a variable can filter the date table as per the user's selection on the report and pass it as an argument to SUMMARIZESCOLUMNS to restrict the formula only for that date. Like GROUPBY, SUMMARIZECOLUMNS excludes column values with no data from the results so it acts as a SQL inner join.

SUMMARIZECOLUMNS should be more efficient than SUMMARIZE because it utilizes the storage engine better. Unfortunately, SUMMARIZECOLUMNS doesn't work in aggregate-over-aggregate measures and in other measures that modify the filter context. For example, you can attempt the following formula:

```
AVERAGEX (
    SUMMARIZECOLUMNS (DimDate[CalendarQuarter],
    "CustomerDCount", DISTINCTCOUNT ( DimCustomer[CustomerAlternateKey] )
    ),
    [CustomerDCount]
)
```

However, you'll get the error "SummarizeColumns() and AddMissingItems() may not be used in this context". Therefore, you must resort to ADDCOLUMNS/SUMMARIZE or GROUPBY for measures that require computing aggregates over aggregates.

15.2 Implementing Grouping Measures

Now that you know about the DAX grouping functions, let's take them for a ride. But before this, I'd like to emphasize when they are not required, and when you can use CALCULATE instead. In this practice, you'll implement a measure to calculate the average order sales amount for orders that have shipped as of the report date.

15.2.1 Using CALCULATE

Requirements can be tricky so make sure you understand what the business rules are and how they are supported by your data. Suppose you are tasked to calculate the average order sales amount by ship date. As you know by now, every row in FactResellerSales represents an order line item. Should you calculate the average *order* amount by just averaging the line items? Or, do you need to calculate the order total before you aggregate? If the former approach is OK, then CALCULATE is all you need.

Practice
Add an AvgOrderRevenue measure to FactResellerSales with the following formula:

```
AvgOrderRevenue =
   CALCULATE (
     AVERAGE ( FactResellerSales[SalesAmount] ),
     USERELATIONSHIP(FactResellerSales[ShipDateKey], DimDate[DateKey])
)
```

Output
To test the measure, create a Table visual with DimDate[CalendarYear] and AvgOrderRevenue, as shown in **Figure 15.1**.

CalendarYear	AvgOrderRevenue
2011	1,926
2012	1,288
2013	1,179
Total	**1,322**

Figure 15.1 The AvgOrderRevenue measure averages the order line item revenue.

Analysis
It's important to understand how this measure works. The AVERAGE function computes a simple average by summing up FactResellerSales[SalesAmount] for each row (order line item) in FactResellerSales whose ship date falls in the period, and then divides the sum by the number or rows. The formula uses USERELATIONSHIP to force the calculation over the FactResellerSales[ShipDateKey] ⇨ DimDate[DateKey] relationship.

What if you need to perform some arithmetic before aggregating the data, such as to compute the fulfillment time as Ship Date – Order Date? Well, the first argument of CALCULATE needs to be a column or a measure. So, you could add a calculated column to FactResellerSales with this formula:

```
FulfilledDuration = DATEDIFF(FactResellerSales[OrderDate], FactResellerSales[ShipDate], DAY)
```

But what if you need to implement multiple measures and creating calculated columns becomes counterproductive? The second option is to switch to AVERAGEX and avoid calculated columns whatsoever. This requires some formula reshuffling.

```
AvgOrderFulfilledTime =
   CALCULATE (
     AVERAGEX (
       FactResellerSales,
```

```
        DATEDIFF ( FactResellerSales[OrderDate], FactResellerSales[ShipDate], DAY )
    ),
    USERELATIONSHIP(FactResellerSales[ShipDateKey], DimDate[DateKey])
)
```

Because AVERAGEX requires a table as a first argument, the formula passes FactResellerSales. The advantage of AVERAGEX is that it can take an expression that is calculated for each row in the table (in the row context). The formula uses the DATEDIFF function to calculate the time difference in days between the line item order date and ship date.

15.2.2 Working with Grouping Functions

Let's move on now to the second version of the average order revenue, which requires an average over the order total. Therefore, you need to aggregate at the order level before computing the average. This requires using one of the aggregation functions I discussed in this lesson.

Practice
First, let's use ADDCOLUMNS/SUMMARIZE for the new version of the AvgOrderRevenue measure. Add a new measure AvgOrderRevenue (o) to FactResellerSales with the following formula

```
AvgOrderRevenue (o) =
AVERAGEX (
  CALCULATETABLE (
    ADDCOLUMNS (
      SUMMARIZE ( FactResellerSales, FactResellerSales[SalesOrderNumber] ),
      "OrderTotal", CALCULATE ( SUM ( FactResellerSales[SalesAmount] ) )
    ),
    USERELATIONSHIP ( FactResellerSales[ShipDateKey], DimDate[DateKey] )
  ),
  [OrderTotal]
)
```

Output
Add AvgOrderRevenue (o) to the report and compare your results with **Figure 15.**.

CalendarYear	AvgOrderRevenue	AvgOrderRevenue (o)
2011	$1,926	$22,041
2012	$1,288	$22,248
2013	$1,179	$20,111
Total	**$1,322**	**$21,194**

Figure 15.2 The AvgOrderRevenue (o) measure computes an average on top of the sales order total.

Analysis
Starting from SUMMARIZE and going outwards, first this formula groups on FactResellerSales [SalesOrderNumber]. Then, ADDCOLUMNS adds an extended column to sum the SalesAmount column. Next, CALCULATETABLE modifies the filter context by using USERELATIONSHIP to navigate the inactive relationship. Since ADDCOLUMNS returns a table, you need CALCULATETABLE (not CALCULATE) to make this change.

Now that you have the summary table, you're ready to compute the average. The formula uses AVERAGEX because it conveniently takes a table as the first argument. The second argument is the extended column added by ADDCOLUMNS.

Practice
The AvgOrderRevenue (o2) measure uses GROUPBY instead of ADDCOLUMNS/SUMMARIZE:

```
AvgOrderRevenue (o2) =
AVERAGEX (
  CALCULATETABLE (
    GROUPBY (
      FactResellerSales,
      FactResellerSales[SalesOrderNumber],
      "OrderTotal", SUMX ( CURRENTGROUP (), FactResellerSales[SalesAmount] )
    ),
    USERELATIONSHIP ( FactResellerSales[ShipDateKey], DimDate[DateKey] )
  ),
  [OrderTotal]
)
```

Analysis

GROUPBY has the same syntax as SUMMARIZE. The difference is that you need to use SUMX and CURRENTGROUP(). Using the profiling techniques you'll learn in the "Queries" part of the book, you can see that this version uses only two queries to the storage engines versus four with ADD-COLUMNS/SUMMARIZE. Therefore, it makes sense to test GROUPBY and use it if it performs better.

15.3 Summary

Most measure requirements can be met with CALCULATE or CALCULATETABLE. Use the DAX grouping functions to aggregate data when you need to produce aggregates over aggregates. Consider GROUPBY when you can use an "X" function for the aggregation. Otherwise, stick to ADD-COLUMNS/SUMMARIZE.

PART 4

Time intelligence

O ne of the most common data analytics tasks is implementing time calculations, such as year-to-date, parallel period, previous period, period-over-period variances, and so on. DAX has about 40 functions for extending your data models with time calculations, but you don't need to know them all.

This part of the book teaches you how to implement time intelligence. Since time intelligence re-quires a date table, it starts by teaching you how to work with built-in and custom date tables. After revisiting quick measures for time intelligence, it shows you how to implement custom formulas for more advanced requirements, such as custom date filters and semi-additive measures. You'll also learn how to centralize time intelligence formulas by using calculation groups.

You'll find the completed exercises and reports for this part of the book in the Adventure Works and Inventory models that are included in the \Source\Part4 folder.

Lesson 16

Working with Date Tables

Time intelligence requires a date table. Otherwise, DAX time intelligence functions won't work, or they will produce wrong results. This lesson starts by explaining what options Power BI supports for date tables. You'll learn the difference between built-in and custom date tables. I'll also share best practices for configuring date tables. You'll find the DAX formulas for this lesson in \Source\Part4\Working with Date Tables.dax.

16.1 Understanding Date Tables

A date table stores a range of dates that you need for data analytics. A data table must meet the following requirements:

- Day granularity – The granularity of the date table must be at a day level.
- Consecutive range – The date table must store a consecutive range of dates. No gaps are allowed.
- Date column – The date table must include a column of a Date data type. This is the only column required but typically a date table includes other columns for flexible exploration, such as CalendarQuarter, CalendarYear, and so on.

16.1.1 Understanding Auto-generated Date Tables

To avoid requiring you to create custom date tables, Power BI Desktop is configured by default to automatically generate date tables and hierarchies. In Power BI Desktop, this is controlled by the Auto Date/Time setting in File ⇨ Options and Settings ⇨ Options (Data Load tab in the Current File section). This feature generates a hidden date table for every column of a Date type. It also adds a hierarchy with Year, Quarter, Month, and Day levels under each date field in the Fields pane.

Understanding advantages of built-in date tables
The obvious advantage of the built-in date tables is that you may not need a custom date table. You can start analyzing your data by using the auto-generated Year, Quarter, Month, and Day levels (also called variations). Time intelligence formulas in quick measures support built-in date tables too.

Understanding disadvantages of built-in date tables
The main disadvantage of the built-in date tables is that they are not flexible. You can't access the actual tables and change them. You can't add additional fields or levels, such as to have a fiscal calendar or a flag to mark workdays. In addition, these can severely bloat your model as you discovered in the "Understanding Storage" lesson. Not only does Power BI generate a table for every date field, but it also adds rows for the entire date range.

For example, let's say you have a date with a minimum value of January 1, 1900 and a maximum value of December 31, 2200. When creating the hidden date table, Power BI will populate it with 109,573 rows. If you have 10 date fields like this, you've now added over one million rows just for date tables! This can severely bloat your data model. Therefore, if you plan to use auto-generated date tables, leave this feature on but monitor the size of your data model.

 TIP As a best practice, have a designated Date table and turn off auto-generated date tables. You can use the Vertipaq Analyzer to check the storage of the built-in date tables (all these tables whose names start with LocalDateTable_<guid>). Consider turning off built-in date tables if they consume excessive storage.

Using built-in date tables
You can use the levels of the built-in date hierarchies like any Power BI hierarchy. For example, you can drag the entire hierarchy or just one level to your visual. The left screenshot in **Figure 16.1** shows how the built-in hierarchies appear in the Fields pane. Power BI automatically generates the hierarchy and names it Date Hierarchy, but you can rename it. The right screenshot shows the hierarchy and its levels (variations) appear in the Values area if you add a date field (DueDate) that has auto-generated hierarchy.

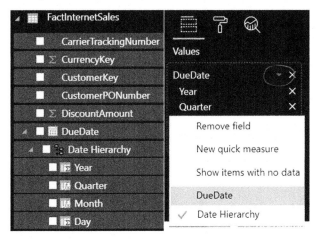

Figure 16.1 You can use auto-generated hierarchies and levels like any other any Power BI hierarchy or field.

Notice that you can remove hierarchy levels in the Visualizations pane if you don't need them on the report. If you only want to see the date field (and not the hierarchy) in your visual, you can expand the dropdown next to the home field in the Visualizations pane and switch from the hierarchy to the date field, as shown in **Figure 16.1**.

Disabling built-in date tables
You can turn off the Auto Date/Time setting in your Power BI Desktop file to disable built-in date tables. You must turn it off for each Power BI Desktop file (currently, there isn't a global default setting). This is what happens when you turn this setting off:

- Power BI deletes all built-in date tables in the model. You can't turn them on and off per field or table.
- If there are existing measures, such as quick measures, that reference the date variations, they will be invalidated. You must change their formulas to reference the corresponding fields in your custom Date table.

Power BI supports special syntax for referencing auto-generated date levels. For example, if you create a quick year-to-date measure that references a date field with an auto-generated date hierarchy, Power BI generates this formula:

```
SalesAmount YTD =
IF(
    ISFILTERED('FactInternetSales'[OrderDate]),
    ERROR("Time intelligence quick measures can only be grouped or filtered by the Power BI-provided
    date hierarchy or primary date column."),
    TOTALYTD(
        SUM('FactInternetSales'[SalesAmount]),
        'FactInternetSales'[OrderDate].[Date]
    )
)
```

'DimDate'[Date].Date references the Date variation of the auto-generated date table for the Fact-InternetSales[OrderDate] field. Once you disable the Auto Date/Time setting, this variation won't exist anymore, and the formula will be invalidated. To fix it, just change the formula to reference the Date column in your Date table as follows (changes are shown in **bold**):

```
SalesAmount YTD =
IF(
    ISFILTERED(DimDate[Date]),
    ERROR("Time intelligence quick measures can only be grouped or filtered by the Power BI-provided
    date hierarchy or primary date column."),
    TOTALYTD(
        SUM('FactInternetSales'[SalesAmount]),
        DimDate.[Date]
    ))
```

16.1.2 Understanding Custom Date Tables

A best practice is to have a separate date table and write time calculations to use this table. This approach is preferable because it's more flexible (you control what fields and hierarchies you want), reduces storage, and centralizes maintaining your date table in one place. A date table typically includes additional columns for flexible time exploration, such as Quarter, Year, Fiscal Quarter, Fiscal Year, Holiday Flag, and so on. It may also include fiscal and manufacturing calendars.

Creating custom date tables
There are a few ways to create a custom date table. You can import it from your corporate data warehouse. You can maintain it in an Excel file and import it from there. As I demonstrated in the lesson "Implementing Calculated Tables", you can also use the CALENDAR and CALENDARAUTO functions to auto-generate a date table. You can even generate it in Power Query using custom code written in the "M" query language.

And, as I explained in the same lesson, you can have more than one date table in your model. This could be useful if you want to aggregate the same fact table by multiple dates, such as order date, ship date, and due date.

Marking a date table
You should go one step further by telling Power BI about your date table(s) by marking as such (right-click the date table in the Fields pane and click "Mark as date table" ⇨ "Mark as date table"). Marking a date table accomplishes several things:

- Disables the Power BI-generated date table for the Date field in the Date table. Note that it doesn't remove the built-in date tables from the other tables unless you disable the Auto Date/Time setting in File ⇨ Options and Settings ⇨ Options (Data Load tab).

- Lets you use your Date table for time calculations in Quick Measures.
- Makes DAX time calculations work even if the relationship between a fact table and the Date table is created on a field that is not a date field, such as a smart integer key in the format YYYYMMDD. If the table is not marked, you must use ALL(DimDate) in your DAX time intelligence formulas to make them work.
- When Analyze in Excel is used, enables special Excel date-related features when you use a field from the Date table, such as date filters.

You can unmark a date table at any time by going through the same steps (right-click the table and then click "Mark as date table" ➪ "Mark as date table"). If you want to change the settings, such as to use a different date column, go to "Mark as date table" ➪ "Date table settings".

What about analysis by time?
One existing limitation of the automatic in-line date hierarchy feature is that it doesn't generate time levels, such as Hour, Minute, and so on. If you require time analysis, create a Time table with the required levels and join it to the fact table. This usually involves the following steps:

1. Create a DimTime table. Typically, this table is grained at a minute level, so it will have 1,440 rows to store all minutes in a day. There are plenty of scripts on the Internet for generating such a table. I recommend the primary key of this table be of the Time data type (so you can join it directly to the corresponding foreign key in the fact table).
2. If this is not done already, in your fact table break the column of the DateTime data type into two columns: one that stores the date and another column that stores the time.
3. Join the two columns to their respective dimension tables. If you need to analyze the data by time, use DimTime, or you can use it together with DimDate to analyze the data by date and time.

16.2   Working with Date Tables

If you haven't done so, let's take a moment to make the necessary configuration changes to the date tables in the Adventure Works model. I'll also show you why leaving the date fields in the fact tables could be beneficial in some cases.

16.2.1 Working with Built-in Date Tables

Because by default Power BI auto-generates date tables, every date field in our model has a hidden date table behind it.

Practice
Let's take a moment to get familiar with the built-in date tables.

1. Open the Adventure Works model in Power BI Desktop.
2. In the Fields pane, expand FactInternetSales, and then expand the OrderDate field. Notice that it has a Date Hierarchy. This tells you that the model has built-in date tables.
3. Right-click the FactInternetSales table and click "New quick measure".
4. Configure the measure as shown in **Figure 16.2** and click OK.

Quick measures

Calculation	Fields
Year-to-date total ▼	🔍 Search

Calculate the total of the base value, starting from the beginning of the current year. Learn more

Base value ⓘ

| Sum of SalesAmount ▼ ✕ |

Date ⓘ

| OrderDate ✕ |

Don't see the calculation you want? Post an idea.

FactInternetSales
- CarrierTrackingNumber
- Σ CurrencyKey
- CustomerKey
- CustomerPONumber
- Σ DiscountAmount
- ▸ 📅 DueDate
- Σ DueDateKey
- Σ ExtendedAmount
- Σ Freight
- ▸ 📅 OrderDate
- Σ SalesAmount

[OK] Cancel

Figure 16.2 You can create quick time intelligence measures using the built-in date tables.

Output
Power BI creates SalesAmount YTD measure in the FactInternetSales table.

1. Add a Table visual and bind it to the FactInternetSales[OrderDate] date hierarchy and the Internet-Sales[SalesAmount YTD] measure. Verify that the measure works as expected.

2. Go to File ⇨ Options and settings ⇨ Settings and turn off the Auto Date/Time setting in Data Load tab (the Current File section). Click OK.

3. Back to the report, notice that the visual fails to render. If you click the detail link, you'll see the error "Column reference in 'OrderDate' in table 'FactInternetSales' cannot be used with a variation 'Date' because it doesn't have any". In addition, there is a warning icon preceding the SalesAmount YTD measure in the Fields pane indicating that the measure is invalidated.

Analysis
I recommend you decide upfront if you'll use a custom date table or built-in date tables. If your reports or measures reference built-in date tables, they will be invalidated once you disable the "Auto Date/Time setting".

16.2.2 Working with Custom Date Tables

In the previous practice, you disabled the built-in date tables because you had a custom DimDate date table. In this practice, you'll mark this table as such to let Power BI validate it. You'll also change the quick measure formula to use the DimDate.

Practice
Star by marking the date table.

1. In the Fields list, right-click the Date table and then click "Mark as date table" ⇨ "Mark as date table".

2. Expand the "Date column" drop-down and select the Date column (you must select a column that has a Date data type), as shown in **Figure 16.3**. Press OK once Power BI validates the date table to ensure that it meets the requirements I listed at the beginning of this lesson.

Mark as date table

×

Select a column to be used for the date. The column must be of the data type 'date' and must contain only unique values. Learn more

Date column

Date ▼

🗑 Validated successfully

ⓘ When you mark this as a date table, the built-in date tables that were associated with this table
are removed. Visuals or DAX expressions referring to them may break.
Learn how to fix visuals and DAX expressions

OK   Cancel

Figure 16.3 Mark your
date table(s) to let Power
BI know about them.

4. Change the formula of the FactInternetSales[SalesAmount YTD] measure to reference DimDate[Date].

Output

The FactInternetSales[SalesAmount YTD] measure validates successfully and the report works again. If you right-click the Date table and then click "Mark as date table" again, you should see a green check mark indicating that the DimDate table is already marked.

Analysis

As I explained, marking a date table has important advantages, including letting Power BI validate its data so that your DAX time intelligence formulas work as expected.

Practice

Now that you have a custom date table, should you leave the date fields behind in the fact table? This will surely confuse the end user as to which date to use. However, having these fields could be very beneficial to overwrite the selection in filters and slicers. Suppose you have a dashboard-looking report that has a slicer to let the user select one or more years by filtering DimDate[CalendarYear]. However, there is a chart that must overwrite the filter selection and show a trend across several years.

1. Add a Column Chart visual and bind it to FactInternetSales[OrderDate] in the Axis area and FactInternetSales[SalesAmount] in the Values area.

2. Add a slicer and bind it to DimDate[CalendarYear], as shown in **Figure 16.4**.

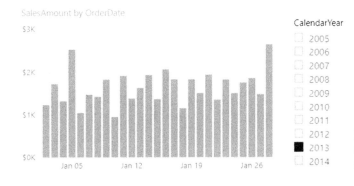

Figure 16.4 You can use
date fields in fact tables to
overwrite global filters.

4. This step is important to prevent the slicer from filtering the chart. Click the slicer to select it. In the Format ribbon, click "Edit interactions". You should see additional icons appearing outside the chart. Click the None icon.

5. Use the Filter pane to apply a chart-level filter, such as to filter OrderDate after January 1, 2014.

Output
The chart has a visual-level filter on OrderDate that works independently from the global filter on CalendarYear, as you can see by changing the year in the slicer. More importantly, the chart can be reconfigured to show sales by any other date field in FactInternetSales, such as DueDate or ShipDate.

Analysis
You can use the date fields in fact tables to overwrite global filters and to allow the user to slice the report by dates that might not even have relationships to your custom date table, such as Order-Date, ShipDate, DueDate. Unfortunately, Power BI doesn't allow you to turn on built-in date hierarchies selectively, such as to enable the Year-Quarter-Month-Day hierarchy on the DueDate field but not for other dates. Hence, if the built-in date tables don't consume too much space, consider leaving them enabled for maximum flexibility.

16.3 Summary

Date tables are very important to any model because almost every model needs time intelligence. In this lesson, you learned about built-in and custom date tables. As a best practice, use a custom date table but consider leaving built-in date tables if you need their auto-generated variations and if they don't bloat the model. Don't forget to mark your custom date table as such.

Lesson 17

Quick Time Intelligence

You've seen how quick measures deliver pre-packaged DAX measure formulas. This lesson continues exploring the quick measures for time intelligence. It will help you understand how time intelligence formulas work, and how you can modify the formulas to tailor them to your needs. You'll find the DAX formulas for this lesson in \Source\Part4\Quick Time Intelligence.dax.

17.1 Understanding Quick Time Intelligence

Currently, Power BI packs seven quick measures specific to time intelligence. **Table 17.1** groups them in three categories: "To-date", "Period-over-period % change", and "Rolling average".

Table 17.1 This table shows the quick time intelligence measures organized in three categories.

Category	Time Intelligence Formulas Used	Description
To-date	TOTALYTD, TOTALQTD, TOTALMTD	Computes the "to-date" value from the first day of the period until the current date.
Period-over-period % change	DATEADD	Computes the % change between two periods.
Rolling average	ENDOFMONTH, STARTOFMONTH, DATESBETWEEN, LASTDATE, DATESINPERIOD	Computes an average over several periods.

17.1.1 Understanding "To-date" Measures

DAX has three functions for computing "to-date" running aggregates: TOTALYTD, TOTALQTD, and TOTALMTD. They have the same syntax with the exception that TOTALYTD has an optional fourth argument to let you specify the year's end date.

TOTALYTD (<Expression>, <Dates> [, <Filter>] [, <YearEndDate>])

Understanding syntax
The first argument is the expression to be evaluated. For example, if you need to compute the sum of FactInternetSales[SalesAmount], you'll pass SUM(FactInternetSales[SalesAmount]). Or, if you have an existing measure, you can specify the measure name in square brackets, such as [NetProfit].

Since your model might have multiple date tables (or multiple built-in date hierarchies), the second argument must reference a column of a Date data type that will be used to evaluate the expression over time, such as DimDate[Date]. If you use a built-in date table, you need to reference the Date variant, such as FactInternetSales[OrderDate].Date.

The Filter argument is optional. Like CALCULATE, you can pass a filter condition or a table to filter the results further. For example, if you don't mark your date table and the relationship to

DimDate is not on a date column, you must pass ALL(DimDate) to the Filter argument for the function to work. However, if the relationship is on a date column and the custom date table is marked, Power BI adds the ALL function in the formula for you and you can omit it.

Lastly, TOTALYTD takes an optional YearEndDate argument, which could be handy for working with fiscal years. For example, if your fiscal year ends in June, you can pass "6/30", "Jun 30", or "30 June", or any string that resolves to a month/day. Unfortunately, you can't pass a measure (you must provide a static string).

 TIP As a best practice, have a designated Date table with the calendars you need, such as regular, fiscal, and manufacturing calendars. If you do this, you have more flexibility and don't have to specify the YearEndDate argument for fiscal years. Not to mention that quarters also need to be offset for fiscal calendars, but TOTALQTD doesn't accept a YearEndDate argument.

Understanding evaluation

The "to-date" functions help you avoid constructing the date ranges for time intelligence measures. For example, TOTALYTD (SUM[FactInternetSales[SalesAmount], DimDate[Date]) is a shortcut to:

```
CALCULATE (SUM ( FactInternetSales[SalesAmount] ),  DATESYTD ( DimDate[Date] ))
```

The DATESYTD function removes any filters from the DimDate table and then applies a filter to select all dates from the beginning of the period until the current date. In the case of TOTALYTD, the filter looks like this:

```
CALCULATE (
    SUM ( FactInternetSales[SalesAmount] ),
    FILTER (
        ALL ( DimDate[Date] ),
        DimDate[Date] <= MAX ( DimDate[Date] ) && YEAR ( DimDate [Date] ) = YEAR ( MAX ( DimDate [Date] ) )
    ))
```

As you know by now, the MAX function returns the largest value in the filter selection. So, if the user sets the report date to July 4, 2013, MAX(DimDate[Date]) will return this date. The FILTER function filters all dates where their year matches the current year and that are before or equal to the current date.

17.1.2 Understanding Variance Measures

There are three variance quick measures for computing period-over-period percentage variance at year, quarter, and month levels. The Quick Measures window allows you to specify the number of periods to lag, such as in the case when you need to calculate the variance between parallel periods.

Understanding syntax

This is what the quick measure formula looks like for Year-over-year change with the default lag of one year and SUM aggregation:

```
SalesAmount YoY%  =
VAR __PREV_YEAR =
    CALCULATE(
        SUM('FactResellerSales'[SalesAmount]),
        DATEADD('DimDate'[Date], -1, YEAR)
    )
RETURN
    DIVIDE(SUM('FactInternetSales'[SalesAmount]) - __PREV_YEAR, __PREV_YEAR)
```

Understanding evaluation

This formula defines a VAR __PREV_YEAR variable which calculates the SUM('FactResellerSales' [SalesAmount]) for the same period last year. Like the "to-date" functions, DATEADD takes a date column as the first argument. If the number of periods is positive, DATEADD adjusts the date filter forward, otherwise it lags the current period with the number of periods specified. Finally, the third argument specifies at what level to lag.

Given the above example and the current month of April 2013, DATEADD with one year to lag returns April 2012. Finally, the formula computes the variance as a percentage by using the DIVIDE function for a safe divide in case the previous year value is zero.

As you can see, the quick calculations are easy to understand. And the best part is that you can change the formulas if needed. The last quick measure type (rolling average) is an interesting calculation which involves several date functions. I'll explain how it works and how to change its behavior in the next section.

17.2 Implementing Rolling Averages

A rolling average measure is typically used to give you a better idea of values in a series by smoothing ups and downs. Suppose you need to implement a rolling average measure over three months (previous, current, and next month), as shown in **Figure 17.1**.

CalendarYear	EnglishMonthName	SalesAmount	SalesAmount rolling average (c)
2010	November		$43,421
2010	December	$43,421	$256,622
2011	January	$469,824	$326,527
2011	February	$466,335	$473,786
2011	March	$485,199	$484,536
2011	April	$502,074	$516,318
2011	May	$561,681	$600,532

Figure 17.1 The "SalesAmount rolling average (c)" measure computes a rolling average over three months.

The highlighted cell for January 2011 is computed as a simple average over the previous month (December 2010), current month (January 2011), and the next month (February 2011). The formula can't just divide the sum by three. Instead, it must divide by the number of periods with data. For example, the November 2010 is computed by dividing the December 2010 value by one since there is data for December only.

17.2.2 Implementing a Quick Measure

The rolling average is one of the quick measures that Power BI supports. If you're excited about quick gains and DAX avoidance, let's take this path to see how far you can get.

Practice

Follow these steps to implement the rolling average as a quick measure:

1. Right-click FactInternetSales in the Fields pane and click "New quick measure".
2. In the "Quick measures" window, expand the Calculation dropdown and select "Rolling average" under the "Time intelligence" section.

3. Drag FactInternetSales[SalesAmount] to the "Base value" field. Notice that the default aggregation is Sum, but you can expand the dropdown and select another standard aggregation function. You can also drag an existing explicit measure.

4. Expand the Period dropdown and select Months to compute the rolling average across months.

5. Leave the "Periods before" and "Periods after" to their default values of 1.

6. If you have followed my advice from the last lesson to remove the built-in date tables, attempt to drag DimDate[Date] to the Date field. Notice that Power BI complains with the following error "Only Power BI-provided date hierarchies are supported". Unfortunately, the rolling average quick measure doesn't work with a custom date table (a custom date table is a best practice).

7. To complete this exercise, click Cancel. Then turn on the Auto Date/Time setting in File ⇨ Options and Settings ⇨ Options (Data Load tab in the Current File section). This will auto-generate date tables for each date field in the model. Don't worry that this is not a best practice. I'll show you how to use a custom date table later.

8. Create a new quick measure and this time, drag FactInternetSales[OrderDate] to the Date field. Compare your setup with **Figure 17.2**. Click OK.

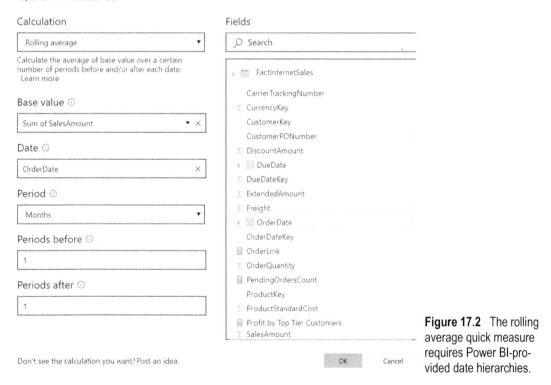

Figure 17.2 The rolling average quick measure requires Power BI-provided date hierarchies.

Output

Power BI adds a "SalesAmount rolling average" to the Fields pane.

1. Rename this measure to *SalesAmount rolling average (q)*.

2. Add a Table visual with FactInternetSales[OrderDate] (Year and Month levels are enough), FactInternetSales[SalesAmount], and FactInternetSales[SalesAmount rolling average (q)] to the Values area. Compare your results to **Figure 17.1**.

Analysis

If you select the "SalesAmount rolling average (q)" measure in the Fields pane, you'll see this rather complicated formula in the formula bar:

```
SalesAmount rolling average (q) =
IF(
    ISFILTERED('FactInternetSales'[OrderDate]),
    ERROR("Time intelligence quick measures can only be grouped or filtered by the Power BI-provided date hierarchy or primary date column."),
    VAR __LAST_DATE = ENDOFMONTH('FactInternetSales'[OrderDate].[Date])
    VAR __DATE_PERIOD =
        DATESBETWEEN(
                'FactInternetSales'[OrderDate].[Date],
                STARTOFMONTH(DATEADD(__LAST_DATE, -1, MONTH)),
                ENDOFMONTH(DATEADD(__LAST_DATE, 1, MONTH))
        )
    RETURN
        AVERAGEX(
                CALCULATETABLE(
                        SUMMARIZE(
                                VALUES('FactInternetSales'),
                                'FactInternetSales'[OrderDate].[Year],
                                'FactInternetSales'[OrderDate].[QuarterNo],
                                'FactInternetSales'[OrderDate].[Quarter],
                                'FactInternetSales'[OrderDate].[MonthNo],
                                'FactInternetSales'[OrderDate].[Month]
                        ),
                        __DATE_PERIOD
                ),
                CALCULATE(
                        SUM('FactInternetSales'[SalesAmount]),
                        ALL('FactInternetSales'[OrderDate].[Day])
                )
        )
)
```

Let's take a moment to understand it, so you can customize it later. The formula starts with an IF statement which uses the ISFILTERED function to ensure that a variation of the built-in OrderDate hierarchy is on the report. Then, it declares a variable VAR __LAST_DATE which uses the ENDOFMONTH to return the last date in the month.

The formula also declares a variable VAR __DATE_PERIOD to store a table of date periods required for the calculation. The variable formula uses the DATESBETWEEN function, which returns a table with one column populated with dates within a given range. In this case, the range starts at the beginning of the previous month (STARTOFMONTH returns the first date in a month). and ends one month after the current month. The net effect is that VAR __DATE_PERIOD has all the dates that span the previous, current, and next month.

The main part of the formula (where RETURN starts) is somewhat convoluted but we can simplify it later. Starting with SUMMARIZE, first the formula groups FactInternetSales by Year, Quarter, and Month levels. Then CALCULATETABLE is used to filter the grouped table only for the dates in the __DATE_PERIOD variable. The net result is that SUMMARIZE will have as many rows as the number of combinations of the grouped fields. In other words, SUMMARIZE will produce a table populated with all months that have sales.

Finally, AVERAGEX is used to produce the simple average over the date table. The simple average will be computed over the sum of FactInternetSales[SalesAmount]. The formula uses CALCULATE to remove the filter context from the Day variation of the built-in OrderDate hierarchy.

17.2.3 Customizing the Quick Measure

In this practice, you'll customize the rolling average formula to use the custom DimDate table and to simplify it.

Practice

Let's create a new measure so you can test the modified formula side by side with the query measure. Add a new measure to FactInternetSales with the following formula:

```
SalesAmount rolling average (c) =
    VAR __LAST_DATE = ENDOFMONTH(DimDate[Date])
    VAR __DATE_PERIOD =
        DATESBETWEEN(
                DimDate[Date],
                STARTOFMONTH(DATEADD(__LAST_DATE, -1, MONTH)),
                ENDOFMONTH(DATEADD(__LAST_DATE, 1, MONTH))
        )
    RETURN
        AVERAGEX(
                CALCULATETABLE(
                        ADDCOLUMNS(
                            SUMMARIZE(
                                DimDate,
                                DimDate[CalendarYear],
                                DimDate[EnglishMonthName]
                            ),
                            "Sales", CALCULATE(SUM('FactInternetSales'[SalesAmount]))
                        ),
                        __DATE_PERIOD
                )
            , [Sales]
        )
```

Output

Change your report as follows:

1. Replace the OrderDate variations from the report with DimDate[CalendarYear] and DimDate[EnglishMonthName].

2. Replace the [SalesAmount rolling average (q)] measure with [SalesAmount rolling average (c)].

The report should produce the same results. As an optional step, disable the built-in date hierarchies to make sure that the formula works without them.

Analysis

This formula reuses the two variables from the quick measure formula, but it makes the following changes:

1. SUMMARIZE groups only at the year and month levels because this combination returns all months within a given year, such as "2010 January", "2010 February", and so on. Note that if you just group by EnglishMonthName, you'll get a table with 12 rows that sum sales across all years (if the year is not on the report), so you need to add the year in the SUMMARIZE function.

2. The formula uses the ADDCOLUMNS/SUMMARIZE pattern to project an extended column "Sales". You can also use GROUPBY. In this case, the ADDCOLUMNS/SUMMARIZE pattern works great because it returns only rows with data (remember that the simple average needs to divide by months with data only).

3. Instead of using CALCULATE, AVERAGEX iterates over the summarized table and produces a simple average over the [Sales] extended column.

17.3 Summary

Quick measures are a great way to get you started with DAX formulas provided by Microsoft. However, they have limitations and you still need to know DAX to tailor them to your needs. Now that you know about time intelligence functions and how they work, let's create custom calculations that go beyond quick measures for time intelligence.

Lesson 18

Custom Time Intelligence

As you've seen, Power BI comes with useful quick measures for basic time intelligence, but the chances are that your time intelligence requirements will go far beyond these metrics. This lesson starts by explaining how to overwrite the date filter context. It walks you through the implementation of custom time intelligence calculations, such as for analyzing data by weeks. You'll find the DAX formulas for this lesson in \Source\Part4\Custom Time Intelligence.dax.

18.1 Understanding Custom Time Intelligence

Custom time intelligence is based on the following tenants:

- Custom date table – As I explained in the lesson "Working with Date Tables", a custom date table is a best practice because you can extend the date table with useful fields, such as fiscal calendars and weeks. You should mark this date table as such so that Power BI can validate it and that time intelligence functions work when they reference this table.

- Date filter context – Depending on your requirements, you need to learn how to modify the date filter context. For example, if you are working on a measure that returns revenue for the current week, you must filter the date table accordingly.

18.1.1 Changing Date Context

As you know by now, once you move beyond basic measures, you need to change the measure filter context in different ways. Custom time intelligence is no exception. At a high level, implementing your own time intelligence may involve two steps. First, try to find a suitable DAX function for the task at hand. If one exists, then use it because it will simplify your formula. For example, it will overwrite the date context for you, so you don't have to ignore it explicitly with the ALL function. If there is no suitable DAX function, then create your own date filter context by using whatever date arithmetic is required. Let's discuss these two steps in more detail.

Understanding the PREVIOUSDAY function
Suppose you're working on a measure that returns the revenue for the previous day, such as to calculate a variance between the current day and previous day. After consulting with the DAX documentation, you come across the PREVIOUSDAY function, which looks promising. It has this syntax:

PREVIOUSDAY (<Dates>)

It takes a single argument, which typically is a reference to a column of a Date data type (or DateTime). DAX transitions the filter context and you don't have to ignore it with the ALL function:

Understanding context transition

Figure 18.1 shows how PREVIOUSDAY changes the filter context. Suppose the user has selected July 4, 2018 in a report slicer or filter. This becomes the "as of" or "current" date that defines the default filter context for all time calculations on the report.

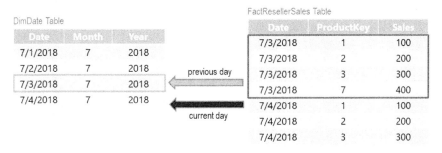

DimDate Table

Date	Month	Year
7/1/2018	7	2018
7/2/2018	7	2018
7/3/2018	7	2018
7/4/2018	7	2018

previous day

current day

FactResellerSales Table

Date	ProductKey	Sales
7/3/2018	1	100
7/3/2018	2	200
7/3/2018	3	300
7/3/2018	7	400
7/4/2018	1	100
7/4/2018	2	200
7/4/2018	3	300

Figure 18.1 DAX functions, such as PREVIOUSDAY, change the filter context on the Date dimension.

If you don't use any time intelligence function that transitions the date filter context, your measures will evaluate formulas as of the current date. Let's say you have the following measure:

PreviousDaySales = CALCULATE(SUM(FactResellerSales[SalesAmount]), PREVIOUSDAY(DimDate[Date]))

When DAX parses PREVIOUSDAY and discovers a reference to a date column, it replaces the reference with the following formula:

CALCULATETABLE (DISTINCT (<Dates>))

The CALCULATETABLE function transitions the filter context on the DimDate table to July 3, 2018 and the measure returns the revenue as of that date.

18.1.2 Creating Custom Date Context

Although DAX packs many time intelligence functions to address common requirements, sometimes you won't find an appropriate function. In this case, you need to filter your date table (or built-in date hierarchy) explicitly to evaluate the formula in the appropriate context.

Filtering the date table

You can use the FILTER function to filter the date table but DATESBETWEEN is specifically designed to work with dates. It has the following definition:

DATESBETWEEN (<Dates>, <StartDate>, <EndDate>)

The first argument is a reference to a column of a Date data type, such as DimDate[Date]. The second and third arguments define the range. If the StartDate is omitted, DATESBETWEEN defaults to the earliest date in the Dates column evaluated in the current context (same as MIN(DimDate[Date]). Similarly, if the EndDate is omitted, DATESBETWEEN will default to the latest date in the Dates column evaluated in the current context (same as MAX(DimDate[Date]).

Using variables

Variables could make the date arithmetic easier to read and maintain, and the resulting formulas might perform better. The rolling average measure you implemented in the previous lesson uses variables to scope the date period.

VAR __LAST_DATE = ENDOFMONTH(DimDate[Date])
VAR __DATE_PERIOD =
    DATESBETWEEN(

```
        DimDate[Date],
        STARTOFMONTH(DATEADD(__LAST_DATE, -1, MONTH)),
        ENDOFMONTH(DATEADD(__LAST_DATE, 1, MONTH))
    )
```

Once you have the filtered date table, you can add it as an argument to CALCULATE or CALCU-LATETABLE to modify the measure filter context.

18.2 Implementing Custom Time Intelligence

Let's put what you've learned about customizing time intelligence into practice. Analyzing data by weeks is a common requirement. However, as you'll quickly discover there are no DAX functions for working with weeks, except WEEKDAY (returns a number identifying the day of the week) and WEEKNUM (returns the week number in the year). In the first practice, you'll add a column to the DimDate table in the format "W <weekstartdate>". In the second practice, you'll implement a rolling variance for comparing the revenue in the last seven days to the revenue in the seven days prior to that.

18.2.1 Adding Weeks to Date Tables

Management has requested the ability to analyze data by weeks. The week name should include the week starting date. You'll implement this requirement by adding a calculated column to DimDate.

Practice
Follow these steps to implement the WeekName calculated column:

1. In the Fields pane (Data View or Report View tab), right-click DimDate and then click "New column".

2. Enter the following formula in the formula bar for the new calculated column:

WeekName = "W " & FORMAT((DimDate[Date] - WEEKDAY(DimDate[Date], 2) + 1), "Short Date")

3. To sort weeks in their chronological order as opposed to an alphanumeric order, add a WeekSort calculated column with this formula:

WeekSort = DimDate[Date] - WEEKDAY(DimDate[Date], 2) + 1

4. In the Data View tab with DimDate selected, select the WeekName column. In the Modeling tab, expand the "Sort By Column" button and select WeekSort.

5. Hide the WeekSort column because it's used just for sorting.

CalendarYear	W 12/27/2010	W 1/24/2011	W 2/28/2011	W 3/28/2011	W 4/25/2011
2010	$489,329				
2011		$1,538,408	$1,165,897	$844,721	$2,324,136
2012					
2013					
Total	**$489,329**	**$1,538,408**	**$1,165,897**	**$844,721**	**$2,324,136**

Figure 18.2 Use the WeekName function to analyze revenue by weeks.

Output
Add a Matrix visual with DimDate[CalendarYear] in the Rows area, DimDate[WeekName] in the Columns area, and FactResellerSales[Amount] in the Values area (see **Figure 18.2**). The date format in the WeekName column may differ from the screenshot because it will reflect your local culture.

Analysis

The formula uses the WEEKDAY function to construct the week name. WEEKDAY returns a number from 1 to 7. The second argument of WEEKDAY is optional, and it allows you to specify the week start day. The default value is one, which means that the week will start on Sunday. The formula passes two to start the week on Monday. The weekday is then subtracted from the Date column so that all days within a week share the same week name. For example, if DimDate[Date] is July 4, 2019 (Thursday), the formula subtracts 4 from that date and it gets Jun 30, 2019. Then it adds one and it gets July 1, 2019, which falls on a Monday.

Then, the formula uses the FORMAT function to format the date. FORMAT supports different format settings for numbers and dates. As a best practice, you use the predefined culture-neutral formats, such as "Short Date", so that Power BI can format the column using your culture settings.

 NOTE The week names may require more complex logic when they span years. This example carries the previous year into the next. For example, the week starting December 29, 2008 is named "W 12/29/2008" but you may need to start every new year with a new week.

18.2.2 Implementing a Rolling Variance

You're tasked to implement a week-over-week (WoW) rolling variance to calculate the change between count of orders submitted in the last 7 days to count of orders submitted in the seven days prior to that. The measure must work as of any date specified by the interactive user.

Practice

Let's go through a couple of implementation options. Start by implementing an explicit measure to return the distinct count of FactInternetSales[SalesOrderNumber] (remember that an order can have several line items so you can't just count SalesOrderNumber).

1.Add a measure FactInternetSales[OrderCount] with the following formula:

```
OrderCount = DISTINCTCOUNT(FactInternetSales[SalesOrderNumber])
```

2.To avoid an overly complex formula that defines two measures and a variance, let's break it up into three measures. First, implement an OrderCount7 measure to count orders placed in the last seven days as of the report date:

```
OrderCount7 =
VAR EOP = MAX ( DimDate[Date] )
VAR BOP = MAX ( DimDate[Date] ) - 6
VAR Period = DATESBETWEEN ( DimDate[Date], BOP, EOP )
RETURN
    CALCULATE ( [OrderCount], Period )
```

Another way to write this measure would be:

```
OrderCount7 =
VAR EOP = MAX ( DimDate[Date] )
VAR BOP = MAX ( DimDate[Date] ) - 6
RETURN
    CALCULATE ( [OrderCount],
    DimDate[Date] >= BOP,
    DimDate[Date] <= EOP )
```

Output

Add a Table visual with DimDate[Date] and InternetSales[OrderCount7] fields (see **Figure 18.3**). Because the OrderCount7 measure is very performance intensive, I suggest you limit the report to filtering only a few days, such as by creating a visual-level filter where Date is on or after January 1, 2014.

Date	OrderCount7
1/1/2014	337
1/2/2014	277
1/3/2014	240
1/4/2014	217
1/5/2014	231

Figure 18.3 The OrderCount7 measure calculates the order count for the past seven days as of the current date.

Analysis

The first OrderCount7 version uses a Period variable to filter the DimDate table between the current date and six days before. This is the implementation approach I discussed at the beginning of this lesson. The second version uses filters in CALCULATE. Interestingly, in this model the first version outperforms the second almost twice!

 TIP This is another example of why performance testing is so important. Different measure versions will perform differently from one model to the next. In this case, the performance impact is caused by the DISTINCTCOUNT function because counting distinct values is very resource intensive. We'll see what you can do about this in Part 5 of this book, but for now remember to try different versions and optimize your measures relentlessly!

Assuming a report date of January 5, 2014, the alternative SQL query would be:

```
SELECT COUNT (DISTINCT SalesOrderNumber)
FROM dbo.FactInternetSales
WHERE OrderDate BETWEEN '12/30/2013' AND '1/5/2014'
```

Practice

Add another measure (OrderCount14) to calculate the order count for the previous seven days.

```
OrderCount14 =
VAR EOP = MAX ( DimDate[Date] ) - 7
VAR BOP = MAX ( DimDate[Date] ) - 13
VAR Period = DATESBETWEEN ( DimDate[Date], BOP, EOP )
RETURN
   CALCULATE ( [OrderCount], Period )
```

Lastly, add another measure "OrderCount WoW" that calculates the change between the OrderCount7 and OrderCount14 measures.

```
OrderCount WoW =
VAR OrderCount7 = [OrderCount7]
VAR OrderCount14 = [OrderCount14]
RETURN
   IF (
     NOT ISBLANK ( OrderCount7 ) && NOT ISBLANK ( OrderCount14 ),
     [OrderCount7] - [OrderCount14]
   )
```

Output

Add the OrderCount14 and OrderCount WoW measures to the report. Compare your results with
Figure 18.4.

Date	OrderCount7	OrderCount14	OrderCount WoW
1/1/2014	337	527	-190
1/2/2014	277	525	-248
1/3/2014	240	516	-276
1/4/2014	217	506	-289
1/5/2014	231	469	-238
1/6/2014	223	431	-208
1/7/2014	217	386	-169

Figure 18.4 The OrderCount WoW measure calculates the variance between the OrderCount7 and OrderCount14 measures.

Analysis

The only difference between OrderCount14 and OrderCount7 is that OrderCount14 changes the
date offset. [OrderCount WoW] calculates the variance if both measures are not blank.

18.3 Summary

This lesson showed you how to use time intelligence functions to modify the filter context. When
there isn't a suitable function, such as in the case of WoW calculations, you can filter your data table (or built-in date hierarchy) and change the filter context as per your requirements. It's important to create and test different measure versions to find which one performs the best.

Lesson 19

Semi-additive Measures

All the measures you've implemented until now aggregate uniformly across all dimensions, including the Date dimension. Sometimes, you might encounter semi-additive measures, such as to handle inventory or account balances. This lesson explains how additivity affects measures and shows you how to implement semi-additive measures for analyzing inventory balances. You'll find the DAX formulas for this lesson in \Source\Part4\Semi-additive Measures.dax.

19.1 Understanding Measure Additivity

The most common usage of data analytics is to aggregate measures across dimensions. When you add an implicit measure to the report, the measure is aggregated according to the aggregate function you specify in the Visualizations pane. The default aggregation is SUM for numeric fields and Count for text fields. Explicit measures, of course, aggregate using the formulas you write.

19.1.1 Understanding Additive Measures

The most useful measures are numeric and additive (also called fully additive in the dimensional modeling terminology), such as the SalesAmount and OrderCount measures. Fully additive measures are also uniform because they can be aggregated across all dimensions. For example, you can sum revenue across any dimension and get the expected total.

Aggregating additive measures
When measures are fully additive, aggregated values can be derived from previously aggregated results. No matter how you slice and dice data, the aggregated measures produce the correct totals without any special intervention. Suppose you create a visual that shows revenue by month. When Power BI receives the query, it calls down the storage engine to get the SalesAmount column aggregated at the month level.

To do this, the storage engine scans the SalesAmount column and rolls it up to months. Then, the formula engine sums the results at a higher grain. For example, if the visual shows yearly totals, Power BI rolls up the monthly values to years.

Understanding additive functions
Most DAX aggregate functions are additive. They perform common aggregation tasks with additive measures. For example, all standard aggregation functions for implicit measures are additive, such as Sum, Min, Max, Count, and Distinct Count. I mentioned before that whenever an "X" function exists, Power BI maps these functions to their "X" counterparts. For example, SUM(table[column]) is internally translated to SUMX(table, SUM(table[column])). So, the extended functions are also additive.

19.1.2 Understanding Semi-Additive Measures

A semi-additive measure typically aggregates the normal way across all dimensions except the Date dimension. For example, although you can sum inventory balances across product, it's meaningless to do so across time.

Aggregating semi-additive measures
To understand how semi-additive measures aggregate, consider the following extract from a hypothetical Inventory fact table (see **Table 19.1**).

Table 19.1 Semi-additive measures don't aggregate over time.

Product	March 1st	March 2nd	Total
Product A	10	15	25 (15)
Product B	20	25	45 (25)
Total by Product	30	40	70 (40)

This fact table stores the closing product quantity at the end of each day. Aggregating the product quantity over the Product dimension produces the correct total. However, summing the product quantity over time is meaningless and wrong. What is really needed is taking the ending balance as of the requested date (the numbers in bold). For example, the product quantity for Product A spanning two subsequent days, March 1st and March 2nd, should show 15.

Understanding semi-additive functions
To support semi-additive measures, Power BI provides several functions, including FIRSTDATE, FIRSTNONBLANK, LASTDATE, LASTNONBLANK, OPENINGBALANCEMONTH, OPENINGBAL-ANCEQUARTER, OPENINGBALANCEYEAR, CLOSINGINGBALANCEMONTH, CLOSINGBAL-ANCEQUARTER, and CLOSINGBALANCEYEAR. As the lesson "Determining Filter Context" demonstrated, more complex requirements that cannot be addressed by the semi-additive functions alone, may require more involved formulas, such as to produce aggregate-over-aggregate results.

Understanding non-additive measures
Lastly, some measures, such as rates and percentages, shouldn't be aggregated with standard aggregation functions at all. For example, the ResellerSales[UnitPriceDiscountPct] stores the discount percent and cannot be meaningfully aggregated across any dimension. However, a calculated column can use this measure to compute the net profit, which can be aggregated. Or, an extended function, such as SUMX can perform the arithmetic for each order line item before the result is rolled up.

19.2 Working with Semi-additive Measures

As a manufacturing company, Adventure Works maintains an inventory. You're tasked to model inventory balances and to produce a measure that returns the product quantity at hand. This will help the Adventure Works management analyze and forecast inventory levels.

19.2.1 Understanding the Schema

You won't use the Adventure Works model for this practice. Instead, I imported the inventory-related tables from the AdventureWorksDW database in the \Source\Part4\Inventory.pbix file. Use this file for the practices in this lesson.

Practice
Let's take a moment to get familiar with the model schema.

1. Open the \Source\Part4\Inventory.pbix file in Power BI Desktop.
2. Switch to the Model View tab to review the model schema, which is shown in **Figure 19.1**.

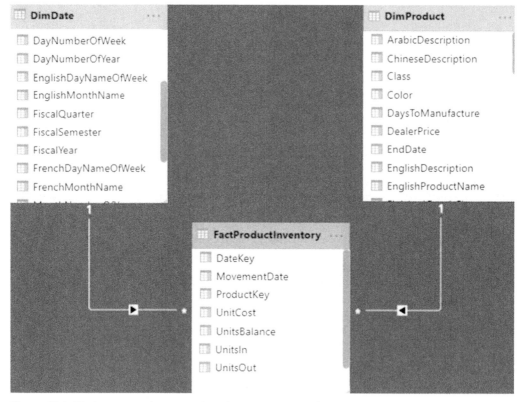

Figure 19.1 The inventory schema consists of three tables (one fact table and two dimension tables).

Analysis
In the corporate data warehouse (AdventureWorksDW database), the inventory subject area is modeled using one fact table and two dimension tables. Let's explain these tables in more detail.

- FactProductInventory – This fact tables captures the inventory movement measures (UnitsIn and UnitsOut) and the closing quantity measure (UnitsBalance) at the end of every day. Dimensional modeling refers to this type of fact table as a *periodic snapshot*.

- DimProduct and DimDate – You're already familiar with these two dimensions from the Adventure Works model. Here, they are used to analyze inventory by date and product. I've renamed the DimDate[FullDateAlternateKey] to *Date*. I've also marked DimDate as a date table and configured DimDate[EnglishMonthName] to sort by the DimDate[MonthNumberOfYear] column so that months are sorted in their chronological order.

19.2.2 Working with Closing Balances

The UnitsIn and UnitsOut measures are additive because they can be summed up across Product and Date. The UnitsBalance measure is not and this will become obvious in a moment.

Practice
Let's create a report to analyze the product closing balances.

1. Add a Matrix visual and bind it to DimProduct[EnglishProductName] in the Rows area, CalendarYear, CalendarQuarter, EnglishMonthName, and Date fields from DimDate in the Columns area, and FactProductInventory[UnitsBalance] in the Values area.

2. Drill down the 2013 year column to expand it to quarters, and then drill down the fourth quarter to expand it to months. Compare your results with **Figure 19.2**.

CalendarYear	2013					Total
CalendarQuarter	4				Total	
EnglishProductName	October	November	December	**Total**		
Adjustable Race	27,125	26,250	27,125	**80,500**	**80,500**	**80,500**
All-Purpose Bike Stand	78	80	93	**251**	**251**	**251**
AWC Logo Cap	-88	-51	137	**-2**	**-2**	**-2**
BB Ball Bearing	21,700	21,000	21,700	**64,400**	**64,400**	**64,400**
Bearing Ball	27,125	26,250	27,125	**80,500**	**80,500**	**80,500**
Bike Wash - Dissolver	-151	-212	27	**-336**	**-336**	**-336**
Blade	21,700	21,000	21,700	**64,400**	**64,400**	**64,400**
Cable Lock	124	120	124	**368**	**368**	**368**
Chain	11,824	11,980	14,384	**38,188**	**38,188**	**38,188**

Figure 19.2 The UnitsBalance measure sums up across any field from DimDate and this is incorrect.

Analysis
While the report sums UnitsBalance over products (as it should), it also sums balances across time and this is incorrect. For example, the fourth quarter ending balance for the first product (Adjustable Race) should be 27,125 (its December balance) and not 80,500 (the sum of the three months).

Practice
Let's fix the closing balances issue by creating a new measure.

1. Add a UnitsAtHand measure to the FactProductInventory table with the following formula:

UnitsAtHand = CALCULATE(SUM(FactProductInventory[UnitsBalance]), LASTDATE(DimDate[Date]))

2. Replace the UnitsBalance field in the Matrix visual with UnitsAtHand.

Output
The report now produces the expected results, as shown in **Figure 19.3**. Please feel free to explore the data in different ways, such as to use ProductLine (instead of EnglishProductName) to aggregate products up.

Analysis
No matter how you slice the data, UnitsAtHand produces the expected results. The formula uses the CALCULATE function to overwrite the filter context by passing the LASTDATE function as the second argument. As its name suggests, LASTDATE returns the last date in the current context of the specified column. For December 2013, the last date is December 31, 2013. The measure gets

the quantity from this date and it applies it to the dimension totals. This is exactly what you need to implement closing balances.

| CalendarYear | 2013 | | | | Total | |
| CalendarQuarter | 4 | | | Total | | |
EnglishProductName	October	November	December	Total		
Adjustable Race	875	875	875	875	875	875
All-Purpose Bike Stand	3	3	3	3	3	3
AWC Logo Cap	3	7	7	7	7	7
BB Ball Bearing	700	700	700	700	700	700
Bearing Ball	875	875	875	875	875	875
Bike Wash - Dissolver	3	2	3	3	3	3
Blade	700	700	700	700	700	700
Cable Lock	4	4	4	4	4	4
Chain	400	464	464	464	464	464

Figure 19.3 The UnitsAtHand measure produces the expected results by showing the last balance in the period.

Practice

If every product has its quantity recorded every day then you're done. Real life is not perfect though and it's possible that there will be days with no recorded quantities. Or, you may not want to wait for the current month to be over to show its balances. What should the measure return then? Should it return the quantity for the last non-blank date? Or, should it return an empty value, such as in the case when the product is discontinued and destroyed? If you use LASTDATE, you'll get the latter outcome.

1. Since Adventure Works has exemplary data quality and it has data for every month and product, I added a calculated column UnitsBalanceOverwrite to FactProductInventory to simulate a missing quantity value. The measure formula follows:

UnitsBalanceOverwrite = IF(FactProductInventory[ProductKey]=1 && FactProductInventory[DateKey] = 20131231,
        BLANK(), FactProductInventory[UnitsBalance])

This formula sets a blank value for the Adjustable Race product and December 31, 2013. You can achieve the same effect if you remove the entire row in Power Query and reload the table.

2. Change the formula of the UnitsAtHand measure to use the UnitsBalanceOverwrite column. Notice that the Matrix visual now shows a blank value in the quarter and year totals for Adjustable Race.

| CalendarYear | 2013 | | | |
| CalendarQuarter | 4 | | | |
EnglishProductName	October	November	December	Total
Adjustable Race	875	875		
All-Purpose Bike Stand	3	3	3	3
AWC Logo Cap	3	7	7	7
BB Ball Bearing	700	700	700	700

Figure 19.4 LASTDATE will return an empty balance if there is balance for the closing period.

If data is not available on the last date, the measure returns a blank value. Assuming you want the totals to show the last non-blank balance instead, change the UnitsAtHand formula as follows:

```
UnitsAtHand =
CALCULATE (
    SUM ( FactProductInventory[UnitsBalanceOverwrite] ),
    LASTNONBLANK (
        DimDate[Date],
        CALCULATE ( SUM ( FactProductInventory[UnitsBalanceOverwrite] ) )
    )
)
```

Output

The Adjustable Race totals should now show 875. This is the November 30th balance, which happens to be the last non-blank date.

Analysis

The LASTNONBLANK function goes back in time to find the last date where the expression passed a second argument has a non-blank value. This function is an iterator and you must use the CALCULATE function to transition the row context to a filter context. Because it iterates back in time, LASTNONBLANK could be slow with many products and dates.

In the case of missing end dates, such as when you have incomplete months, you might get much better performance if you use this formula:

```
UnitsAtHand (a) =
VAR LASTNONBLANKDATE = CALCULATE ( MAX ( DimDate[Date] ), ALL ( DimProduct ) )
RETURN
    CALCULATE (
        SUM ( FactProductInventory[UnitsBalanceOverwrite] ),
        DimDate[Date] = LASTNONBLANKDATE
    )
```

The new version uses a LASTNONBLANKDATE variable to store the last date with data across all products. Then, it calculates the closing balance as of that date. However, this measure won't work (it will return blank values) for products with missing quantities. It also won't work if the balance dates differ across products, such as when the quantity of some products is recorded on December 15 and for others it's recorded on December 16.

19.3 Summary

You'll encounter semi-additive measures when you must calculate closing balances (both finance and inventory), and when you need to return the last recorded value, such as when you work with exchange rates. DAX has functions to calculate the values at the period start and end dates. This lesson showed you how the semi-additive functions work and how to use them to calculate closing balances.

Lesson 20

Centralizing Time Intelligence

Your model could include many time intelligence measures and maintaining all these formulas might become a maintenance liability. Calculation groups can help you centralize time intelligence formulas in one place and this lesson shows you how. As of the time of writing, Power BI Desktop doesn't yet support calculation groups (I'll use Analysis Services Tabular), so you might not be able to practice this feature right away. You'll find the DAX formulas for this lesson in \Source\Part4\Calculation Groups.dax.

20.1 Understanding Calculation Groups

To understand calculations groups, you need to understand what problem they solve. It's not uncommon for Power BI models to have many measures. It's also not uncommon for a measure to have various time intelligence variants. For example, SalesAmount might have several time intelligence measures, such as SalesAmount YTD, SalesAmount QTD, SalesAmount YTD, SalesAmount YoY, SalesAmount YoY%, and so on.

If you multiply the number of time intelligence variants by the number of other measures that need the same formulas, you might end up with hundreds of measures. This is a measure explosion! Typing and maintaining all these formulas one by one in the rudimentary Power BI Desktop formula editor could be very time consuming and there is always the risk of "forgetting" to apply changes and bug fixes. Calculation groups help you overcome this issue.

20.1.1 What is a Calculation Group?

Like field groups (see the "Grouping and Binning" lesson), which consolidate column values, a calculation group consolidates measure formulas so that they can be maintained in one place.

How calculation groups are presented
Power BI presents calculation groups as a single table in the Fields pane. This table has a single column. The users can add this column to a report filter or slicer and select which time intelligence feature they need. Consider the Matrix report shown in **Figure 20.1**. Suppose you have implemented calculation groups as a table called "Time Intelligence" and the column is called "Time Measure".

In this case, the user has added a slicer bound to the Time Measure column, which has formulas for the current value of the measure, mount-to-date (MTD), quarter-to-date (QTD), and YTD (year-to-day) time intelligence variants. The visual is bound to the Reseller Total Sales measure in the Values area, Time Measure in the Columns area, and Calendar Year and Month Name in the Rows area. The user has selected QTD and YTD values in the slicer. The report shows QTD and YTD values. The user can add more measures to the report and get time intelligence for all the measures on the report. The model doesn't need a separate formula for each time intelligence variation and each measure.

Calendar Year	QTD	YTD	Total
2010	**$489,329**	**$489,329**	**$489,329**
December	$489,329	$489,329	**$489,329**
2011	**$5,664,610**	**$18,192,803**	**$18,192,803**
January	$1,538,408	$1,538,408	**$1,538,408**
February	$1,538,408	$1,538,408	
March	$3,549,026	$3,549,026	**$2,010,618**
April		$3,549,026	
May	$4,027,080	$7,576,107	**$4,027,080**
June	$4,027,080	$7,576,107	
July	$713,117	$8,289,223	**$713,117**
August	$4,069,186	$11,645,293	**$3,356,069**
September	$4,952,086	$12,528,193	**$882,900**
October	$2,269,117	$14,797,309	**$2,269,117**
November	$3,270,920	$15,799,113	**$1,001,804**
December	$5,664,610	$18,192,803	**$2,393,690**
2012	**$7,534,276**	**$28,193,632**	**$28,193,632**

Time Measure

☐ Current
☐ MTD
☑ QTD
☑ YTD

Calendar Year ▾ ✕

Month Name ▾ ✕

Columns

Time Measure ▾ ✕

Values

Reseller Total Sales ▾ ✕

Figure 20.1 The user can select specific time intelligence measures on the report.

When to use calculation groups?

Consider calculation groups in the following scenarios:

- Centralizing time intelligence – This is the most important reason to use calculation groups. You can define all time intelligence formulas in calculation groups so if you need to make changes, you can do it in one place.

- Reducing number of time intelligence measures – Calculation groups can help you avoid creating separate time intelligence measures if the users are willing to forgo some flexibility. For example, they must filter the measures they need, and they can't insert another measure in between the time intelligence columns (time intelligence variations are kept together on the visual).

 REAL LIFE Calculation groups alone may lead to more rigid report layouts that end users might not tolerate well. Analysis Services Multidimensional has a similar feature that allows models to implement "shell" time dimensions that work in the same way. However, most real-life models might still require exposing time intelligence calculations as separate measures for maximum flexibility. So, calculation groups might not help you reduce the number of measures, but they can help centralizing the formulas.

Understanding limitations

As of the time of writing, calculation groups have certain limitations specific to Power BI. They don't support Power BI implicit measures, so you must use only explicit measures (another good reason to have explicit measures even for standard aggregations). Continuing the list of limitations, the MDX query interface doesn't support them so they won't work in Excel or other MDX clients. Row level security (RLS) is not supported. Lastly, dynamic format strings (produced by measures) are not supported but are on the short-term roadmap.

20.1.2 Implementing Calculation Groups

Once you have your time-intelligence formulas, implementing calculation groups is easy thanks to several DAX functions that Microsoft added specifically for calculation groups.

Understanding calculation group functions

Table 20.1 shows the DAX functions for calculation groups.

Table 20.1 DAX has three functions that are specifically designed for calculation groups.

Function	Description
SELECTEDMEASURE	Returns a reference to the measure that is in the current context of the calculation group.
SELECTEDMEASURENAME	Returns the name of the measure that is in the current context of the calculation group.
ISSELECTEDMEASURE(M1, M2,..Mn)	Returns TRUE if one of the specified measures is in the current context of the calculation group.

Understanding calculation group precedence

You can have more than one calculation group and a calculation group doesn't have to handle only time intelligence. This opens interesting scenarios for reusing programming logic. For example, you may have a calculation group with different formulas for computing averages, as shown in **Table 20.2**.

Table 20.2 A sample calculation group for calculating averages.

Calculation Item	Formula
Current	SELECTEDMEASURE
Simple Average	DIVIDE(SELECTEDMEASURE(), COUNTROWS(DimDate))
3-mo Average	CALCULATE (AVERAGEX (VALUES(DimDate[EnglishMonthName]), [Sales]), DATESINPERIOD (DimDate[Date], MAX (DimDate[Date]), -3, MONTH))

Then, you might have another calculation group for time intelligence, and you want the time intelligence functions to apply also to the averages. This requires the time intelligence calculation group to have a higher evaluation order than the averages calculation group. Each calculation group has a Precedence property to let you specify the execution order. For example, you can leave the precedence of the averages group to its default value of zero and increase the precedence of the other group to 10.

Understanding implementation steps

Here are the high-level steps for implementing calculation groups:

1. Create DAX formulas for each type of time intelligence you plan to support, such as YTD, QTD, and so on.

2. Add a special Calculation Group table to the model, such as Time Intelligence.

3. Rename the single calculation group attribute to whatever column name you want your users to see, such as Time Measure.

4. Create a calculated item for each time intelligence type and enter the appropriate formula.

20.2 Working with Calculation Groups

As I mentioned, the Power BI Tabular backend-service supports calculation groups, but Power BI Desktop currently has no user interface for you to configure them. Nor does the SQL Server Data Tools (SSDT) tool. Microsoft is currently working on providing write access to the XMLA endpoint of the Tabular backend service. Once this is in place, you'll have at least two options to implement calculation groups:

- Use Tabular Editor to make and publish the changes to Power BI.
- Script the Power BI published dataset in SQL Server Management Studio (SSMS) and apply the necessary changes.

20.2.1 Creating Calculation Groups

I'll use the first approach for this practice, and I'll use the excellent community tool Tabular Editor (https://tabulareditor.github.io), which I typically use to design Analysis Services Tabular models. Calculation groups are supported in SQL Server 2019 and I used a community technology preview (CTP) build. Since the Power BI XMLA endpoint is not currently write-enabled, I deployed the changes to an Analysis Services Tabular model. Again, you won't be able to do this practice in Power BI Desktop, but it will help you understand how this important feature works so you can use it once it's enabled in Power BI.

Practice
Let's follow the above steps to create a calculation group in Tabular Editor.

1. I'll use the following formulas for MTD, QTD, and YTD calculations, which you're already familiar with:

```
TOTALMTD(SELECTEDMEASURE(), 'Date'[Date])
TOTALQTD(SELECTEDMEASURE(), 'Date'[Date])
TOTALYTD(SELECTEDMEASURE(), 'Date'[Date])
```

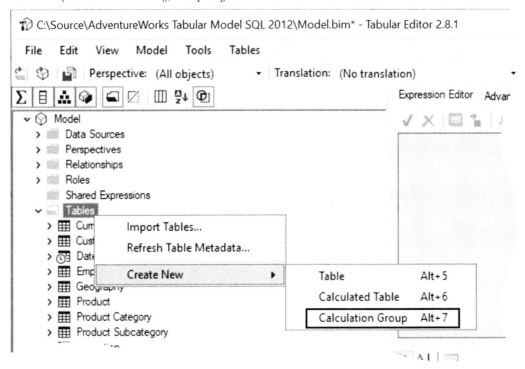

Figure 20.2 Tabular Editor supports calculation groups.

2. Open Tabular Editor and then open the Analysis Services Tabular *.bim file (unlike Power BI Desktop, Tabular saves the model metadata into a *.bim file). Right-click the Tables node and click Create New ⇨ Calculation Group (see **Figure 20.2**). This will add a new special table called New Calculation Group to the list of tables. Rename the table to *Time Intelligence*.

 NOTE While you are in the table properties, notice that a calculation group has a numeric Precedence property with the default value of zero. As I explained before, you can increase it to a higher value when you have multiple and intra-dependent calculation groups.

3. Rename the single attribute of the Time Intelligence table to *Time Measure*.

4. Right-click the Time Intelligence table and click New Calculation Item for each of the calculation items you need. Enter the DAX formula for each calculation item, as shown in **Table 20.3**.

Table 20.3 A sample calculation group for calculating averages.

Calculation Item	Formula	Description
Current	SELECTEDMEASURE()	No time intelligence, just return the current measure value
MTD	TOTALMTD(SELECTEDMEASURE(), 'Date'[Date])	Calculates month-to-date
QTD	TOTALQTD(SELECTEDMEASURE(), 'Date'[Date])	Calculates quarter-to-date
YTD	TOTALYTD(SELECTEDMEASURE(), 'Date'[Date])	Calculates year-to-date

Analysis
At the end of this practice the Time Intelligence calculation group should look like **Figure 20.3**.

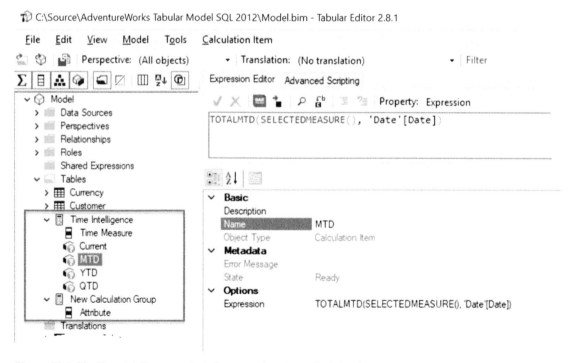

Figure 20.3 The Time Intelligence calculation group has four calculation items.

1. Save and deploy your changes. This is where you need the write connectivity to Power BI so you can apply the changes directly to the published dataset while waiting for Power BI Desktop to catch up and provide user interface.

2. (Optional) To support more flexible report layouts, consider creating separate measures that use the Time Intelligence calculation group to "flatten" measures, such as:

```
[Sales YTD] = CALCULATE ([Sales] ), 'Time Intelligence'[Time Measure] = "YTD")
[Sales QTD] = CALCULATE ([Sales] ), 'Time Intelligence'[Time Measure] = "QTD")
```

20.2.2 Using Calculation Groups

As I explained before, calculation groups don't work with implicit measures. Therefore, your Power BI visual must use explicit measures.

Practice

Let's test the changes in Power BI Desktop by creating a report that looks like the one shown in **Figure 20.1**.

1. Add a Matrix visual and bind it to the Reseller Total Sales measure in the Values area, 'Time Intelligence'[Time Measure] in the Columns area, and Calendar Year and Month Name in the Rows area.

2. Add a slicer and bind it to the 'Time Intelligence'[Time Measure] field.

3. Select all the calculated items. Then select only a few calculated items.

4. (Optional) Add another measure to the report.

Analysis

Notice that the report creates a time intelligence column for each calculated item. Calculated groups are very handy but not so flexible when it comes to report layouts. For example, you can't reorder the columns, such as to place the Current variation at the end of the list. You also can't add measures to the report that are outside the time intelligence section.

Although the calculated item formula can check for specific measures using SELECTEDMEAS-URENAME and set them to empty values, the measure will still be repeated for each calculated item in the report. Therefore, I recommend creating separate measures that piggyback on the calculation group variations.

20.3 Summary

Calculation groups are convenient for centralizing management of common DAX formulas. Although not specific to just time intelligence, calculation groups are especially useful to centralize time intelligence calculations because they tend to cause many measures. If users are OK with less flexible report layouts, then you can also avoid having a separate measure per each field that requires time intelligence formulas. Otherwise, create measures that "flatten" the calculation group.

PART 5

Queries

Besides calculated columns and measures, you can use DAX to query Power BI and Tabular models. In fact, when you interact with a report, Power BI generates DAX queries and sends them to the backend Analysis Services Tabular service. You can create your own DAX queries. This brings several benefits, such as testing measures outside Power BI Desktop, exploring the model data, and implementing reports with other tools that require you to specify a dataset query, such as Power BI Report Builder.

This part of the book introduces you to DAX queries. You'll learn how to create and test measures and variables, and how to identify and address performance bottlenecks. You'll also implemented a paginated report with Power BI Report Builder. You'll find the completed exercises for this part of the source code included in the \Source\Part5 folder.

Lesson 21

Introducing DAX Queries

Analysis Services Tabular, which is the backend service that hosts your local and published Power BI models, provides two external query interfaces: Multidimensional Expressions (MDX) and Data Analysis Expressions (DAX). MDX clients, such as Microsoft Excel, can query the model with MDX, while DAX-aware clients can send DAX queries. Since DAX is the native expression language of Power BI and Tabular, the DAX interface is usually more efficient, so use DAX instead of MDX.

This chapter introduces you to DAX queries. You'll learn how to create basic DAX queries and how to test them. I'll also show you how to auto-generate DAX queries in SQL Server Management Studio (SSMS). You'll find the DAX formulas for this lesson in \Source\Part5\Introducing DAX Queries.dax.

21.1 Understanding DAX Queries

When you interact with reports, Power BI generates DAX queries for you, but you never see them. Behind the scenes, there is a query behind every visual on the report. Each time you make data changes to the visual, such as adding or removing fields, filtering, or sorting, Power BI generates and runs a new DAX query. You can create your own DAX queries to:

- Create and test measures – Let's face it. The formula editor in Power BI Desktop is improving but it could be tedious. Once you get more proficient with DAX, you might prefer to test your measures outside Power BI Desktop.

- Profile measure performance – DAX Studio includes features for evaluating the measure performance, such as to check if the measure is storage engine-bound.

- Create paginated reports – Some reporting tools, such as Power BI Report Builder, requires you to specify a query for every dataset. When connecting to Power BI and Tabular models, it makes sense to use DAX, as it's the native Power BI language.

To create your custom queries, you need to understand the query syntax first.

21.1.1 Understanding Query Syntax

Power BI supports a DAX query syntax centered on the EVALUATE clause.

```
[DEFINE {  MEASURE <tableName>[<name>] = <expression> }
    { VAR <name> = <expression>}]
EVALUATE <table>
[ORDER BY {<expression> [{ASC | DESC}]}[, ...]
[START AT {<value>|<parameter>} [, ...]]]
```

Don't worry if the query syntax looks intimidating because many of the clauses are optional (that's why they are surrounded with square brackets). Just like measures and calculated columns, the query syntax is not case-sensitive, and you can use upper or lower case, such as *EVALUATE* or *evaluate*. Let's explain this syntax one step at a time.

Understanding the DEFINE clause

The DEFINE clause is an optional clause that allows you to define query-scoped measures or variables using DAX formulas. Similar to explicit measures, you can specify a query-scoped measure by using the TableName[MeasureName] syntax and by entering an expression that returns a single scalar value. A query-scoped measure can reference other query-scoped measures defined before or after that measure.

 NOTE A DAX query can define query-scoped measures and variables only. You can't define calculated columns. Calculated columns must be created in Power BI Desktop at design time.

Understanding the EVALUATE clause

The EVALUATE clause is the only mandatory clause. A query can have only one EVALUATE clause. Think of EVALUATE as the SELECT statement in the SQL language. EVALUATE must be followed by a single table or an expression that produces a table. The expression can reference query-scoped measures or table variables that were previously introduced with the DEFINE clause.

Understanding ORDER BY and START AT clauses

An optional ORDER BY clause can be added to sort the results. The optional START AT clause provides a mechanism to request the results at a spot in the ordered set. The ORDER BY and START AT clauses are closely related, and you can't use START AT without using ORDER BY. Each item following the START AT clause maps to one of the ORDER BY expressions. The query might specify either a starting value or the name of a parameter that will contain the starting value, such as @Month.

21.1.2 Choosing a Query Tool

Microsoft has extended SQL Server Management Studio (SSMS) with DAX query capabilities. There is also DAX Studio - a community tool designed to help you test DAX queries. **Table 21.1** compares the two tools side by side based on their support for DAX queries.

Table 21.1 This table compares SSMS and DAX Studio for working with DAX queries.

Feature	SSMS	DAX Studio
Installation	Standalone desktop app	Standalone desktop app, Excel add-in
Syntax coloring	Yes	Yes
Intellisense	Yes	Yes
Auto-generating DAX	No	Yes
Defining and expanding measures	No	Yes
Profiling performance	No	Yes
Tracing queries	No (need to use SQL Profiler)	Yes
Integrated function reference	No	Yes
Integrated Data Management Views (DMVs)	No	Yes

Using SSMS

SSMS is the Microsoft premium tool for all tasks related to SQL Server (not just DAX). SSMS has two features that are specifically designed to help you work with DAX queries:

- ■ DAX Query Editor – Once you connect to a Power BI or Tabular model, right-click the database and click New Query ⇨ DAX. To connect to a Power BI Desktop model, in Object Explorer connect to Analysis Services using the localhost:port connection string (you can obtain the port from DAX Studio as the lesson "Understanding storage" demonstrated). This opens a new query editor, where you can type and execute your DAX query.
- ■ DAX Query Designer – Right-click the database but instead of New Query, click Browse. This opens the same DAX Query Designer that is available in Power BI Report Builder. It can auto-generate DAX queries as you drag and drop fields. I'll demonstrate this feature in the "Using Power BI Report Builder" lesson.

Using DAX Studio

DAX Studio is a free community tool, created and maintained by the community, including prominent Microsoft Most Valuable Professionals (MVPs). It's specifically designed for working with DAX and it has features that SSMS doesn't have, such as analyzing the query performance and formatting DAX code. Because of this, I recommend you use DAX Studio.

21.2 Working with Basic Queries

In this practice, I'll introduce you to DAX Studio IDE and how you can use it for testing custom DAX code. Then, you'll execute a few sample DAX queries.

21.2.1 Getting Started with DAX Studio

You can download and install the latest version of DAX Studio from https://daxstudio.org/. By default, the tool saves query files with a *.dax file extension, which are just text files that you can open with any text editor.

Practice

Let's open an existing *.dax file in DAX Studio and get familiar with its environment.

1. Open Power BI Desktop and load the Adventure Works file that you worked on in Part 4 of this book or use the one included in the \Source\Part5 folder.

2. Open DAX Studio and click Cancel in the connection window.

3. Click File ⇨ Open, and then open the Source\Part5\Introducing DAX Queries.dax file.

4. When prompted to connect, choose the "PBI / SSDT" option and connect to the Adventure Works model.

Once DAX Studio connects, it displays the model metadata in the left Metadata pane (see **Figure 21.1**). The Metadata pane has three tabs. The Metadata tab fulfills a similar role as the Fields pane in Power BI Desktop, but it also shows hidden objects, such as the Power BI auto-generated date tables. The Functions tab lists the DAX functions organized by categories. You can drag a function and drop it in the query to see its syntax.

Output

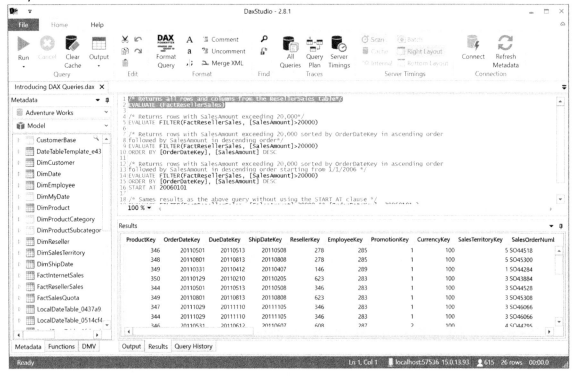

Figure 21.1 DAX Studio is specifically designed for working with DAX queries.

The DMV tab lists dynamic management views (DMVs). Analysis Services provides dynamic management views (DMVs) to help administrators monitor the health of a server instance, to diagnose problems, and to tune performance. You can use SQL-like SELECT statements to query these views just like you can query a SQL Server relational table. The views are documented at https://docs.microsoft.com/sql/analysis-services/instances/use-dynamic-management-views-dmvs-to-monitor-analysis-services.

 TIP Looking for a quick way to get a list of all measures, their formulas, and other metadata, such as display folders? Just drag the MDSCHEMA_MEASURES DMV and drop it in the query. Then, run the resulting SELECT statement.

The right pane is where your DAX queries go. You can have multiple files open and you can have multiple queries in a file. If you press the Run button in the ribbon, DAX Studio runs all the queries in the file loaded in the active tab. Or, you can select a query and click Run (or F5) to run just this query. There are three tabs in the bottom of the query pane:

- Output – Gives you high-level execution statistics, such as the count of rows in the query results and the query execution time. This tab also shows the error text if a formula generates an error or the query syntax is incorrect.

- Results – By default, the query results are shown in a grid in the Results tab. But you can use the Output ribbon button to save the results in a tab-delimited text file if you prefer.

- Query History – Lists previously run queries. You can double-click a query to load it in the query pane.

Many other features are available in the ribbon, such as formatting queries, commenting, and analyzing the query performance.

Analysis
DAX Studio can connect to models hosted in Analysis Services Tabular or Power BI Desktop. You must have your file open in Power BI Desktop in order for DAX Studio to connect to its backend Analysis Services Tabular instance when querying Power BI Desktop models.

21.2.2 Running DAX Queries

Next, you'll execute a few basic DAX queries in DAX Studio to get familiar with both the tool and the query syntax.

Practice
You'll start with a barebone DAX query and enhance it. Select the following query and click F5 to run it.

EVALUATE FactResellerSales

Output
The query will run for a few seconds due to the large number of rows. Once it's done, the Results tab shows all rows and columns from the FactResellerSales table.

Analysis
EVALUATE <table> is equivalent to SELECT * FROM <table> in SQL.

Practice
The EVALUATE clause can use any function that returns a table, such as the FILTER function. The following query returns the rows with SalesAmount exceeding 20,000:

EVALUATE FILTER(FactResellerSales, [SalesAmount] > 20000)

The following query adds the ORDER BY clause to sort the results by OrderDateKey in an ascending order, followed by SalesAmount in a descending order:

EVALUATE FILTER(FactResellerSales, [SalesAmount]>20000)
ORDER BY [OrderDateKey], [SalesAmount] DESC

The following query uses the START AT clause to limit the results to start at January 1st, 2013 just like a SQL query can use a WHERE clause to filter the output:

EVALUATE FILTER(FactResellerSales, [SalesAmount]>20000)
ORDER BY [OrderDateKey], [SalesAmount] DESC
START AT 20130101

The following query returns the same results without using the START AT clause.

EVALUATE FILTER(FactResellerSales, [SalesAmount]>20000 && [OrderDateKey] >= 20130101)
ORDER BY [OrderDateKey], [SalesAmount] DESC

21.3 Summary

You use the EVALUATE statement with optional clauses to define a custom DAX query. Both SSMS and DAX Studio can execute DAX queries, but I recommend you use DAX Studio because it has more features and it's specifically designed for working with DAX.

Lesson 22

Creating and Testing Measures

As you become more proficient with DAX, you might find the Power BI Desktop formula editor is somewhat tedious. One of the main benefits of custom DAX queries is to create and test measures outside of the Power BI Desktop. This way you can quickly make changes and ensure that the measure returns the expected results.

This lesson teaches you how to work with measures and variables in custom queries. It shows you how to create queries to test measures. You'll find the DAX queries in the \Source\Part5\Creating and Testing Measures.dax file.

22.1 Getting Started with Query Measures

You already know how measures work and you've created various explicit measures in the previous lessons. You just need to learn a few more things to transition your knowledge to custom queries. In Power BI Desktop, you test measures by creating reports, which in turn auto-generate and execute DAX queries. In DAX Studio, you're responsible for creating the query, so let's start there.

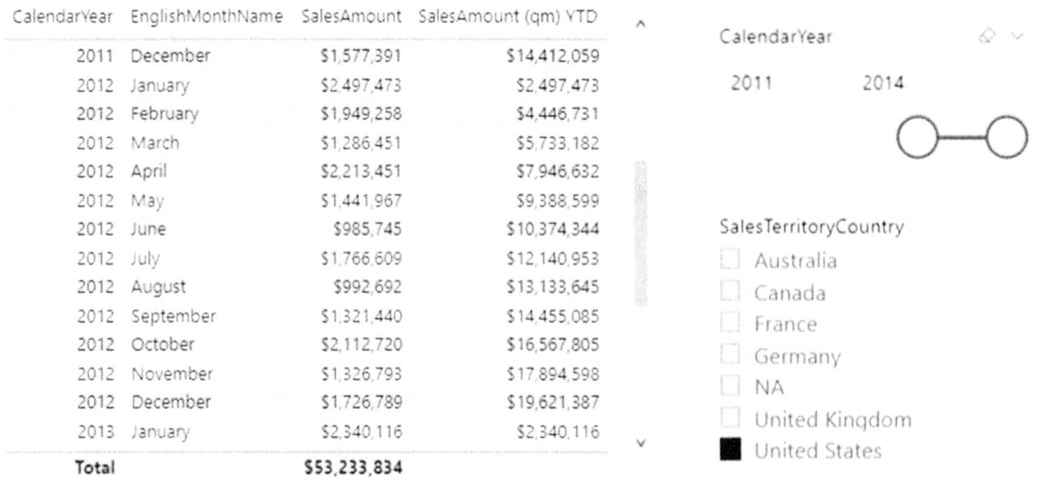

CalendarYear	EnglishMonthName	SalesAmount	SalesAmount (qm) YTD
2011	December	$1,577,391	$14,412,059
2012	January	$2,497,473	$2,497,473
2012	February	$1,949,258	$4,446,731
2012	March	$1,286,451	$5,733,182
2012	April	$2,213,451	$7,946,632
2012	May	$1,441,967	$9,388,599
2012	June	$985,745	$10,374,344
2012	July	$1,766,609	$12,140,953
2012	August	$992,692	$13,133,645
2012	September	$1,321,440	$14,455,085
2012	October	$2,112,720	$16,567,805
2012	November	$1,326,793	$17,894,598
2012	December	$1,726,789	$19,621,387
2013	January	$2,340,116	$2,340,116
Total		**$53,233,834**	

CalendarYear

2011   2014

SalesTerritoryCountry
- [ ] Australia
- [ ] Canada
- [ ] France
- [ ] Germany
- [ ] NA
- [ ] United Kingdom
- [x] United States

Figure 22.1 You can use a similar report to generate a test query.

22.1.1 Capturing Test Queries

Unfortunately, DAX Studio doesn't provide a query template, so you need to fill in this gap by creating a query to test your measure(s). In the first lesson "Introducing DAX", I showed you how to capture queries using the Performance Analyzer feature in Power BI Desktop. DAX Studio has a similar feature. Let's try it to capture a query generated by Power BI Desktop so you can use it as a query template for testing.

Practice

In this practice, you'll capture and examine a DAX query from Power BI Desktop.

1. Open the \Source\Part5\Adventure Works.pbix file in Power BI Desktop.

2. In Report View, select the "Creating and Testing Measures" tab to view the report shown in **Figure 22.1**. This report has a Matrix visual and two slicers.

3. Open DAX Studio. Choose the "PBI/SSDT Model" connectivity option and select the Adventure Works model. If you don't see it in the dropdown list, make sure that Power BI Desktop is open with the Adventure Works model loaded. Click Connect.

4. In the DAX Studio ribbon, click the "All Queries" button to capture queries sent from Power BI Desktop to the backend Analysis Services Tabular instance. This adds another tab "All Queries" to the query pane.

5. In Power BI Desktop, change a slicer. For example, drag the CalendarYear slicer to expand or narrow the filter selection. This will cause Power BI to generate and execute a DAX query.

6. In DAX Studio, click the "All Queries" tab to select it. You should see two queries (one resulting from the slicer change and another that provides data to the visual).

7. Usually, the visual query has a longer duration. Double-click that query to load it in the query pane.

Output

The query behind the Matrix visual should look like this:

```
DEFINE
 VAR __DS0FilterTable = FILTER(KEEPFILTERS(VALUES('DimDate'[CalendarYear])), 'DimDate'[CalendarYear] >= 2011)
 VAR __DS0FilterTable2 = TREATAS({"United States"}, 'DimSalesTerritory'[SalesTerritoryCountry])

EVALUATE
 TOPN(502,
  SUMMARIZECOLUMNS(
   ROLLUPADDISSUBTOTAL(
     ROLLUPGROUP('DimDate'[CalendarYear], 'DimDate'[EnglishMonthName],
     'DimDate'[MonthNumberOfYear]), "IsGrandTotalRowTotal" ),
   __DS0FilterTable,
   __DS0FilterTable2,
   "SumSalesAmount", CALCULATE(SUM('FactResellerSales'[SalesAmount])),
   "SalesAmount__qm__YTD", 'FactResellerSales'[SalesAmount (qm) YTD]
  ),
  [IsGrandTotalRowTotal], 0,
  'DimDate'[CalendarYear], 1,
  'DimDate'[MonthNumberOfYear], 1,
  'DimDate'[EnglishMonthName], 1
 )
ORDER BY
 [IsGrandTotalRowTotal] DESC,
 'DimDate'[CalendarYear],
 'DimDate'[MonthNumberOfYear]
```

Analysis

The query uses the DEFINE clause to declare two table variables that correspond to the two slicers. Although the second variable uses a different syntax (TREATAS), the exact syntax doesn't matter.

What matters is that these variables apply filters (think of the WHERE clause in a SQL SELECT statement) that return a subset of the data for testing. To make things simple, forget about TREATAS and use just the FILTER function.

> **NOTE** Although not required for a simple filter, the KEEPFILTERS function preserves any previous filters so that both the new and previous filters are applied. Suppose you want to filter the table T on the column C. The following expression returns rows from T where [C] = 1 or [C] = 2. Although there is filter T[C]=3, only the latest (innermost) filter takes effect: CALCULATETABLE(CALCULATETABLE (T, T[C]=1 || T[C]=2), T[C]=2 || T[C]=3)
>
> Whereas, the next formula returns rows from T where [C]=2. In other words, KEEPFILTERS returns the intersection of both filters: CALCULATETABLE(CALCULATETABLE(T, KEEPFILTERS(T[C]=1 || T[C]=2)), T[C]=2 || T[C]=3)

Next, EVALUATE marks the start of the main query. EVALUATE needs to be followed by a table expression. Power BI uses the TOPN function to return data in chunks of 502 rows at a time. As you scroll down the visual, Power BI fetches more rows as needed. Nested in TOPN is SUMMA-RIZECOLUMNS that returns the data grouped by the fields in the data visual: CalendarYear, EnglishMonthName, and MonthNumberOfYear.

SUMMARIZECOLUMNS accepts additional constructs, such as ROLLUPGROUP, to generate totals. It also projects the two measures added to the Values area of the visual: SumSalesAmount (an implicit measure so Power BI generates its aggregation formula), and Sales_Amount_qum__YTD (an existing measure). Notice that the table variables are passed as filter arguments to SUMMA-RIZECOLUMNS to evaluate the measures only for a subset of data. Lastly, the query orders the results using the ORDER BY clause.

22.1.2 Creating a Test Query Template

Although you can run the query as it is, it might make be preferable to simplify it and save it so that you can reuse it as a template for testing measures in DAX.

Practice
Here is the simplified version:

```
DEFINE
    VAR __DS0FilterTable =  FILTER ( KEEPFILTERS ( VALUES ( 'DimDate'[CalendarYear] ) ),
        'DimDate'[CalendarYear] >= 2011  )
    VAR __DS0FilterTable2 =  TREATAS ( { "United States" }, 'DimSalesTerritory'[SalesTerritoryCountry] )
EVALUATE
SUMMARIZECOLUMNS (
  'DimDate'[CalendarYear],
  'DimDate'[EnglishMonthName]
  __DS0FilterTable,
  __DS0FilterTable2,
  "SumSalesAmount", CALCULATE ( SUM ( 'FactResellerSales'[SalesAmount] ) ),
  "SalesAmount__qm__YTD", 'FactResellerSales'[SalesAmount (qm) YTD])
```

> **TIP** To format your query nicely so you can read it better, select all the text of the query and click the Format Query button in the ribbon. You can also use this feature to ensure that the query is syntactically correct because the formatter validates the query and it will show errors in the Output tab in case of syntax errors.

Output
Select all the text of the simplified query and run it. Compare your results with **Figure 22.2**.

CalendarYear	EnglishMonthName	SumSalesAmount	SalesAmount_qm_YTD
2011	January	1221427.2382	1221427.2382
2011	March	1570069.9481	2791497.1863
2011	May	3386610.98	6178108.1663
2011	July	549336.8611	6727445.0274
2011	August	2744093.6988	9471538.7262
	··mber		10126370.9351

Figure 22.2 The results generated by the simplified query.

Analysis
This query removes the total rollup, the MonthNumberOfYear column (not needed unless you want to sort the results by it), and the ORDER BY clause. To recap, the important steps for creating a query to test measures are:

1. Define the appropriate filters as table variables depending on how you want to filter the data.
2. Use SUMMARIZECOLUMNS to group by the appropriate fields.
3. Pass the table variables as filter arguments to SUMMARIZECOLUMNS.
4. Project the measures you want to test as extended columns in SUMMARIZECOLUMNS.

Now you have a generic query that you can reuse to create and test your measures!

22.2 Working with Measures

You can add your explicit measures in the DEFINE portion of the query. You can also retrieve the definition of existing measures in the model so that you can work on or reuse their formulas. The following practices demonstrate both approaches.

22.2.1 Retrieving Measure Formulas

Suppose you want to make changes to an existing measure formula. You'll use DAX Studio to go through several iterations. You might find this approach more convenient than using the Power BI Desktop formula bar and waiting for the report to refresh every time you make a change.

Practice
DAX Studio can retrieve the formula for existing measures.

1. In DAX Studio, click the magnifying glass in the metadata pane and type *YTD*. DAX Studio searches the model metadata and shows all fields whose name contains "YTD".
2. Right-click the SalesAmount (qm) YTD measure and click Define Measure.

Output
DAX obtains the measure formula and immediately adds it below the DEFINE clause in the first query in the active query pane.

```
DEFINE
---- MODEL MEASURES BEGIN ----
MEASURE FactResellerSales[SalesAmount (qm) YTD] = IF(
    ISFILTERED('DimDate'[Date]),
    ERROR("Time intelligence quick measures can only be ...."),
    TOTALYTD(SUM('FactResellerSales'[SalesAmount]), 'DimDate'[Date])
)
```

Analysis
Recall that all measures defined in a query are scoped to that query only. Therefore, a query-scoped measure overshadows a measure with the same name in the model. This is great because you can change and finetune the measure formula in DAX Studio. Once you're satisfied with the changes, you can copy the formula (after the equal sign) and paste it in Power BI Desktop to apply the changes to the model.

22.2.2 Creating Custom Measures and Variables

Now that you know how DAX queries work, you're ready to create and test your own measures in DAX Studio.

Practice
The following query defines a PendingOrderCount measure that returns the count of open orders for the first five days in January 2013.

```
DEFINE
  MEASURE FactInternetSales[PendingOrdersCount] =
    VAR EOP = MAX ( DimDate[Date] )
    RETURN
      CALCULATE (
        DISTINCTCOUNT ( FactInternetSales[SalesOrderNumber] ),
        FactInternetSales[ShipDate] >= EOP,
        FactInternetSales[OrderDate] <= EOP,
        ALL ( DimDate )
      )
  VAR DateFilter =
    FILTER (
      KEEPFILTERS ( VALUES ( 'DimDate'[Date] ) ),
      'DimDate'[Date] >= DATE ( 2013, 1, 1 ) && 'DimDate'[Date] <= DATE ( 2013, 1, 5 )
    )
EVALUATE
SUMMARIZECOLUMNS (
  'DimDate'[Date],
  DateFilter,
  "PendingOrdersCount", FactInternetSales[PendingOrdersCount])
```

Output
Select the entire query text (including comments is OK) and press the Format Query button in the ribbon to format the query and ensure that there are no syntax errors. Then, click the Run Query button (or F5) to execute the query. Compare your results (Results tab) with **Figure 22.3**.

Date	PendingOrdersCount
1/1/2013	116
1/2/2013	109
1/3/2013	119
1/4/2013	124
1/5/2013	132

Figure 22.3 The results of the query with the PendingOrdersCount query-scoped measure.

Analysis

The query starts by defining the measure formula immediately after the DEFINE statement (you can define variables before measures if you prefer). Because you want to group results by just one field (DimDate[Date]), there is no need for a second table variable to filter data further. To make it more intuitive, I renamed the first table variable to DateFilter and changed the filter expression to filter the first five days in January 2013.

If you need more explanation about how the PendingOrderCount measure works, refer to the "Changing Filter Context" lesson. To recap, the measure declares an EOP variable that returns the last date in the current date context (this will be the date that appears in each row in the query results). Then, the measure calculates the distinct count of the SalesOrderNumber column values where the current date falls between the order date and ship date.

22.3 Summary

You can use DAX Studio to create and test measures and variables. This lesson introduced you to the query capabilities of DAX Studio. It showed you how to retrieve the measure formulas from the model and how to work with custom measures. One of the most useful features of DAX Studio is that it can help you profile the query performance, and this is the subject of the next lesson.

Lesson 23

Optimizing Query Performance

The Power BI in-memory engine (xVelocity) gives your reports a significant performance boost because the computer memory is the fastest storage medium. However, every technology has a limit and xVelocity is no exception. Inefficient DAX measures can slow down your reports and slow reports annoy end users.

This lesson shares practical tips to help you troubleshoot and optimize your DAX measures. I'll show you how to find which visual slows down a report and how to analyze the query performance. I'll also share best practices for optimizing DAX measures and I'll show you how to apply them to optimize a slow measure. You'll find the query examples in \Source\Part5\Optimizing Query Performance.dax.

23.1 Understanding DAX Performance

"This report is slow!" I hope you never hear this, but the chances are that you will sooner or later. No one likes watching a spinning progress indicator and waiting for the report to show up. DAX calculated columns, implicit measures, and simple "wrapper" measures are unlikely to impact performance. Not so much, however, about more complex explicit measures.

23.1.1 Understanding Query Execution

Understanding the query execution requires understanding where the query time is spent. Analysis Services Tabular (the backend service that hosts Power BI models) has two engines: a formula engine and a storage engine.

About the formula engine
When Analysis Services Tabular receives a DAX query, its formula engine parses the query, evaluates the formulas, and creates an execution plan. The formula engine can also take over more complicated computation tasks. If the formula engine determines that a calculation can be run more efficiently (for example, an IF function or the LASTDATE function), it adds a callback to itself in the storage engine query, so that it can process some of the work. Though the formula engine is single threaded per query, it can be called in parallel from the multiple threads in the storage engine.

About the storage engine
The xVelocity storage engine (often referred to by its old name VertiPaq) is designed to efficiently scan the in-memory data. The lesson "Understanding storage" covered the xVelocity storage engine in more detail. The execution plan produced by the formula engine will likely require many queries for data retrieval that the formula engine sends in parallel to xVelocity. The storage engine also supports basic aggregates and predicates, such as WHERE, SUM, and GROUP BY.

TIP As a general best practice, try to rewrite your DAX measures in such a way that they push as much work to the storage engine as possible. Because the storage engine is highly parallel, queries typically benefit from more CPU cores, faster memory, and more CPU cache. Of course, when you publish your models to Power BI, you have no control over the hardware, unless your organization is on Power BI Premium.

23.1.2 Understanding Optimization Steps

In general, DAX performance optimization involves four high-level steps:

1. Identify slow queries
2. Identify slow measures
3. Find the source of performance degradation
4. Apply optimizations and retest

Identifying slow queries

It's best to analyze the query performance in an isolated environment. For Power BI, this means opening the model locally in Power BI Desktop as opposed to testing a published model. In the previous lesson, I showed you how to capture the queries behind the report visuals in DAX Studio (recall that you can also use the Power BI Desktop Performance Analyzer to get the queries). Once you capture the queries, you can pinpoint the slow queries by analyzing their duration.

If you can't obtain the Power BI Desktop file, you might still be able to profile a published report if it's deployed to a workspace in a Power BI premium capacity. To do so, you can connect DAX Studio (or SQL Server Profiler) to the XMLA endpoint of that workspace.

Be aware of the internal caching that Power BI uses to cache query results both in Power BI Desktop and Power BI Service. For example, if you select another report page and go back to the previous page, you may not capture any queries because Power BI reuses identical query results.

TIP Suppose you have a report with multiple pages and one of the pages is slow to load. You can select another report page and close Power BI Desktop. Then, open Power BI Desktop and load the file. Power BI Desktop should load the last active page. Once you set up DAX Studio for tracing, click the slow page to capture its queries.

Identifying slow measures

A visual can have multiple measures. The principle of elimination is the best way to find which measures deteriorate performance the most. Once you capture the query, load the query in DAX Studio (or SSMS), and comment its measures one by one to exclude them from the query. Then, execute the DAX query and see if it runs any faster.

NOTE Analysis Services also has caches and it may service queries from the cached results. When testing DAX queries, it's important to clear these internal caches before executing the query to avoid skewed results. If you expand the Run button in the DAX Studio, you'll see a "Clear Cache and Run" option, which will clear the cache and run the query in one step. Or, you can click the "Clear Cache" ribbon button before you run the query.

Finding the source for performance degradation

This is the most important step. Start by finding in DAX Studio if the query is formula engine or storage engine bound. You can also examine the physical and logical plans by enabling the Query Plans button, but these plans are very verbose and difficult to interpret. You'd probably find yourself alternating between this step and the next one until you pinpoint the performance culprit.

Applying optimizations

This step is more art than science. Here are some general best practices for optimizing DAX:

1. Optimize storage – Focus on optimizing storage if the most time is spent in the storage engine. Use the VertiPaq Analyzer (see Lesson 3) to understand column cardinality and consumed storage. Remove unused high-cardinality columns. Use a good star schema with limited snowflaking. Disable built-in date tables if you don't use them and they consume a lot of storage. Use more compact data types, such as Whole Number instead of Decimal Number, if you don't need decimals. Consider denormalizing commonly used fields from large dimensions into the fact tables.

 TIP Relationships on high-cardinality columns, such as Sales[CustomerKey] ⇨ Customer[CustomerKey] could be expensive with millions of rows. Consider eliminating these joins by duplicating commonly used dimension columns into the fact table so that the entire query can be answered by just one table.

2. Materialize when possible – Instead of a performance intensive measure, consider materializing the whole measure or a part of its formula as a calculated column or a custom column in Power Query or SQL. You'll see an example of this technique in a moment.

3. Use CALCULATE filters --- Instead of using the FILTER function to filter entire tables, use filters in CALCULATE. For example, instead of writing CALCULATE(<expression>, FILTER (<table>, <criteria>)), use CALCULATE(<expression>, <criteria>). Refer to Lesson 7 for examples illustrating this approach.

4. Use variables – Variables are evaluated once. This results in a faster execution plan when the same expression appears multiple times in a formula.

23.2 Finding and Fixing Performance Issues

Now that you know the essentials of DAX performance optimization, let's put what you've learned into practice. The "Optimizing Query Performance" page in the \Source\Part5\Adventure Works.pbix file is slow. You need to investigate the performance degradation and, if possible, fix it.

23.2.1 Identifying Slow Queries

This report page has two visuals. To start with, you'll use DAX Studio to identify which query slows down the overall report execution.

Practice
To avoid dealing with cached queries, make sure that Power BI Desktop opens with another page selected.

1. Open the \Source\Part5\Adventure Works.pbix file in Power BI Desktop.

2. Select another page, such as the "Creating and Testing Measures" page. Remember to save the file and close Power BI Desktop.

3. Open Power BI Desktop again and load the Adventure Works.pbix file. The Report View should open with the "Creating and Testing Measures" page active.

4. Open DAX Studio and connect to the Adventure Works model using the PBI/SSDT connectivity option.

5. Click the All Queries button in the ribbon.

6. Switch to Power BI Desktop and select the "Optimizing Query Performance" page. Wait for the page to load.

7. Back to DAX Studio, select the All Queries tab in the query pane. You should see two queries captured. One of the queries has a significantly higher duration (about 10 seconds).

To make sure Power BI Desktop doesn't cache queries, you need to open it with another page (you can add a blank page if you prefer). Once DAX Studio captures the queries, you can quickly identify the slowest queries so you can focus on them.

23.2.2 Identifying Slow Measures

Next, if the query has multiple measures, you need to identify which one(s) are the most performance intensive.

Practice

1. Double-click the slow query to load it in the query pane. You should see this DAX code:

```
DEFINE VAR __DS0FilterTable =
  FILTER( KEEPFILTERS(VALUES('DimDate'[Date])),  'DimDate'[Date] >= DATE(2014, 1, 1) )
EVALUATE
  TOPN(502,
    SUMMARIZECOLUMNS(
      ROLLUPADDISSUBTOTAL('DimDate'[Date], "IsGrandTotalRowTotal"),
      __DS0FilterTable,
      "OrderCount_WoW", 'FactInternetSales'[OrderCount WoW],
      "OrderCount7", 'FactInternetSales'[OrderCount7],
      "OrderCount14", 'FactInternetSales'[OrderCount14]
    ),
    [IsGrandTotalRowTotal],  0,
    'DimDate'[Date],  1  )
ORDER BY [IsGrandTotalRowTotal] DESC, 'DimDate'[Date]
```

2. Comment OrderCount7 and OrderCount14 measures by typing a double hyphen (--) in front of the corresponding lines so that only the OrderCount_WoW measure will be used. Remove the comma at the end of the line for this measure.

3. Expand the Run button in the ribbon and select "Clear Cache then Run". Click the Run button to clear the cache and run the query.

Analysis

By isolating measures, you determine that the "OrderCount WoW" measure is the slowest (it takes about 5 seconds to execute). You used the "Clear Cache then Run" option to clear all runtime caches so that the query executes without caching.

23.2.3 Finding the Source

Next, you need to find which specific DAX formula is the performance culprit. Start with a high-level analysis of where the query time is spent.

Practice

Let's execute the query again but this time you'll enable the Server Timings feature in DAX Studio.

1. If the All Queries button is pressed, press it to stop tracing queries.

2. Click the Server Timings button in the ribbon. This adds a new "Server Timings" tab in the query pane.

3. Click the Run button again to run the query. Once the results come back, switch to the Server Timings tab (see **Figure 23.1**).

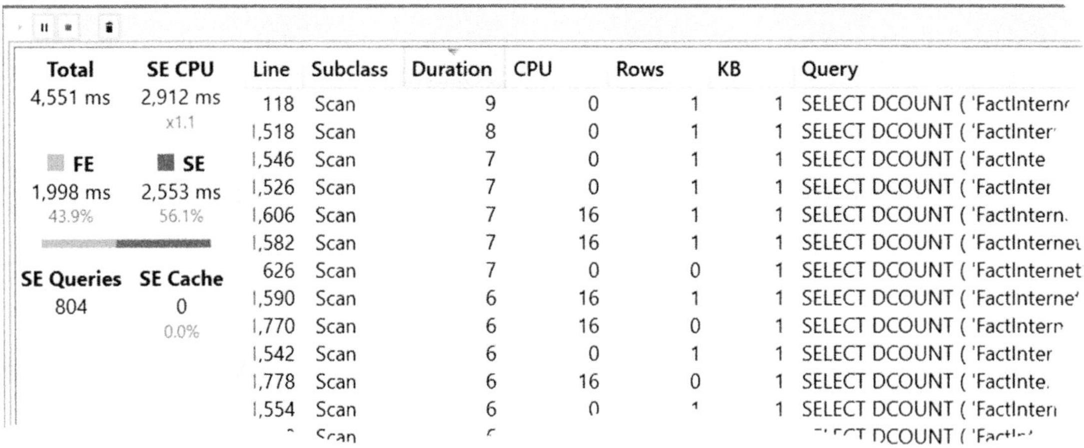

Total
4,551 ms
SE CPU
2,912 ms
x1.1
FE
1,998 ms
43.9%
SE
2,553 ms
56.1%
SE Queries
804
SE Cache
0
0.0%
Line Subclass Duration CPU Rows KB Query
118 Scan 9 0 1 1 SELECT DCOUNT ('FactIntern
1,518 Scan 8 0 1 1 SELECT DCOUNT ('FactInter
1,546 Scan 7 0 1 1 SELECT DCOUNT ('FactInte
1,526 Scan 7 0 1 1 SELECT DCOUNT ('FactInter
1,606 Scan 7 16 1 1 SELECT DCOUNT ('FactIntern.
1,582 Scan 7 16 1 1 SELECT DCOUNT ('FactInterne
626 Scan 7 0 0 1 SELECT DCOUNT ('FactInternet
1,590 Scan 6 16 1 1 SELECT DCOUNT ('FactInterne
1,770 Scan 6 16 0 1 SELECT DCOUNT ('FactIntern
1,542 Scan 6 0 1 1 SELECT DCOUNT ('FactInter
1,778 Scan 6 16 0 1 SELECT DCOUNT ('FactInte.
1,554 Scan 6 0 1 1 SELECT DCOUNT ('FactInteri

Figure 23.1 Use the Server Timings tab to get an idea of where the query time is spent.

Analysis
The Server Timings tab reveals important information about the query execution. The metrics on the left side are:

- Total – the total execution query time.
- SE CPU – The estimated storage engine time if the query was executed on a single thread.
- FE – The query time spent in the formula engine.
- SE – The query time spent in the storage engine.
- SE Queries – The number of queries sent to the storage engine.
- SE Cache – The percentage of queries that were answered by the storage engine cache.

In this case, most of the query time was spent in the storage engine, which is preferable. The query resulted in 804 queries to the storage engine. In the right pane, you can see the actual storage engine queries and sort them by duration. Most of these queries uses the DCOUNT function to count distinct orders.

23.2.4 Applying Optimizations

Distinct count is a very expensive operation and the best way to optimize is to avoid it if possible. Let's see how this approach could work in this case.

Practice
Let's add the definition of the "OrderCount WoW" measure to the query.

1. In the Metadata pane, hover over the magnifying class and type *WoW* to locate the measure.
2. Right-click the "Order Count WoW" measure and click "Define and Expand Measure". This adds the definition of this measure and all dependent measures in the DEFINE query clause. Now you can see that "OrderCount WoW", OrderCount7, and OrderCount14 measures use the OrderCount measure which has this formula:

```
MEASURE FactInternetSales[OrderCount] = DISTINCTCOUNT(FactInternetSales[SalesOrderNumber])
```

3. Replace the DISTINCTCOUNT function with this formula which uses SUMX.

```
MEASURE FactInternetSales[OrderCount] = SUMX(FactInternetSales, IF(FactInternetSales[SalesOrderLineNumber] = 1, 1))
```

4. Run the query again with Server Timings enabled. Now the query executes in only 87 milliseconds!

Analysis

Instead of counting distinct orders, the formula checks if the current row in FactInternetSales is the first order line item and returns one if this is the case (otherwise the IF statement returns a blank value). Then, SUMX sums the result to count the first line items in every order that's in the filter scope. You can now update the OrderCount measure in the Adventure Works model with this formula and the report will run instantaneously.

23.3 Summary

DAX can humble even experienced developers. Slow reports are typically caused by inefficient DAX formulas. Instead of throwing in more hardware (if this is even an option), plan to analyze and optimize your DAX measure relentlessly using the techniques you learned in this lesson. DAX Studio can help you analyze the query performance and test different measure versions to find the one that performs the best.

Lesson 24

Using Power BI Report Builder

One of the most prominent Power BI architectural strengths is that it doesn't lock you into just one reporting tool. Besides Power BI, you can use a reporting tool of your choice, such as Excel, Power BI Report Builder, or any MDX or DAX-aware third-party tool, to analyze your data. Some reporting tools, however, are less interactive and might require a query for each dataset. In this lesson, you'll learn how to create and parameterize a DAX query in a Power BI Report Builder report. You'll find the query examples in \Source\Part5\Using Power BI Report Builder.dax.

24.1 Understanding Power BI Report Builder

Long before Power BI was Microsoft SQL Server Reporting Services (SSRS) – the Microsoft flagship reporting tool for creating paginated reports. Paginated reports are traditional, paper-oriented reports that are designed to be printed or exported. Although lacking in interactivity, SSRS reports have always excelled in extensibility. You'll be hard pressed to find a requirement that you can't meet with SSRS reports, although creating paginated reports is not as easy as Power BI reports and requires specific report authoring skills.

24.1.1 When to Use Report Builder

Microsoft provides two designers for authoring paginated reports. The SQL Server Data Tools (SSDT) Report Designer integrates with Visual Studio and targets BI professionals. Report Builder is for business users willing to create and test reports outside Visual Studio. In April 2019, Microsoft introduced a special version of this tool called Power BI Report Builder that's optimized for creating paginated reports from published Power BI datasets and deploying these reports to Power BI. This is conceptually like how you can use the Power BI Analyze in Excel feature to create Excel reports from published datasets.

Understanding usage scenarios
In a nutshell, consider using Report Builder when paginated reports might be preferable compared to Power BI reports. Here are the main reasons:

- More demanding reporting requirements – Power BI reports are very easy to create but they are also somewhat simplistic. Report Builder supports more sophisticated report layouts, such as nesting report items (a chart repeated for each row in a table).

- Better control over the report layout – As I mentioned, paginated reports are designed to pixel-perfect. Every organization requires a list of standard reports that don't require too much interactivity and are designed to be printed or exported.

- Extensibility – Almost every aspect of paginated reports can be customized or extended, including plugging in custom data sources, subscription delivery channels, export formats, and even implementing custom security.

NOTE I've been privileged to contribute to and witness the evolution and success of Microsoft SQL Server Reporting Services since its debut in 2004. SSRS is Microsoft's most mature and extensible reporting platform. Although written more than a decade ago, my book "Applied Microsoft SQL Server 2008 Reporting Services" (768 pages) should help you appreciate the breath of its features.

Understanding Power BI limitations

As of the time of writing, Power BI paginated reports are a preview feature that requires Power BI Premium. Many of the SSRS features are not available but Microsoft is working hard to migrate them to Power BI. For example, Power BI supports only a subset of the SSRS data sources, and it doesn't support shared data sources and datasets, subreports and drillthrough reports, as well as management features, such as report caching. For more information about existing limitations, read the article "What are paginated reports in Power BI Premium?" at https://docs.microsoft.com/-power-bi/paginated-reports-report-builder-power-bi.

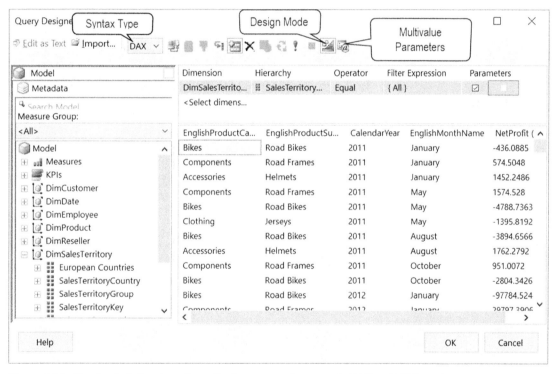

Figure 24.1   The Analysis Services Query Designer can auto-generate DAX and MDX queries.

24.1.2 Understanding the Analysis Services Query Designer

Like Power BI, Report Builder has the concept of datasets. However, a Report Builder dataset always connects directly to the data source (the data is not imported). Report Builder requires you to specify a query for each dataset. It includes graphical query designers to help you auto-generate queries for some Microsoft data sources, such as SQL Server and Analysis Services. The Analysis Services Query Designer (see **Figure 24.1**) deserves more attention because it can generate DAX queries.

NOTE Besides Report Builder, you'll find the Analysis Services Query Designer in SQL Server Management Studio (SSMS), when you browse a Tabular model or a Power BI model. One notable difference is that SSMS doesn't support parameterizing the query (only Power BI Report Builder supports it).

Understanding connectivity options

You can connect Report Builder to any of the Analysis Services data sources (published reports require a Power BI gateway to connect to on-prem data sources):

- Published Power BI datasets – Currently, this option requires the dataset to be hosted in a premium workspace. Use the XMLA endpoint syntax to connect to the workspace:

  powerbi://api.powerbi.com/v1.0/myorg/[your workspace name]

- Analysis Services Multidimensional or Tabular models – This includes SQL Server Analysis Services (Multidimensional and Tabular) and Azure Analysis Services Tabular.

- Published Power Pivot models – You can also connect to Power Pivot models deployed to SharePoint Server.

Auto-generating queries

A unique feature of this designer is that it can autogenerate MDX and DAX queries (recall that Analysis Services supports these two query interfaces). You can toggle the Syntax Type drop-down to select a query type. Then, just drag fields from the left Metadata pane into the right query pane. Click the Exclamation button to run the query and see the results. To see the query text, toggle the Design Mode button. Remember that you can customize and optimize the query in Text Mode, such as to use variables, but you can't switch back to the graphical interface (Design Mode) without losing your changes.

You can also parameterize your queries. To do so, drag one or more fields to the Filter pane (above the query pane), specify an operator, and a default value. To promote the filter to a parameter, don't forget to check the Parameters checkbox. The query designer will auto-generate a hidden dataset for each parameter, and it will make the necessary changes to the main dataset.

Sales Summary

Category	Subcategory	2010 Total	2011 Total	2012 Total	2013 Total	Total
⊟ Accessories	Bike Racks			3,164	30,524	**33,688**
	Bottles and Cages			115	1,233	**1,349**
	Cleaners			232	1,769	**2,002**
	Helmets	563	11,113	17,242	20,563	**49,482**
	Hydration Packs			1,128	9,905	**11,034**
	Locks		295	2,881		**3,176**
	Pumps		255	2,416		**2,672**
	Tires and Tubes			29	145	**174**
	Total	563	11,664	27,208	64,140	103,576
⊞ Bikes	Total	12,864	(90,049)	129,235	(448,300)	(396,250)
⊞ Clothing	Total	(108)	7,744	103,915	38,983	150,535
⊞ Components	Total	663	121,752	371,011	191,870	685,297
Total		**13,982**	**51,112**	**631,370**	**(153,306)**	**543,158**

Figure 24.2 The Sales Summary paginated report connects to a Power BI model.

24.2 Creating a Paginated Report

Next, you'll practice using the Power BI Report Builder to create a paginated report that uses a DAX query to retrieve the data. The Sales Summary crosstab report (see **Figure 24.2**) sources data from a Power BI model. I included the report definition in the \Source\Part5 folder.

24.2.1 Getting Started with Power BI Report Builder

Let's start by installing the Power BI Report Builder and using one of its wizards to quickly create the report layout. As a prerequisite, if you want to connect to a published Power BI model, deploy the Adventure Works model to a premium workspace (in the Power BI portal, premium workspaces have a diamond icon next to their names). If you don't have access to a premium workspace, you can follow along by connecting to your local Power BI Desktop model.

Practice
Follow these steps to install Power BI Report Builder:

1. Open your web browser and navigate to powerbi.com. Log in with your credentials.

2. In the Power BI portal, click the Download menu in the top right corner and then click "Paginated Report Builder". This navigates you to the Microsoft Power BI Report Builder download page. Download and install the setup program.

3. Open Power BI Report Builder on the desktop. In the Getting Started splash screen, choose "Table or Matrix Wizard".

4. In the "Choose the dataset" step, select the "Create a dataset" option to set up a new dataset.

5. In the "Choose a connection to a data source" step, click New. In the "Data Source Properties" window, rename the data source from DataSource1 to *AdventureWorks*. Expand the "Select connection type" dropdown and choose "Microsoft SQL Server Analysis Services". Currently, you must use this data source to connect to published models although Microsoft has indicated that they plan to introduce a data source for published datasets). Click the Build button.

6. In the Connection Properties window, enter one of the following in the "Server name" field:

   ■ The XMLA endpoint address – In case you connect to a published Power BI model, enter the XMLA endpoint address for the premium workspace. Power BI Report Builder will ask you to provide your credentials to log in to Power BI.

   ■ The local Tabular instance address behind the Power BI Desktop model – Once you open the Adventure Works model in Power BI Desktop, use DAX Studio to get this address, which will be in the format *localhost:port*. This option won't ask you to authenticate because it will use your Windows identity. You can use this connectivity option to test Power BI Report Builder if you don't have access to Power BI Premium, but remember that it will work only on your desktop (a published report won't be able to connect).

7. In the Connection Properties window, expand the "Connect to a database" dropdown and select your Power BI Desktop file. If you connect to the local Tabular instance, you'll see only one item with a system-generated Global Unique Identifiers (guid) name.

8. Click "Test Connection" to test connectivity. If all is well, click OK to return to the "Data Source Properties" window. The "Connection string" field should now be populated. Click OK. Then, click Next to advance to the wizard's "Design a query" step.

Analysis

Currently, Report Builder comes in two flavors: SQL Server Reporting Services and Power BI. The former is designed to work with an SSRS report server and supports all SSRS features. The latter is designed to integrate with Power BI and support only paginated report features that are compatible with Power BI. Both versions produce paginated reports described in a documented Report Definition Language (RDL) specification.

Given the subject of this book, the most interesting connectivity options for the reader would be connecting to Analysis Services Tabular and Power BI models, and then publishing the report to Power BI. Currently, paginated reports are a Power BI Premium feature.

24.2.2 Working with DAX Queries

The "Design a query" step is where you design the DAX query using the Analysis Services Query Designer. Let's quickly create and examine the generated DAX query.

Practice

Instead of creating the query from scratch, you'll auto-generate it by dragging and dropping fields. Notice that the query designer supports only explicit measures. Unlike Power BI, you can't create implicit measures.

1. In the Metadata pane, expand the Measures folder and then expand the FactResellerSales folder. Drag the "Net Profit (m)" measure and drop it in the query pane. Or, right-click the measure and then click "Add to Query". The order you add the query fields in is insignificant.

2. Expand the DimProduct table and add EnglishProductCategoryName and EnglishProductSubcategoryName to the query.

3. Expand the DimDate table and add CalendarYear and EnglishMonthName fields to the query.

4. To parameterize the report by country, expand DimSalesTerritory and drag SalesTerritoryCountry to the filter pane above the query pane. Expand the Operator field and choose the "Equal" operator. Expand the Filter Expression field and check the All item to default the parameter to all countries. To promote the filter to a report parameter, check the Parameters checkbox.

5. Click the Execute Query (the exclamation point button) to run the query. Compare your results with **Figure 24.1**.

6. Toggle the Design Mode button to switch to text mode. Notice that the tool has generated the following DAX query:

```
DEFINE
  VAR DimSalesTerritorySalesTerritoryCountry1 =
    IF (
      PATHLENGTH ( @DimSalesTerritorySalesTerritoryCountry ) = 1,
      IF (
        @DimSalesTerritorySalesTerritoryCountry <> "",
        @DimSalesTerritorySalesTerritoryCountry,
        BLANK ()    ),
      IF (
        PATHITEM ( @DimSalesTerritorySalesTerritoryCountry, 2 ) <> "",
        PATHITEM ( @DimSalesTerritorySalesTerritoryCountry, 2 ),
        BLANK ()    )
    )
  VAR DimSalesTerritorySalesTerritoryCountry1ALL =
    PATHLENGTH ( @DimSalesTerritorySalesTerritoryCountry ) > 1
      && PATHITEM ( @DimSalesTerritorySalesTerritoryCountry, 1, 1 ) < 1
```

```
EVALUATE
SUMMARIZECOLUMNS (
   'DimProduct'[EnglishProductCategoryName],
   'DimProduct'[EnglishProductSubcategoryName],
   'DimDate'[CalendarYear],
   'DimDate'[EnglishMonthName],
   FILTER (
      VALUES ( 'DimSalesTerritory'[SalesTerritoryCountry] ),
      ( ( DimSalesTerritorySalesTerritoryCountry1ALL
         || 'DimSalesTerritory'[SalesTerritoryCountry] = DimSalesTerritorySalesTerritoryCountry1 ) )
   ),
   "NetProfit (m)", [NetProfit (m)])
```

7. Click Next to advance to the next step. In the Arrange Fields step, drag the EnglishProductCategoryName and EnglishProductSubcategoryName fields to the "Row group" area, CalendarYear and EnglishMonthName fields to the "Column groups" area, and NetProfit_m field to the Values area.

8. Accept the defaults in the next steps and then click Finish. Power BI Report Builder generates the report definition and opens the report in design mode.

9. Click the Run button (or press F5) to run and test the report. It should look like **Figure 24.2**, although I've made a few layout tweaks to polish the report appearance a bit.

Analysis

By default, the query designer creates multivalue parameters, but the query syntax doesn't support them. For example, if you select multiple countries and run the report, you'll get a "Type mismatch" error. To avoid this, you must toggle the Multi-value Parameters button in the Analysis Services Query Designer in DAX mode, which rewrites the query completely and uses an undocumented RSCustomDaxFilter function.

 TIP You don't have to stick to the auto-generated DAX queries and their limitations. My blog "SSRS Multivalue Parameters in DAX" (https://prologika.com/ssrs-multivalue-parameters-in-dax/) shows you how to modify the query to handle multivalue parameters and simplify its syntax. Unfortunately, once you take the custom query path, you can't use the graphical query designer and its drag-and-drop feature anymore.

The query starts by declaring two variables for detecting the parameter selection. The first variable, DimSalesTerritorySalesTerritoryCountry1, detects the selected country. The second variable is to detect if all countries or the "All" value are selected. To understand these variables better, exit the query designer, right-click the Datasets node in the Report Data pane, and then click "Show Hidden Datasets". You'll see another dataset that the query designer has generated for the parameter's available values. This dataset uses this DAX query:

```
EVALUATE
SELECTCOLUMNS (
   ADDCOLUMNS (
      SUMMARIZECOLUMNS (
         ROLLUPADDISSUBTOTAL ( 'DimSalesTerritory'[SalesTerritoryCountry], "h0" )
      ),
      "ParameterLevel", IF ( [h0], 0, 1 )
   ),
   "ParameterCaption", SWITCH (
      [ParameterLevel],
      1, "" & 'DimSalesTerritory'[SalesTerritoryCountry],
      "All"
   ),
```

"ParameterValue", [ParameterLevel] & "|" & 'DimSalesTerritory'[SalesTerritoryCountry],
"ParameterLevel", [ParameterLevel],
"'DimSalesTerritory'[SalesTerritoryCountry]", 'DimSalesTerritory'[SalesTerritoryCountry])

Figure 24.3 shows you the results from this query.

SalesTerritoryCountry	ParameterCaption	ParameterValue	ParameterLevel
(null)	All	0|	0
Australia	Australia	1|Australia	1
Canada	Canada	1|Canada	1
France	France	1|France	1
Germany	Germany	1|Germany	1
NA	NA	1|NA	1
United Kingdom	United Kingdom	1|United Kingd...	1
United States	United States	1|United States	1

Figure 24.3 This dataset is used for the parameter's available values.

The query constructs a ParameterValue column. Does its syntax look familiar? It complies with the output of the DAX PATH function. And the ParameterLevel column returns the value level (indentation) with the All value being at level 0 and other values at level 1 (a hierarchy may have more levels).

Going back to the main query, @DimSalesTerritorySalesTerritoryCountry represents the parameter value that the report passes to the query. You can see this placeholder defined on the dataset properties page (Parameters tab). The variables use the PATHLENGTH and PATHITEM functions to detect the parameter level and the actual value. Finally, like Power BI-generated queries, SUMMARIZECOLUMNS is used to group the query and filter the results for the selected parameter value.

24.3 Summary

Some reporting tools, such as Power BI Report Builder, can't auto-generate DAX when you interact with the report and require you to specify dataset queries. Power BI Report Builder includes an Analysis Services Query Designer that can generate DAX queries at design time. You can also use the knowledge from this book to customize the generated DAX queries or replace them with your own queries.

Advanced DAX

N ow that you know how to create the three DAX constructs (calculated columns, measures, and queries), you're ready to tackle more advanced scenarios with DAX. This part of the book starts by showing you how DAX can help you work with different types of joins, including recursive (parent-child), many-to-many, inner, outer, and other joins.

If you need to restrict certain users to a subset of the data, you need data security. I'll show you how to implement row-level security (RLS) with DAX. You'll also learn how to handle more complicated security policies, such as by externalizing the secured entities in a separate table.

You'll find the completed exercises and reports for this part of the book in the Adventure Works and Bank models that are included in the \Source\Part6 folder.

Lesson 25

Recursive Relationships

So far, you've created DAX calculations that work with regular relationships where a dimension (lookup) table joins to the fact table directly. In this lesson, you'll learn how to work with recursive relationships, which DAX doesn't support natively, but it has functions that are specifically designed for this relationship type. You'll find the DAX formulas in \Source\Part6\Recursive Relationships.dax.

25.1 Understanding Recursive Relationships

A recursive (also known as parent-child) relationship represent is a hierarchical relationship formed between two entities with an arbitrary number of levels. Common examples of parent-child relationships include an employee hierarchy, where a manager has subordinates who in turn have subordinates, and an organizational hierarchy, where a company has divisions, offices, and branches.

25.1.1 Modeling Recursive Hierarchies

In a regular hierarchy, each level has a separate column and usually the number of levels is small. A recursive hierarchy on the other hand is a hierarchy formed by two columns that define a recursive relationship among the hierarchy members.

EmployeeKey	ParentEmployeeKey	FirstName	LastName
1	18	Guy	Gilbert
2	7	Kevin	Brown
3	14	Roberto	Tamburello
4	3	Rob	Walters
5	3	Rob	Walters
6	267	Thierry	D'Hers
7	112	David	Bradley
8	112	David	Bradley
9	23	JoLynn	Dobney
10	189	Ruth	Ellerbrock
11	3	G·¨	¨·ickson

Figure 25.1 The ParentEmployeeKey column contains the identifier for the employee's manager.

Modeling parent-child columns
The EmployeeKey and ParentEmployeeKey columns in the DimEmployee table have a parent-child relationship, as shown in **Figure 25.1**. Specifically, the ParentEmployeeKey column points to the

EmployeeKey column (the primary key of the DimEmployee table) to identify the employee's manager. For example, Kevin Brown (EmployeeKey = 2) has David Bradley (EmployeeKey=7) as a manager, who in turn reports to Ken Sánchez (EmpoyeeKey=112). (Ken is not shown in the screenshot.) Ken Sánchez's ParentEmployeeKey is blank, which means that he's the top manager.

Recursive hierarchies might have an arbitrary number of levels. Such hierarchies are called *unbalanced* hierarchies. For example, Kevin is a marketing manager and his branch in the organizational chart may consist of only two levels. However, James Hamilton, who's a vice president of production and also reports to Ken, might have a deeper hierarchy.

When to use recursive hierarchies

A recursive hierarchy is typically used to model deep relationships, such as a manager-subordinate relationship, that may require many levels and creating a column for each level might be limiting and impractical. To model a recursive hierarchy as a regular hierarchy you need to estimate the maximum number of levels. Then, you'd probably increase that number to accommodate the case where the hierarchy levels increase in the future. Recursive hierarchies solve this issue elegantly by requiring only two columns.

All popular relational database management systems (RDBMS) support parent-child relationships. They may also enforce constraints to prevent deleting a parent, which may lead to orphan members.

25.1.2 Handling Recursive Relationships in DAX

Unfortunately, DAX doesn't natively support recursive relationships. It doesn't have functions to traverse hierarchies either, such as to find the ancestor or descendants of a current member. However, it has functions to "flatten" the levels in a recursive hierarchy to columns and to return the path to each member (see **Table 25.1**)

Table 25.1 DAX has specific functions for recursive hierarchies.

Function	Syntax	Description
PATH	PATH (<PrimaryColumn>, <ParentColumn>)	Returns the entire path to the current member as a delimited list starting from the top
PATHLENGTH	PATHLENGTH (<Path>)	Returns the number of levels before and including the current member
PATHITEM	PATHITEM (<Path>, <Position> [, <Type>])	Returns the item at a specified position starting from the left of the delimited list produced by the PATH function
PATHITEMREVERSE	PATHITEMREVERSE (<Path>, <Position> [, <Type>])	Same as PATHITEM but going in reverse (from lower to higher levels)
PATHCONTAINS	PATHCONTAINS (<Path>, <Item>)	Returns TRUE if the specified item exists in the delimited list produced by the PATH function

All these functions are designed to work in the row context, so you'll use them to add calculated columns to the table containing the recursive hierarchy.

Functions for hierarchy paths

The mother of all DAX recursive functions is PATH. This function produces the hierarchy path as a delimited string from the top member to the current member. For example, a path of "112|7|2" means that the top member is 112, the immediate descendant is 7, and 2 is the identifier of the current member.

You can use PATHLENGTH to find how many levels a given member has. For example, PATH-LENGHT("112|7|2") returns 3. This function could be useful to find the number of ancestors by subtracting one from the return value.

Functions for locating members

You can locate a member by using the PATHITEM item function and specifying a starting position and offset. For example, PATHITEM ("112|7|2", 1, 0) returns 112 because this member is at the top. The third argument (Type) specifies the data type of the output and it takes one of these two values: 0 (returns the member identifier as a number) and 1 (returns the identifier as text). And PATHITEMREVERSE works the same way but in the opposite direction.

PATHCONTAINS checks if a member identifier is in the hierarchy path. You'll use this function later in this part of the book to implement a row-level security filter that restricts the user to see only his sales and the sales of his subordinates.

25.2 Working with Recursive Relationships

Next, you'll practice the DAX functions for handling recursive relationships. You'll use the DimEmployee table in the Adventure Works model for this practice. You'll start by creating a hierarchy to drill down the organizational chart. Then, I'll show you how to hide members that don't have data.

25.2.1 Creating a Recursive Hierarchy

Before you can create an organizational hierarchy to analyze sales by the manager-subordinate relationship, you must first flatten the recursive relationship into levels.

Practice

As a first step, use the PATH function to return the hierarchy path for each employee.

1. If you don't have a FullName calculated column in the DimEmployee table, add a calculated column FullName to this table with the following formula:

FullName = [FirstName] & " " & [LastName]

2. Add a Path calculated column to the Employee table with the following formula:

Path = PATH([EmployeeKey], [ParentEmployeeKey])

> **NOTE**   You may get the following error with your real-life models when you use the PATH function: "The columns specified in the PATH function must be from the same table, have the same data type, and that type must be Integer or Text". The issue could be that the parent key column is of a Text data type. This might be caused by a literal text value "NULL" in the ParentEmployeeKey, while it should be a blank (null) value. To fix this, open the Power Query Editor (right-click the table and click Query Editor), right-click the text column, and then click Replace Values. In the Replace Value dialog, replace NULL with blank. Then, in the Power Query Editor (Home ribbon tab), change the column type to Whole Number and click the "Close & Apply" button.

The formula uses the PATH function, which returns a delimited list of IDs (using a vertical pipe as the delimiter) starting with the top (root) of a parent-child hierarchy and ending with the current employee identifier.

The next step is to flatten the parent-child hierarchy by adding a column for each level. This means that you need to know beforehand the maximum number of levels that the employee hierarchy might have. To be on the safe side, add one or two more levels to accommodate future growth.

3. Add a Level1 calculated column that has the following formula:

Level1 = LOOKUPVALUE([FullName], [EmployeeKey], PATHITEM ([Path],1,1))

This formula uses the PATHITEM function to parse the Path calculated column and return the first member identifier as a number (notice that the third argument is 1), which is 112. Then, it uses the LOOKUPVALUE function to return the full name of the corresponding employee, which in this case is Ken Sánchez.

4. Add five more calculated columns for Levels 2-6 that use similar formulas to flatten the hierarchy all the way down to the lowest level. Compare your results with **Figure 25.2**.

Path	Level1	Level2	Level3	Level4	Level5	Level6
112|23|18|1	Ken Sánchez	Peter Krebs	Jo Brown	Guy Gilbert		
112|7|2	Ken Sánchez	David Bradley	Kevin Brown			
112|14|3	Ken Sánchez	Terri Duffy	Roberto Tamburello			
112|14|3|4	Ken Sánchez	Terri Duffy	Roberto Tamburello	Rob Walters		
112|14|3|5	Ken Sánchez	Terri Duffy	Roberto Tamburello	Rob Walters		
112|14|3|267|6	Ken Sánchez	Terri Duffy	Roberto Tamburello	Ovidiu Cracium	Thierry D'Hers	
112|7	Ken Sánchez	David Bradley				
112|8	Ken Sánchez	David Bradley				
112|23|9	Ken Sánchez	Peter Krebs	JoLynn Dobney			
112|23|189|10	Ken Sánchez	Peter Krebs	Andrew Hill	Ruth Ellerbrock		
112|14|3|11	Ken Sánchez	Terri Duffy	Roberto Tamburello	Gail Erickson		
112|23|189|12	Ken Sánchez	Peter Krebs	Andrew Hill	Barry Johnson		
	Ken Sánchez	Terri D...	...amburello	Jossef Goldh...		

Figure 25.2   Use the PATHITEM function to flatten the parent-child hierarchy.

5. Hide the Path column in the Employee table as it's not useful for analysis.
6. Create an Employees hierarchy consisting of six levels based on the six columns you just created. To create the hierarchy, right-click the DimEmployee[Level1] column in the Fields pane, and then click "New Hierarchy". Rename the new hierarchy to *Employees*. Then, right-click the remaining Level2 to Level6 columns one by one and then click "Add to hierarchy ⇨ Employees".

Output
Let's create a quick report to test the results.

1. Add a Matrix visualization to analyze sales by the Employees hierarchy. To do so, add the Employees hierarchy to the Row area and ResellerSales[SalesAmount] to the Values area.
2. Right-click Ken Sanchez and click Expand ⇨ All. Compare your results with **Figure 25.3**.

Analysis
Going back to the Data View tab, notice that most of the cells in the Level 5 and Level 6 columns are empty, and that's okay because only a few employees have more than four indirect managers. However, what doesn't look right are the empty cells in the Matrix visual which are the byproduct of the missing levels.

For example, Joe Pak reports to Amy Alberts and he is at Level 4 in the organizational hierarchy. His levels 5 and 6 are empty and the report shows them as empty cells.

Level1	SalesAmount
Ken Sánchez	$80,450,597
Brian Welcker	$80,450,597
Amy Alberts	$15,535,946
	$732,078
	$732,078
	$732,078
Jae Pak	$8,503,339
	$8,503,339
	$8,503,339
Rachel Valdez	$1,790,640
	$1,790,640
	$1,790,640
Ranjit Varkey Chudukatil	$4,509,889

Figure 25.3 The empty members correspond to blank levels in the Employees hierarchy.

25.2.2 Refining a Recursive Hierarchy

Unfortunately, Power BI doesn't make it easy to hide these blank members. The backend Tabular server has a HideMembers property, but it's not yet exposed in Power BI Desktop. Of course, this presents another opportunity to hone in your DAX skills.

Practice
Let's add a calculated column and a new measure to handle the blank members.

1. Add a LevelNumber calculated column to the DimEmployee table with the following formula:

LevelNumber = PATHLENGTH ([Path])

2. Add a SalesAmount (h) measure to DimEmployee table with the following formula:

```
SalesAmount (h) =
VAR MemberLevel = ISFILTERED(DimEmployee[Level1]) + ISFILTERED(DimEmployee[Level2]) +
    ISFILTERED(DimEmployee[Level3]) + ISFILTERED(DimEmployee[Level4]) +
    ISFILTERED(DimEmployee[Level5]) + ISFILTERED(DimEmployee[Level6])
VAR TotalLevels = MAX ( DimEmployee[LevelNumber] )
RETURN
if(MemberLevel > TotalLevels, BLANK(), SUM(FactResellerSales[SalesAmount]))
```

Output
Replace the ResellerSales[SalesAmount] measure in the Matrix report with the DimEmployee-[SalesAmount (h)] measure. Now the report doesn't show empty cells. Compare your results with **Figure 25.4**.

Analysis
The SalesAmount (h) measure "fixes" the report and removes the blank members. Let's analyze how it works. The LevelNumber calculated column uses the PATHLENGTH function to return the number of levels in the hierarchy. For example, LevelNumber returns 4 for Jae Pack because Jae's path is "112|277|290|291" (has four segments).

The MemberLevel variable in the SalesAmount (h) measure calculates the current level in the report. When used in arithmetic calculations, TRUE is treated as 1 so the variable adds 1 to calculate the level for each member in the report, including empty members. The TotalLevels variable returns the LevelNumber value associated with the employee. Because it's a measure, it must use an aggregate function. There will be only one row in the filter scope of each cell and MAX (DimEmployee[LevelNumber]) returns that value (you can also use the MIN function).

Level1	SalesAmount (h)
Ken Sánchez	$80,450,597
Brian Welcker	$80,450,597
Amy Alberts	$15,535,946
Jae Pak	$8,503,339
Rachel Valdez	$1,790,640
Ranjit Varkey Chudukatil	$4,509,889
Stephen Jiang	$63,320,315
David Campbell	$3,729,945
Garrett Vargas	$3,609,447
Jillian Carson	$10,065,804
José Saraiva	$5,926,418

Figure 25.4 The SalesAmount (h) measure removes the blank members from the report.

The measure then checks if the current level is greater than the total levels. This condition will return TRUE only for blank members. If that's the case, the measure returns an empty (blank) value. Because by default Power BI visuals remove blank values, the net effect is that the blank members are excluded from the report.

25.3 Summary

Recursive relationships are typically used to model deep unbalanced hierarchies. DAX doesn't support them natively and it doesn't have functions for navigating hierarchies. However, DAX has functions to flatten the recursive relationship into columns for each level. Currently, preventing blank members from showing up in reports requires changing the measures formulas.

Lesson 26

Many-to-Many Relationships

Another advanced relationship type that you might encounter is a many-to-many relationship. This lesson teaches you how to model many-to-many relationships declaratively and programmatically. You'll find the DAX formulas in \Source\Part6\ Many-to-Many Relationships.dax. and you'll use the \Source\Part6\Bank.pbix model for this practice.

26.1 Understanding Many-to-Many Relationships

A many-to-many relationship models a many-to-many cardinality between two tables. This occurs when a row in the dimension table relates to many rows in the fact table, and vice versa. Common real-life examples of many-to-many relationships are joint bank accounts (one customer can have multiple accounts and a joint account has multiple customers) and student course enrollment (a student can enroll in multiple courses and a course has multiple students).

26.1.1 Modeling Many-to-Many Relationships

Usually, a dimension table joins a fact table directly because the cardinality between the two tables is one-to-many. Many-to-many relationships are often tricky to represent and may require an intermediate table to break the "many-to-many" relationship into two "one-to-many" relationships.

Understanding bridge tables
The Bank.pbix file demonstrates a simplified version of a popular many-to-many scenario involving joint bank accounts. Open it in Power BI Desktop and select the Model View tab to see the table diagram (see **Figure 26.1**).

The Customer dimension table stores the bank's customers. The Account dimension table stores the bank accounts. The Balances fact table records the account balances every month and it's joined to the Date table. A customer might have multiple bank accounts, and a single account might be owned by two or more customers.

To resolve the Customer-Account many-to-many relationship, the model introduces an intermediate CustomerAccount table. This table is also referred to as a bridge table. In its simplest version, it may have only two columns: Customer and AccountNumber. Each row represents an account ownership, as shown in **Table 26.1** (notice that the A1 joint account is repeated).

Table 26.1 The CustomerAccount bridge table stores the many-to-many combinations.

Customer	AccountNumber
Teo	A1
Maya	A1
Teo	A2

For example, Teo owns two accounts (A1 and A2) and account A1 is joined by Teo and Maya. So, this table will have duplicated customers (if the customer owns multiple accounts) and duplicated account numbers in the case of joint accounts.

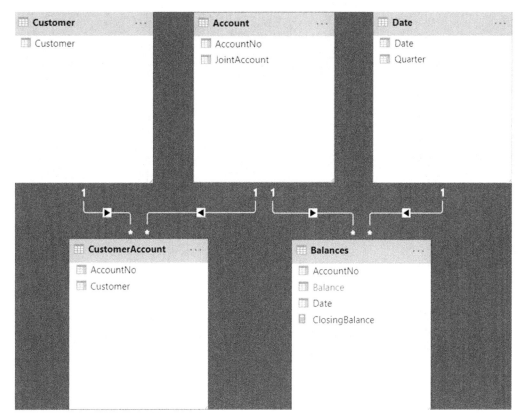

Figure 26.1 The CustomerAccount bridge table resolves the many-to-many relationship.

When to use bridge tables

Large bridge tables (over one million rows) could negatively impact the performance of your reports. Don't model every many-to-many scenario with bridge tables. A bridge table is required to represent the many-to-many relationship between a dimension table and a fact table. You might be able to avoid it with a many-to-many relationship between two dimension tables.

For example, consider Product and Promotion dimensions. A product could be on multiple promotions and a promotion can span multiple products. So, this is a many-to-many relationship. But you can resolve this relationship in the sales fact table by simply joining it to the Product and Promotion dimensions with regular many-to-one relationships. When a sales transaction is posted, the row records the associated product and promotion. In this case, there is no need for a bridge table.

But what if a sales transaction can be associated with multiple promotions? Now you have a many-to-many relationship between the Promotion dimension table and the Sales fact table. This requires a bridge table. In fact, the AdventureWorksDW database models the same scenario with the FactInternetSalesReason bridge table to represent the many-to-many relationship between Dim-Promotion and FactInternetSales.

26.1.2 Handling Many-to-Many Relationships

By default, a many-to-many relationship will produce wrong report results, as you'll see when you go through the practice steps. In general, there are two ways to handle many-to-many relationships with bridge tables in Power BI. The first requires reconfiguring the relationship between the fact table and affected dimension table, while the other requires DAX formulas.

Using bidirectional filtering

If your schema allows it, you should reconfigure the relationship from unidirectional to bidirectional because that's the easiest way to handle many-to-many relationships. How do you know which relationship to reconfigure? Going back to **Figure 26.1**, let's trace the path from the Dim-Customer dimension to the Balances fact table. Specifically, you're examining the direction of the relationship arrow.

The Customer ⇨ CustomerAccount relationship has an arrow pointing to CustomerAccount. This means when the query involves any field from the Customer table, the filter context will propagate to CustomerAccount, such as to filter the accounts that belong to a given customer. This is the behavior you want, so you don't need to modify this relationship.

The next relationship is Account ⇦ CustomerAccounts. Now the relationship path reverses the direction. This means that the filter won't propagate from CustomerAccounts to Customer. For example, a balance report by customer will produce wrong results because the filtered accounts in the CustomerAccounts table from the first relationship won't filter the accounts in the Account table. This is the relationship that deserves special attention.

 TIP Don't turn on bidirectional filtering on every relationship to "fix" the report because this may introduce redundant paths with more complicated schemas that Power BI will disallow. Instead, trace the relationship path and turn on bidirectional filtering on the relationship that reverses the path.

To reconfigure the relationship filter direction, open the relationship properties and change the "Cross filter direction" property to Both.

Using DAX

Sometimes, you may not have an active relationship or Power BI might reject a bidirectional relationship if it detects redundant or ambiguous paths. In this case, you can force the measures to be evaluated over the bridge table, using this syntax:

Measure = CALCULATE (<expression>, <bridge_table>)

Or, this syntax:

Measure = CALCULATE (<expression>, SUMMARIZE(<bridge_table>, <column_name>))

The second formula might give you a better performance. Translated to the Bank model, the second formula will look like this:

CALCULATE (<expression>, SUMMARIZE(CustomerAccount, Account[AccountNo]))

This formula filters the Account[AccountNo] values to those that exist in the CustomerAccount table by using the SUMMARIZE function. The net effect is the same as using a bidirectional relationship.

DAX also has a CROSSFILTER function to programmatically turn on bidirectional filtering. This function has the following syntax:

CROSSFILTER(<column1>, <column2>, <direction>)

Column1 typically represents the column on the many side of the relationship, which in our case is CustomerFilter[AccountNo], while Column2 represents the column on the one side of the relationship (Account[AccountNo]). But don't worry if you switch the columns as the function will internally swap them for you. Finally, the direction argument can have one of three values:

- One – the dimension table filters the fact table (default).
- Both – configures the relationship as bidirectional
- None – no cross-filtering occurs in this relationship

26.2 Working with Many-to-Many Relationships

You're back to the Bank model in Power BI Desktop. In this exercise, you'll practice different ways to handle many-to-many relationships so that reports return expected results. You'll practice once more handling semi-additive measures because account balances don't sum across time.

26.2.1 Using Declarative Approach

The Bank model is very simple as it has only five tables. It's a good candidate for the declarative approach to handle many-to-many relationships, where you'll reconfigure the relationships without using DAX.

Practice
Before making any changes, let's see what a balance by customer report would look like.

1. In the Fields pane, click the Balances[ClosingBalance] measure to examine its formula in the formula bar.
2. Add a Matrix visual and bind it to Customer[Customer] in the Rows area, Date[Quarter] and Date[Date] fields in the Columns area, and the Balances[ClosingBalance] measure in the Values area.
3. Compare your results with **Figure 26.2**.

Quarter	Q1 2011				Q2 2011			
Customer	1/1/2011	2/1/2011	3/1/2011	**Total**	4/1/2011	5/1/2011	**Total**	**Total**
Alice	700	1000	400	**400**	200	50	**50**	**50**
Bob	700	1000	400	**400**	200	50	**50**	**50**
John	700	1000	400	**400**	200	50	**50**	**50**
Sam	700	1000	400	**400**	200	50	**50**	**50**
Total	**700**	**1000**	**400**	**400**	**200**	**50**	**50**	**50**

Figure 26.2 This report produces wrong balances per customer.

Analysis
Like the inventory example in the lesson "Semi-additive measures", the ClosingBalance measure uses the LASTNONBLANK function:

```
ClosingBalance = CALCULATE(SUM(Balances[Balance]),
LASTNONBLANK('Date'[Date], CALCULATE(SUM(Balances[Balance]))))
```

Consequently, the quarter total shows the last balance recorded for that quarter and this works as expected. However, the report shows repeating balances across customers, which is wrong. If you replace Customer[Customer] with Account[AccountNo], the report shows correct results.

Practice

The wrong report results are caused by the many-to-many relationship between the Customer and Account tables. Specifically, the CustomerAccounts[AccountNo] ⇨ Account[AccountNo] reverses its direction when navigating the Customer ⇨ CustomerAcount ⇨ Account path.

1. In the Model View, double click the CustomerAccounts[AccountNo] ⇨ Account[AccountNo] relationship. Alternatively, click the Manage Relationships button in the ribbon which is available in any view. Then, select the CustomerAccounts[AccountNo] ⇨ Account[AccountNo] relationship and then click Edit.

2. In the "Edit relationship" window, expand the "Cross filter direction" dropdown and select Both. Click OK.

Output

Once you apply the relationship changes, Power BI refreshes the report, which now should look like the one in **Figure 26.3**.

Quarter	Q1 2011				Q2 2011			
Customer	1/1/2011	2/1/2011	3/1/2011	Total	4/1/2011	5/1/2011	Total	Total
Alice	100	200	300	300				300
Bob	600	700	300	300				300
John	100	200		200				200
Sam		100	100	100	200	50	50	50
Total	700	1000	400	400	200	50	50	50

Figure 26.3 This report produces correct results after reconfiguring the relationship cross-filter direction.

Analysis

The report now shows the correct balances. Because the CustomerAccounts[AccountNo] ⇨ Account[AccountNo] relationship is bidirectional (the Model View tab shows a double arrow), the filter context on the CustomerAccounts table transfers to the Account table, which in turn applies it to the Balances table to produce the balance per customer. Therefore, the filter context propagates from the Customer table all the way to the Balances table.

26.2.2 Using Programmatic Approach

By default, Power configures all relationships as unidirectional. Suppose you can't turn on bidirectional filtering (presumably because it results in ambiguous or redundant paths). Power BI will detect such conflicts and disallow them. However, you can use DAX formulas.

Practice

Handling many-to-many relationships in DAX requires changing the formulas of all measures that will be analyzed by any field in the Customer table.

1. Deactivate the CustomerAccounts[AccountNo] ⇨ Account[AccountNo] relationship (or change its cross-filtering property back to Single).

2. Add a new measure ClosingBalance (a) with the following formula:

```
ClosingBalance (a) = CALCULATE(SUM(Balances[Balance]),
    LASTNONBLANK('Date'[Date], CALCULATE(SUM(Balances[Balance]))),
    CustomerAccount)
```

Output

Replace the ClosingBalance measure in the report with ClosingBalance (a). Notice that the report produces the same results.

Analysis

The formula passes the CustomerAccount table as a filter argument to the CALCULATE function. This forces DAX to evaluate the formula for only accounts that exist in the CustomerAccount bridge table. You can also use this formula:

```
ClosingBalance (b) =
CALCULATE (
    SUM ( Balances[Balance] ),
    LASTNONBLANK ( 'Date'[Date], CALCULATE ( SUM ( Balances[Balance] ) ) ),
    SUMMARIZE ( CustomerAccount, Account[AccountNo] ))
```

Lastly, suppose that you prefer the CustomerAccounts[AccountNo] ⇨ Account[AccountNo] to be unidirectional by default, but you want to turn on bidirectional cross-filtering only for specific measures. You can accomplish this by using the CROSSFILTER function.

```
ClosingBalance (c) = CALCULATE(SUM(Balances[Balance]),
LASTNONBLANK('Date'[Date], CALCULATE(SUM(Balances[Balance]))),
CROSSFILTER(CustomerAccount[AccountNo]
, Account[AccountNo]
, Both)
)
```

This measure uses the CROSSFILTER function to achieve the same effect as turning on bidirectional filtering in the relationship properties, but it applies the configuration only for this measure.

26.3 Summary

You'll encounter many-to-many relationships when a many-to-many data cardinality exists between a dimension table and a fact table. When modeling many-to-many relationships, you should always favor active or inactive relationships because you'll get better performance and you don't have to change the measure formulas. When this is not an option, DAX has functions to achieve the same behavior programmatically.

Lesson 27

Joins with Existing Relationships

If you're familiar with SQL, you know that it supports various types of joins to relate and join tables. This lesson recaps and expands your knowledge of implementing similar joins in DAX, including inner and outer joins. I recommend you run the sample DAX queries in \Source\Part6\Joins with Existing Relationships.dax either using DAX Studio or SQL Server Management Studio (SSMS) to examine the effect of the different join operations. If you need help with DAX queries, review the first lesion in Part 5.

27.1 Implementing Inner Joins

An inner join retains only the column values that result in a match. Values that don't match, such as years without sales, are removed from the result.

Table 27.1 lists the DAX functions you can use to implement inner or outer joins when active or inactive relationships exist between the joined tables.

Table 27.1 DAX functions for implementing inner and outer joins with existing relationships.

Function	Join Type	Function	Join Type
SUMMARIZECOLUMNS	INNER	SUMMARIZE / VALUES	OUTER
GROUPBY	INNER	RELATED / RELATEDTABLE (no grouping)	OUTER
NATURALINNERJOIN (no grouping)	INNER	NATURALLEFTOUTERJOIN (no grouping)	OUTER

27.1.1 Inner Joins with Grouping

Recall from the lesson "Grouping Data" that the SUMMARIZECOLUMNS and GROUPBY functions eliminate column values with no data. Therefore, you can use these functions to implement inner joins. Run the following query to return aggregated reseller and Internet sales by calendar year:

```
EVALUATE
    CALCULATETABLE (
      SUMMARIZECOLUMNS (
        DimDate[CalendarYear],
        "ResellerSales", SUM ( FactResellerSales[SalesAmount] ),
        "InternetSales", SUM ( FactInternetSales[SalesAmount] )
    ))
```

CalendarYear	ResellerSales	InternetSales
2010	489328.5787	43421.0364
2011	18192802.7143	7075525.9291
2012	28193631.5321	5842485.1952
2013	33574834.1572	16351550.34
2014		45694.72

Figure 27.1 SUMMARIZECOL-UMNS acts as an inner join and eliminates years with no data.

Analysis

The SUMMARIZECOLUMNS function groups by DimDate[CalendarYear] and adds an extended column to aggregate sales from two tables on the many side of the relationship. Years without sales are eliminated from the results (although 2014 doesn't have reseller sales, it has Internet sales and it's retained). The equivalent SQL query would be:

```
select d.CalendarYear, SUM (frs.SalesAmount), SUM (fis.SalesAmount)
from DimDate d inner join FactInternetSales fis on fis.OrderDateKey = d.DateKey
inner join FactResellerSales frs on frs.OrderDateKey = d.DateKey
group by d.CalendarYear
```

SUMMARIZECOLUMNS also works with inactive relationships. For example, the following query works without using the USERELATIONSHIP function although the DimEmployee[SalesTerritoryKey] ⇨ DimSalesTerritory[SalesTerritoryKey] relationship is inactive.

```
EVALUATE
SUMMARIZECOLUMNS (
    DimEmployee[FullName],
    DimSalesTerritory[SalesTerritoryCountry],
    "Sales", SUM ( FactResellerSales[SalesAmount] )
)
```

Practice

GROUPBY also acts as an inner join but remember that it requires an extended "X" function for aggregating data in the extended columns.

```
EVALUATE
    GROUPBY( FactResellerSales,
        DimDate[CalendarYear],
        "ResellerSales", SUMX( CURRENTGROUP(), FactResellerSales[SalesAmount])
    )
```

Output

CalendarYear	ResellerSales
2011	18192802.7143
2012	28193631.5321
2013	33574834.1572
2010	489328.5787

Figure 27.2 GROUPBY also acts as an inner join but only one table can be aggregated on the many side of the join.

Analysis

Notice that the first argument of GROUPBY is the table on which the extended column operates. Unlike SUMMARIZECOLUMNS, GROUPBY is designed to aggregate data from a single table on the many side of the relationship by columns from one or more dimension tables on the one side of the relationship.

27.1.2 Inner Joins Without Grouping

DAX also provides a NATURALINNERJOIN function for joining tables at the table grain that doesn't requires grouping the data. You can use this function to join the data first, before performing other operations on top of the joined data, such as counting or aggregating the data in measures.

Practice
If you need to join two tables before grouping the results, you can use the NATURALINNERJOIN function which has the following syntax: NATURALINNERJOIN (<LeftTable>, <RightTable>)

```
EVALUATE
TOPN (
  5,
  SELECTCOLUMNS (
    NATURALINNERJOIN ( DimDate, FactResellerSales ),
    "Date", DimDate[Date],
    "SalesAmount", FactResellerSales[SalesAmount]
  ))
```

Output

Date	SalesAmount
1/29/2011 12:00:00 AM	874.794
1/29/2011 12:00:00 AM	419.4589
1/29/2011 12:00:00 AM	183.9382
1/29/2011 12:00:00 AM	2146.962
1/29/2011 12:00:00 AM	20.1865

Figure 27.3 NATURALINNERJOIN joins two tables with an inner join.

Analysis
When there is an active relationship, NATURALINNERJOIN uses the relationship to qualify rows where the column values in both tables match. To avoid returning all columns from both tables, the query uses the SELECTCOLUMNS function to select only two columns. It also uses the TOPN function to restrict the output to the first five rows. Notice that the results are not grouped which conceptually is like how a SQL join without GROUP BY aggregation would work.

27.2 Implementing Outer Joins

An outer join retains all column values in one of the tables irrespective if there is a match in the other table. The SQL language distinguishes between left and right outer join depending on which side of the join retains all values.

27.2.1 Outer Joins with Grouping

You can use the ADDCOLUMNS/SUMMARIZE pattern or the VALUES function to implement outer joins and group the data.

Practice

The following query using the SUMMARIZE function to simulate a left outer join between Fact-ResellerSales and DimDate and between FactResellerSalea and DimProduct.

```
EVALUATE
ADDCOLUMNS (
  SUMMARIZE (
    FactResellerSales,
    DimDate[CalendarYear],
    DimProduct[EnglishProductCategoryName]
  ), "ResellerSales", CALCULATE ( SUM ( FactResellerSales[SalesAmount] ) ))
```

Output

CalendarYear	EnglishProductCategoryName	ResellerSales
2010	Clothing	2875.1536
2011	Clothing	136624.1404
2012	Clothing	759490.3014
2013	Clothing	878851.2437
2010	Accessories	1695.666
2011	Accessories	45596.7872
2012	Accessories	145107.4903

Figure 27.4 SUMMARIZE and VALUES retain column values with no data.

Analysis

Notice that because the query groups sales by year and product category (two dimensions are involved), the first argument (base table) passed to the SUMMARIZE function is the fact table because it's related to both dimensions. The output represents the aggregated sales, irrespective of if they have associated years or products (FactResellerSales doesn't have unrelated rows so no empty column values show up). Attempting to group on a column that doesn't have an active relationship to the base table results in the error "column 'name' specified in the 'SUMMARIZE' function was not found in the input table".

You can use CALCULATE or CALCULATETABLE to navigate inactive relationships. For example, this query uses CALCULATETABLE to navigate the FactResellerSales [ShipDateKey] ⇨ DimDate[DateKey] relationship with the USERELATIONSHIP function

```
EVALUATE
CALCULATETABLE (
  ADDCOLUMNS (
    SUMMARIZE (
      FactResellerSales,
      DimDate[CalendarYear],
      DimProduct[EnglishProductCategoryName]
    ),
    "ResellerSales", CALCULATE ( SUM ( FactResellerSales[SalesAmount] ) )
  ) , USERELATIONSHIP ( FactResellerSales[ShipDateKey], DimDate[DateKey] ))
```

27.2.2 Outer Joins without Grouping

Like inner joins, there are DAX functions for looking up or relating data that don't eliminate values if there is no match.

Practice

You can use the RELATED function to look up values from a table on the one side of the relationship.

```
EVALUATE
TOPN (5,
  SELECTCOLUMNS (
    ADDCOLUMNS ( FactResellerSales, "Date", RELATED ( DimDate[Date] ) ),
    "OrderDate", [Date],
    "SalesAmount", [SalesAmount]
  ))
```

Analysis

This query looks up the value of the DimDate[Date] and ADDCOLUMNS adds it to FactReseller-Sales aliased as "Date". Then, SELECTCOLUMNS return only two columns: Date aliased as Order-Date and SalesAmount aliased as SalesAmount.

Practice

When grouping is not required, you can use NATURALLEFTJOIN to implement a left join.

```
EVALUATE
TOPN (5,
  SELECTCOLUMNS (
    NATURALLEFTOUTERJOIN ( DimDate, FactResellerSales ),
    "Date", DimDate[Date],
    "SalesAmount", FactResellerSales[SalesAmount]   ))
```

Analysis

NATURALLEFTOUTERJOIN returns all values from DimDate[Date] irrespective of if they have sales or not. SELECTCOLUMNS returns only the two specified columns from the results and TOPN filters the first five rows.

27.3 Summary

Although not as feature rich as SQL, DAX has a comprehensive list of functions that allow you to simulate left and outer joins over existing relationships. The function choice depends on whether you want the results to be grouped and if you want empty values to be eliminated.

Lesson 28

Virtual Relationships

Sometimes, you may need to relate tables that don't have a physical relationship. A "virtual" relationship is a runtime join that doesn't use an existing active or inactive relationship. This lesson reviews different ways to implement virtual relationships. You'll also learn how to implement more involved joins, such as cross joins and unions. As with the previous lesson, I recommend you run the sample DAX queries in \Source\Part6\Virtual Relationships.dax either using DAX Studio or SQL Server Management Studio (SSMS) to see the effect of the different join operations.

28.1 Implementing Virtual Relationships

You can use the functions shown in **Table 28.1** to implement simple lookups and virtual joins when physical relationships don't exist.

Table 28.1 DAX functions for joining tables without relationships.

Function	Join Type	Function	Join Type
LOOKUPVALUE	OUTER	NATURALINNERJOIN	INNER
NATURALLEFTOUTERJOIN	OUTER	INTERSECT	INNER
TREATAS	OUTER	CROSSJOIN	INNER (with filter)

28.1.1 Implementing Virtual Outer Joins

Next, you'll practice the LOOKUPVALUE and NATURALLEFTOUTERJOIN functions to implement simple lookups and SQL-style outer joins that retain all values from one of the tables.

Practice
Previously, I've shown you how to use LOOKUPVALUE to implement calculated columns. You can also apply this function to measures, such as when the formula uses an iterator function.

```
EVALUATE
TOPN (5,
  SELECTCOLUMNS (
    ADDCOLUMNS ( FactResellerSales, "Date",
    LOOKUPVALUE ( DimDate[Date],  DimDate[Date], FactResellerSales[OrderDate] ) ),
    "OrderDate", [Date],
    "SalesAmount", [SalesAmount]
  ))
```

Analysis

Like the similar example in the previous lesson, this query returns a table with two columns but it uses the LOOKUPVALUE function to look up the DimDate[Date] column that matches the Order-Date column. This works because ADDCOLUMNS is an iterator that passes the row context to LOOKUPVALUE.

Practice

You can use the NATURALLEFTOUTERJOIN function for outer virtual relationships, but the current implementation of the "natural" functions is very restricted. Microsoft hasn't implemented these functions as value-based joins but as dictionary-based joins to deliver the fastest performance. Therefore, the joined columns not only must have the same name, but also must have the same data lineage so that they share the same dictionary.

 NOTE Think of the column data lineage as an additional metadata attached to the column, such as references to the original columns in the data model.

The following query uses NATURALLEFTOUTERJOIN to join DimDate and Customer base tables in order to calculate the overall customer count by date.

```
EVALUATE
GROUPBY (
  NATURALLEFTOUTERJOIN (
    SELECTCOLUMNS (
      DimDate,
      "Date", DimDate[Date] + 0,
      "CalendarYear", DimDate[CalendarYear]
    ),
    SELECTCOLUMNS (
      CustomerBase,
      "Date", CustomerBase[MonthJoined] + 0,
      "CustomerCount", CustomerBase[CustomerCount]
    )
  ),
  [Date],
  "CustomerCount", SUMX ( CURRENTGROUP (), [CustomerCount] ))
```

Output

Date	CustomerCount
12/31/2010 12:00:00 AM	14
10/31/2011 12:00:00 AM	221
11/30/2011 12:00:00 AM	208
12/31/2011 12:00:00 AM	222
~ ~/2011 12:0~ ~M	188

Figure 28.1 You can use NATURALLEFTOUTERJOIN to implement virtual outer joins.

Analysis

Using NATURALLEFTOUTERJOIN requires some preparation. First, the query wraps both Dim-Date and CustomerBase tables with SELECTCOLUMNS so they both have a column called Date. Notice that when projecting the Date column, the query uses an expression-based column to calculate a bogus expression that adds zero to the date. It does this to remove the data lineage from the column so that both date columns have an identical (in this case empty) data lineage.

At this point, the query will return all dates from the DimDate table (with or without customers) which is the expected result from a left outer join. Lastly, the GROUPBY function is used to group by the Date column and remove dates with no data (in order words, to convert the join to an inner join).

Practice

Suppose you have an app that prompts the user to specify a subset of customers and as-of dates for each customer. Your query needs to calculate certain metrics, such as Sales, for these customers but as of the user-specified date for each customer. If the tables don't have physical relationships, you might get the best performance if you use TREATAS, which has the following syntax:

TREATAS (<Expression>, <ColumnName> [, <ColumnName> [, ...]])

The first argument (Expression) is a table-producing expression that returns columns to be mapped from the source table followed by the columns in the target table. Matching is done on column names so the joined columns must have identical names.

```
DEFINE
  VAR _filter =
    DATATABLE (
      "Customer Id", STRING,
      "Date", DATETIME,
      { { "AW00011000", "1/19/2011" }, { "AW00011001", "1/15/2010" } }
    )
EVALUATE
ADDCOLUMNS (
  TREATAS ( _filter, DimCustomer[CustomerAlternateKey], 'DimDate'[Date] ),
  "Sales", CALCULATE ( SUM ( FactInternetSales[SalesAmount] ) ),
  "Quantity", CALCULATE ( SUM ( FactInternetSales[OrderQuantity] ) )
)
```

Output

CustomerAlternateKey	Date	Sales	Quantity
AW00011000	1/19/2011	3399.99	1
AW00011001	1/15/2010		

Figure 28.2 Using TREATAS to propagate filters.

Analysis

DAX supports static tables using the DATATABLE function, but the resulting data table is very limited in features. First, you can't name the table in your query, so you need to resort to using a variable. More importantly, many DAX operations that reference columns, such as attempting to compute MAX of a table column to get the "current" value, will error with "Table variable '_filter' cannot be used in current context because a base table is expected". You can't create physical relationships to a custom data table either.

However, you can use TREATAS to establish virtual relationships based on the input parameters in the data table. The query has a _filter variable that points to a custom data table with two customers and corresponding as-of dates. Then, the query uses TREATAS to evaluate the sales and order quantity for each customer as of the specified date. One cautionary note I need to warn you about is that the cost of such "per-row" virtual relationships could be expensive.

28.1.2 Implementing Virtual Inner Joins

Virtual inner joins can be implemented with NATURALINNERJOIN, INTERSECT, and CROSS-JOIN. NATURALINNERJOIN works the same way as NATURALLEFTOUTERJOIN except that it retains only column values that match.

Practice
INTERSECT returns column values from one table that match column values in another table. It has the following syntax:

INTERSECT (<LeftTable>, <RightTable>)

Both arguments must return tables with the same number of columns that will be joined. You can think of INTERSECT like EXISTS in SQL. The following query returns the DimDate[Date] and DimDate[CalendarQuarter] columns only for the dates that exist in the CustomerBase[Month-Joined] column.

```
EVALUATE
CALCULATETABLE (
  SELECTCOLUMNS(DimDate, "Date", DimDate[Date], "Year", DimDate[CalendarYear]),
  INTERSECT (
    ALL(DimDate[Date]),
    VALUES(CustomerBase[MonthJoined] )
  )
))
```

Output

Date	Year
12/31/2010 12:00:00 AM	2010
10/31/2011 12:00:00 AM	2011
11/30/2011 12:00:00 AM	2011
12/31/2011 12:00:00 AM	2011
'20'	1:00	01'

Figure 28.3 Using INTERCEPT to implement SQL-like EXISTS joins.

Analysis
The query uses the INTERSECT function to find a subset of the DimDate[Date] column values that match Customer[MonthJoined]. Instead of ALL, you can use VALUES(DimDate[Date]), but you may still need ALL to ignore the filter context if the first column comes from a fact table.

To finish with INTERSECT, another DAX function EXCEPT works in the same way but returns only rows from the left-side table that are not in the right-side table.

28.2 Implementing Other Joins

DAX has a few more functions for working with joins that deserve attention. They allow you to cross join, merge, and generate tables.

28.2.1 Implementing Cross Joins

The CROSSJOIN function returns all the combinations (a cross join) between two or more tables, and it has this syntax:

CROSSJOIN (<Table> [, <Table> [, ...]])

Together with FILTER, CROSSJOIN can be used to implement a virtual inner join.

Practice
The following query returns the same results as the INTERSECT query:

```
EVALUATE
CALCULATETABLE (
  SELECTCOLUMNS ( DimDate, "Date", DimDate[Date], "Year", DimDate[CalendarYear] ),
  FILTER (
    CROSSJOIN ( ALL ( DimDate[Date] ), VALUES ( CustomerBase[MonthJoined] ) ),
    DimDate[Date] = CustomerBase[MonthJoined]
  ))
```

Analysis
The CROSSJOIN function returns all combinations between the DimDate[Date] and CustomerBase [MonthJoined] columns. Then, the FILTER function limits the results to only values where the two dates match.

28.2.2 Merging Tables

The DAX UNION function can fulfill a similar role as the SQL UNION ALL function. It returns the union of the two or more tables whose columns match. UNION has the following syntax:

UNION (<Table> [, <Table> [, ...]])

Practice
The following query appends selected columns from FactInternetSales and FactResellerSales and then computes the sum of sales by source.

```
EVALUATE
GROUPBY (
  UNION (
    SELECTCOLUMNS (
      FactInternetSales, "Source", "Internet", "Date", FactInternetSales[OrderDate],
      "ProductKey", FactInternetSales[ProductKey], "Sales", FactInternetSales[SalesAmount]
    ),
    SELECTCOLUMNS (
      FactResellerSales, "Source", "Resale", "Date", FactResellerSales[OrderDate],
      "ProductKey", FactResellerSales[ProductKey], "Sales", FactResellerSales[SalesAmount]
    )
  ),
  [Source]
  ,"TotalSales", SUMX ( CURRENTGROUP (), [Sales] ))
```

Output

Source	TotalSales
Internet	29358677.2207
Resale	80450596.9823

Figure 28.4 UNION combines columns from the FactInternetSales and FactResellerSales tables.

Analysis

This query combines column values ("rows") from the two fact tables. It adds a column "Source" to indicate the source table. Then, it uses GROUPBY to group the Source column and sum sales.

28.2.3 Generating Tables

Like CROSSJOIN, the GENERATE function cross joins two tables, but it also evaluates the right-side table in the context of each row in the left-side table.

Practice

Suppose you have a list of dates and for each date you want to get the orders that are open as of that date. The following query does this (to avoid many rows, it returns only the first 10 orders).

```
EVALUATE
TOPN (10,
  SELECTCOLUMNS (
    GENERATE (
      FactInternetSales,
      FILTER (DimDate,
        AND (DimDate[Date] >= FactInternetSales[OrderDate], DimDate[Date] <= FactInternetSales[ShipDate] )
      )
    ),
    "Date", DimDate[Date],
    "Order Number", FactInternetSales[SalesOrderNumber]
  ))
```

Output

Date	Order Number
12/29/2010...	SO43700
12/29/2010...	SO43699
12/29/2010...	SO43698
12/29/2010...	SO43697
3/29	043°

Figure 28.5 Using GENERATE to return a list of orders that are open as of each date in a list of dates.

Analysis

The query passes FactInternetSales as the first argument of the GENERATE function and a filtered list of DimDate that contains only the dates where the date is between the order date and ship date. This works because when GENERATE iterates each row in FactInternetSales, it passes the row context to the second table. As a result, only the sales orders that are open as of that date are filtered. Another DAX function GENERATEALL, can be used as a left join to retain rows from the right-side table if the evaluated expression results in an empty value.

28.3 Summary

For best performance, you should always create physical (active or inactive) relationships. Power BI maintains internal structures and indexes to optimize joins over physical relationships. However, the model complexity might sometimes preclude physical relationships. In this case, you can use the DAX functions discussed in this lesson to implement virtual joins, ranging from looking up values to more complicated joins.

Lesson 29

Applying Data Security

Do you have a requirement to allow certain users (internal or external) to see only a subset of data that they're authorized to access? For example, as a model author you have access to all the data you imported. However, when you publish the model to Power BI Service, you want other users to see only sales for a specific geography. Or, you might want to restrict external partners to access only their data in a multi-tenant model that you published to powerbi.com. This is where the Power BI data security (also known as row-level security or RLS) can help, and this lesson shows you how.

29.1 Understanding Data Security

Data security is supported for models that import data and that connect live to data, except when connecting live to Analysis Services, which has its own security model. At a high level, implementing data security is a two-step process:

- Modeling step – This involves defining roles and table filters inside the model to restrict access to data. Table filters are implemented as DAX formulas.

- Operational step – Once the security roles are defined, you need to publish the model to Power BI Service to assign members to roles. Configuring membership is the operational aspect of RLS that needs to be done in Power BI Service (powerbi.com).

It's important to understand that data security is only enforced in Power BI Service, that is when the model is published and shared with other users who have view-only rights (they don't have Admin or Edit Content permissions to a workspace) to shared content. Such users won't be able to access any data unless they are assigned to a role. However, if you share the Power BI Desktop file with another user and he opens it in Power BI Desktop, data security is *not* enforced.

29.1.1 Understanding Roles

Setting up data security requires implementing roles and table filters. A role allows you to grant other users restricted access to data in a secured model. A table filter limits the data the user can see in a table and its related tables.

Setting up roles
Figure 29.1 is meant to help you visualize a role. In a nutshell, a role gives its members permissions to view the model data. To create a new role, click the Manage Roles button in the ribbon's Modeling tab. Then, click the Create button in the "Manage roles" window and name the role. As I mentioned, after you deploy the model to Power BI Service, you must assign members to the role. You can type in email addresses of individual users, security groups, and workspace groups.

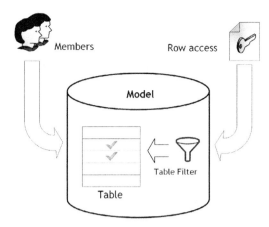

Members   Row access

Model

Table Filter

Table

Figure 29.1 A role grants its members permissions to a table, and it optionally restricts access to table rows.

Understanding role additivity

Roles are additive. If a user belongs to multiple roles, the user will get the superset of all the role permissions. For example, suppose the user is a member of both the Sales Representative and Marketing roles. The Sales Representative role grants him rights to United States, while the Marketing role grants him access to all countries. Because roles are additive, he can see data for all countries.

 TIP As it stands, Power BI doesn't support object security to hide entire tables. Even if the table filter qualifies no rows, the table will show in the model metadata. The simplest way to disallow a role from viewing any rows in a table is to set up a table filter that returns FALSE(). If no table filter is applied to a table, TRUE() is assumed and the user can see all of its data.

29.1.2 Understanding Table Filters

By default, a role can access all the data in all tables in the model. However, the whole purpose of implementing data security is to limit access to a subset of data, such as to allow some users to see only sales for the United States. This is achieved by specifying one or more table filters. As its name suggests, a table filter defines a filter expression that evaluates which table rows the role can see. To set up a row filter in Role Manager, enter a DAX formula next to the table name.

Understanding filter formulas

The DAX formula must evaluate to a Boolean condition that returns TRUE or FALSE. For example, when the user connects to the published model and the user is a member of the role, Power BI applies the row filter expression to each row in the DimSalesTerritory table. If the row meets the criteria, the role is authorized to see that row. For example, **Figure 29.2** shows that the "US" role applies a row filter to the SalesTerritory table to return only rows where the SalesTerritoryCountry column equals "United States".

How table filters affect related tables

From an end-user perspective, rows the user isn't authorized to view and their related data in tables on the many side of the relationship simply don't exist in the model. Imagine that a global WHERE clause is applied to the model that selects only the data that's related to the allowed rows of all the secured tables.

Given the US role setup shown in **Figure 29.2**, the user can't see any other sales territories in the DimSalesTerritory table except "United States". Moreover, because of the DimSalesTerritory ⇨ FactResellerSales filter direction, the user can't see sales for these territories in the FactResellerSales table or in any other tables that are directly or indirectly (via cascading relationships) related to the DimSalesTerritory table if the filter direction points to these tables. In other words, Power BI propagates data security to related tables following the filter direction of the existing relationships.

Figure 29.2 This table filter grants the US role access to rows where SalesTerritoryCountry is United States.

What about other dimension tables, such as DimReseller? Should the user see only resellers with sales in the United States? Again, the outcome depends on the relationship cross-filter direction. If it's Single (there is a single arrow pointing from DimReseller to FactResellerSales), the security filter is *not* propagated to the DimReseller table and the user can see all resellers. To clarify, the user can see the list of all resellers, but he can see only sales for the US resellers because sales come from the filtered ResellerSales table.

However, if the relationship cross-filter direction is Both (a bidirectional relationship) and the "Apply security filter in both directions" setting on the relationship properties is checked, then data security propagates to DimReseller table and the user can see only resellers with sales in the United States.

29.2 Implementing Basic Data Security

In the exercise that follows, you'll add a role that allows the user to view only sales in the United States. Then, I'll show you how to test the role on the desktop and how to add members to the role after you deploy your model to Power BI Service.

29.2.1 Changing the Model

Remember that setting up the security role and table filters are done in the Power BI Desktop.

Practice
Start by creating a new role in the Adventure Works model.

1. In the ribbon's Modeling tab, click the Manage Roles button.
2. In the Manage Roles window, click the Create button. Rename the new role to *US*.

3. Click the ellipsis button next to the DimSalesTerritory table, and then click "Add filter…" ⇨ [SalesTerritoryCountry] to filter the values in this column.

4. Change the "Table Filter DAX Expression" content with the following formula:

[SalesTerritoryCountry] = "United States"

5. Click Save.

> **TIP** Consider adding an Open Access role that doesn't have any table filter. This role is for users who need full access to data. Recall that by default a role has unrestricted access unless you define a table filter.

Output
You don't have to deploy the model to Power BI Service to test the role. Power BI Desktop lets you do this conveniently on the desktop. This allows you to test the role as though you're a user who is a member of the role.

1. In the ribbon's Modeling tab, click the "View as Roles" button.

2. In the "View as roles" window, check the US role. Click OK.

3. You should see a status bar showing "Now viewing report as: US". Create a report that includes the SalesTerritoryCountry column from the DimSalesTerritory table, such as the one shown in **Figure 29.3**. The report should show only data for US.

Now viewing report as: US		Stop viewing	
SalesTerritoryCountry	2005	2006	
United States	$6,552,075.85	$17,622,549.51	$20,071,1
Total	**$6,552,075.85**	**$17,622,549.51**	**$20,071,1**

Figure 29.3 The report shows only data for United States.

4. (Optional) Add a Table visualization showing the ResellerName column from the DimReseller table. You should see all resellers. However, if you add a measure from the FactResellerSales table, you should see only resellers with sales in the US. If you want to prevent the role from seeing non-US resellers, change the cross-filter direction of the FactResellerSales[ResellerKey] ⇨ DimReseller[ResellerKey] relationship to Both.

Analysis
When you browse the data as a member of the US role, you can see only United States in DimSalesTerritory. Moreover, you can see only sales transactions associated with this country. Data security automatically propagates to all fact tables related to the secured dimension table. It's also possible to propagate data security to dimension tables.

29.2.2 Defining Role Membership

Now that the role is defined, it becomes a part of the model, but its setup is not complete yet. Next, you'll deploy the model to Power BI Service and add members to the role.

Practice
Let's deploy the Adventure Works model to powerbi.com to finalize the security setup.

1. In the ribbon's Home tab, click Publish. If prompted, log in to Power BI and deploy the Adventure Works model to My Workspace.

2. Open your browser and navigate to Power BI Service (powerbi.com). Click My Workspace.

3. In the workspace content page, click the Datasets tab. Click the ellipsis button next to the Adventure Works dataset, and then click Security from the drop-down menu.

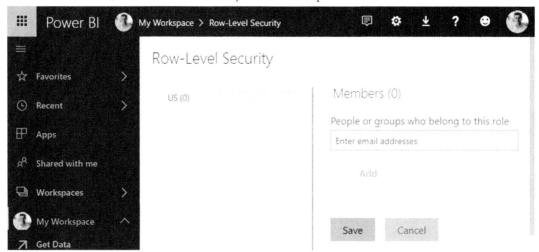

Figure 29.4 You set up the role membership in Power BI Service.

4. In the "Row-Level Security" window, add the emails of individuals or groups who you want to add to the role (**Figure 29.4**). You can also add external users that you have previously shared content with as members to the role. Click Save.

Output
It's always a good idea to check data security with other users to ensure it works.

1. Create a report that uses visualizations from the Adventure Works report and share it with users who belong and don't belong to the role (you and the recipients must have Power BI Pro or Power BI Premium subscriptions). Ask them to view the dashboard and report their results.

2. (Optional) Republish the Adventure Works model. Power BI Desktop will ask you to replace the dataset. In Power BI Service, go to the Adventure Works dataset security settings and notice that the role membership is preserved. That's because the role membership is external to the Adventure Works model and republishing the file doesn't overwrite it. However, if you delete the dataset in Power BI Service, you'll lose its role membership.

NOTE As a model author, you always have admin rights to model so don't be surprised that you see all the data irrespective of your role membership. If you publish the model to a workspace, the workspace administrators and members who can edit content also gain unlimited access.

Analysis
Once data security is enabled, users can't see the model data by default. Although the user has rights to run the report, data security will prevent the user to see any data unless the user is a member of the security role that grants the user data access.

29.3 Summary

Power BI has various security checks to ensure that the user is authorized to view reports and dashboards. Row-level security (RLS) is the most granular because it restricts the user to see a subset of the model data. You use DAX formulas to define table filters at design time and add role members in Power BI Service.

Lesson 30

Implementing Dynamic Security

The row filter in the previous lesson returns a fixed (static) set of allowed rows. This works well if you have a finite set of unique permissions. For example, if there are three regions, you can build three roles. Static filters are simple to implement and work well when the number of roles is relatively small. However, suppose you must restrict managers to view only the sales data of the employees that are reporting directly or indirectly to them. If static filters were the only option, you'd have no choice except to set up a database role for each manager. This might lead to a huge number of roles and maintenance issues. Therefore, Power BI supports dynamic data security. You'll find the DAX formulas for this lesson in \Source\Part6\Implementing Dynamic Security.dax.

30.1 Understanding Dynamic Data Security

Dynamic security relies on the identity of the interactive user to filter data. For example, if I log in to Power BI as teo.lachev@adventure-works.com, a role can filter the Employee table to me and my subordinates. Instead of creating a role per user, you need only a single role with the following table filter applied to the Employee table:

```
PATHCONTAINS(DimEmployee[Path],
LOOKUPVALUE(DimEmployee[EmployeeKey], DimEmployee[EmailAddress], USERPRINCIPALNAME()))
```

30.1.1 Authenticating the Interactive User

The cornerstone of dynamic data security is obtaining the identity of the interactive user and applying security policies based on that identity.

Obtaining the user identity
The above formula uses the USERPRINCIPALNAME() DAX function (specifically added to support Power BI) which returns the user principal name (UPN) in both Power BI Service and Power BI. If you have set up dynamic security with Analysis Services Multidimensional or Tabular, you have probably used the USERNAME() function. However, this function returns the user domain login in Power BI Desktop (see **Figure 30.1**). You can use the WhoAmI.pbix Power BI Desktop file in the \Source\Part6 folder to verify the results.

Figure 30.1 USERPRINCIPALNAME() and USERNAME() return different results in Power BI Desktop.

To avoid using an OR filter to support both Power BI and Power BI Desktop, use USERPRINCIPAL-NAME() but make sure that the EmailAddress column stores the user principal name (typically but not always UPN corresponds to the user's email address) and not the user's Windows login (domain\login).

Authorizing access
To explain the rest of the filter, the DAX expression uses the LOOKUPVALUE function to retrieve the value of the EmployeeKey column that's matching the user's login. Then, it uses the PATH-CONTAINS function to parse the Path column in the Employee table in order to check if the parent-child path includes the employee key. If this is the case, the user is authorized to see that employee and his associated sales because the user is the employee's direct or indirect manager.

 NOTE If your computer is not joined to a domain, both USERPRINCIPALNAME() and USERNAME() would return your login (NetBIOS name) in the format MachineName\Login in Power BI Desktop. In this case, you'd have to use an OR filter so that you can test dynamic security in both Power BI Service and Power BI Desktop.

30.1.2 Implementing Organizational Security

I'll walk you through the steps required to implement dynamic data security for the manager-subordinate scenario we just reviewed.

Practice
Start by creating a new role that filters the DimEmployee table.

5. In the ribbon's Modeling tab, click Manage Roles.

6. In the "Manage roles" window create a new *Employee* role.

7. In the Table section, select the Employee table. Enter the following expression in the "Table Filter DAX Expression" field (recall that you implemented the Path column in the "Recursive Relationships" lesson):

```
PATHCONTAINS(DimEmployee[Path],
LOOKUPVALUE(DimEmployee[EmployeeKey], DimEmployee[EmailAddress], USERPRINCIPALNAME()))
```

8. Click the checkmark button in the top right corner of the window to check the expression syntax. If there are no errors, click Save to create the role.

Output
Now that the Employee role is in place, let's make sure it works as expected.

1. In the ribbon's Modeling tab, click "View As Roles" (see **Figure 30.2**).

Figure 30.2 The "View as roles" window lets you test specific roles and impersonate users.

2. In the "View as roles" window, check the "Other user" checkbox and type in *stephen0@adventure-works.com* to impersonate this user. As a result, USERPRINCIPALNAME() returns Stephen's login.

3. Check the Employee role to test it as though Stephen is a member of the role. Click OK.

4. (Optional) Create a Matrix report that uses the Employees hierarchy (or Level1-Level6 fields) and the DimEmployee[Sales Amount (h)] measure you implemented in the "Recursive Relationships" lesson, as shown in **Figure 30.3**.

Organizational Security	
Level1	SalesAmount (h)
Ken Sánchez	$63,320,315
Brian Welcker	$63,320,315
Stephen Jiang	$63,320,315
David Campbell	$3,729,945
Garrett Vargas	$3,609,447
Jillian Carson	$10,065,804
José Saraiva	$5,926,418
Linda Mitchell	$10,367,007
Michael Blythe	$9,293,903
Pamela Ansman-Wolfe	$3,325,103
Shu Ito	$6,427,006
Tete Mensa-Annan	$2,312,546
Tsvi Reiter	$7 171 013
Total	$63,320,315

Figure 30.3 This report shows only Stephen Jiang and his direct or indirect subordinates.

Analysis

The report lets you access only Stephen Jiang and his direct or indirect subordinates. When you run the report, Power BI normally obtains the identity of the interactive user, but you overwrote it with Stephen's login. The DAX formula in the Employee role applies a filter to DimEmployee to filter only Stephen and his subordinates. Notice that the report also shows Stephen's direct and indirect managers (otherwise, there won't be a way to drill down to Stephen), but their totals are filtered to include only Stephen's team contribution.

30.2 Externalizing Security Policies

The final progression of data security is externalizing security policies in another table. Suppose that Adventure Works uses a master data management application, such as Master Data Services (MDS), to associate a sales representative with a set of resellers that she oversees. Your task is to enforce a security role that restricts the user to see only her resellers. This would require importing a table that contains the employee-reseller associations.

 REAL LIFE This approach builds upon the factless fact table implementation that I demonstrated in my "Protect UDM with Dimension Data Security, Part 2" article (http://bit.ly/YBcu1d). I've used this approach in real-life projects because of its simplicity, performance, and ability to reuse the security filters across other applications, such as across operational reports that source data directly from the data warehouse.

30.2.1 Implementing a Security Policy Table

A new SecurityFilter table is required to store the authorized resellers for each employee (see **Figure 30.4**). This table is related to the Reseller and Employee tables. If an employee is authorized to view a reseller, a row is added to the SecurityFilter table. In real life, business users or IT pros will probably maintain the security associations in a database or external application.

Figure 30.4 The SecurityFilter bridge table stores the authorized resellers for each employee.

Importing the security policy table

For the sake of simplicity, you'll import the security policies from a text file (you can also enter the data directly using the Enter Data button in the ribbon's Home tab).

1. In the ribbon's Home tab, click Get Data. Choose Text/CSV.

2. Navigate to the \Source\Part6 folder and select the SecurityFilter.csv file. Click Open.

5. Preview the data and compare your results with **Figure 30.5**. Click Load. Power BI Desktop adds a SecurityFilter table to the model.

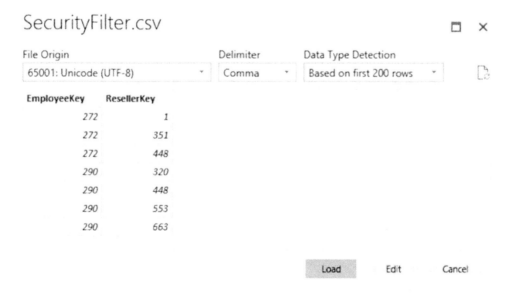

Figure 30.5 The SecurityFilter file includes the allowed resellers that an employee can access.

6. Because users shouldn't see this table, right-click the SecurityFilter table in the Fields pane (Data View) and click "Hide in Report View".

Creating relationships

Next, relate the SecurityFilter table to the appropriate dimensions.

1. In the Relationships View, double-click the FactResellerSales[ResellerKey]⇨DimReseller[ResellerKey] relationship. If the "Apply security filter in both directions" checkbox is checked, uncheck it because it will conflict with the new relationships.

2. In the Relationships View, verify that the SecurityFilter[EmployeeKey]⇨DimEmployee[Employ-eeKey] and SecurityFilter[ResellerKey]⇨DimReseller[ResellerKey] relationships exist and that they are active. If that's not the case, make the necessary changes to create these two relationships.

> **REAL LIFE** Although in this case the SecurityFilter table is related to other tables, this is not a requirement. DAX is flexible and it allows you to filter tables using the FILTER function even if they can't be related. For example, a real-life project required defining application security roles and granting them access to any level in an organization hierarchy. The DAX row filter granted the role access to a parent without explicit access to its children. The security table didn't have relationships to the fact table.

30.2.2 Implementing External Security

Now that the security policy table is in place, the next step is to implement the role and set up a table filter that will authorize the user to see only the permitted resellers.

Practice
Next, you'll add a role that will enforce the security policy. Follow these steps to set up a new Reseller role:

1. In the ribbon's Modeling tab, click Manage Roles.

2. In the "Manage roles" window create a new *Reseller* role.

3. In the Table section, select the DimReseller table.

4. Enter the following expression in the "Table Filter DAX Expression" field:

```
CONTAINS(RELATEDTABLE(SecurityFilter), SecurityFilter[EmployeeKey],
LOOKUPVALUE(DimEmployee[EmployeeKey], DimEmployee[EmailAddress], USERPRINCIPALNAME()))
```

Output
Let's follow familiar steps to test the role:

1. In the ribbon's Modeling tab, click "View As Roles". In the "View as roles" window, check the "Other user" option and enter *stephen0@adventure-works.com* as before.

2. Check the Reseller role and click OK.

3. Create a Table report that uses the ResellerName field from the Reseller table. The report should show only the three resellers associated with Stephen.

4. (Optional) In the Home ribbon, click the Publish button. Deploy the Adventure Works model to Power BI Service. Add members to the Employee and Reseller roles. Ask the role members to view reports and report results.

Analysis
Examining the table filter formula, the LOOKUPVALUE function is used to obtain the employee key associated with the email address. Because the table filter is set on the Reseller table, for each reseller, the CONTAINS function attempts to find a match for that reseller key and employee key combination in the SecurityFilter table. Notice the use of the RELATEDTABLE function to pass the current reseller. The net effect is that the CONTAINS function returns TRUE if there is a row in the SecurityFilter table that matches the ResellerKey and EmployeeKey combination.

30.3 Summary

Power BI supports flexible data security that can address various security requirements, ranging from simple filters, such as users accessing specific countries, to externalizing security policies and dynamic security based on the user's identity. The cornerstone of dynamic security is obtaining the user identity by using the USERPRINCIPALNAME function. You define security roles and table filters in Power BI Desktop and role membership in Power BI Service (powerbi.com).

Appendix A

Glossary of Terms

The following table lists the most common terms and acronyms used in this book.

Term	Acronym	Description
Analysis Services Tabular		An instance of SQL Server Analysis Services that's configured in Tabular mode to host Power BI models and organizational semantic models.
Analysis Services Multidimensional		An instance of SQL Server Analysis Services that's configured in Multidimensional mode to host Power BI models and organizational semantic models (OLAP cubes).
Business Intelligence Semantic Model	BISM	A unifying name that includes both Multidimensional (OLAP) and Tabular (relational) features of Microsoft SQL Server Analysis Services.
Calculated column		A DAX expression-based column added to a table in the data model.
Calculated table		A table that is produced with a DAX expression.
Composite model		A data model with hybrid (import and DirectQuery) storage.
Cube		An OLAP structure organized in a way that facilitates data aggregation, such as to answer queries for historical and trend analysis.
Data Analysis Expressions	DAX	An Excel-like formula language for defining custom calculations and for querying tabular models.
Data model		A BI model designed with Power BI Desktop or Analysis Services.
Data security		Implemented as DAX row filters, data security restricts access to data in the model.
Dataset		The definition of the data that you connect to in Power BI, such as a dataset that represents the data you import from an Excel file.
Date table		A table that stores a consecutive range of dates to fulfill the role of a Date dimension table.
DAX Studio		A community tool for working with DAX queries (https://daxstudio.org)
DirectQuery		A data connectivity configuration that allows Power BI to generate and send queries to the data source without importing the data.
Dimension (lookup) table		A table that represents a business subject area and provides contextual information to each row in a related fact table, such as Product, Customer, and Date.
Extraction, transformation, loading	ETL	Processes extract from data sources, clean the data, and load the data into a target database, such as data warehouse.
Explicit measure		A DAX measure that you create by entering a DAX formula.
Implicit measure		A DAX measure that is created automatically when you add a field to the visual's Values area.

Fact table		A table that keeps a historical record of numeric measurements (facts), such as the FactResellerSales table in the Adventure Works model.
Filter context		Typically used by measures, represents the scope in which the measure formula is executed.
Key Performance Indicator	KPI	A key performance indicator (KPI) is a quantifiable measure that is used to measure the company performance, such as Profit or Return on Investment (ROI).
M		The expression-based language of Power Query
Measure		A business calculation that is typically used to aggregate data, such as SalesAmount, Tax, and OrderQuantity.
Multidimensional		The OLAP path of BISM that allows BI professionals to implement multidimensional cubes.
Multidimensional Expressions	MDX	A query language for Multidimensional for defining custom calculations and querying OLAP cubes.
Online Analytical Processing	OLAP	A system that is designed to quickly answer multidimensional analytical queries to facilitate data exploration and data mining.
Paginated report		A standard, paper-oriented report that is one of the report types supported by SSRS
Power BI		A data analytics platform for self-service, team, and organizational BI that consists of Power BI Service, Power BI Desktop, Power BI Premium, Power BI Mobile, Power BI Embedded, and Power BI Report Server products.
Power BI Desktop		A free desktop tool for creating Power BI reports and self-service data models.
Power BI Premium		A Power BI Service add-on that allows organizations to purchase a dedicated environment.
Power BI Report Server		An extended edition of SSRS that supports paginated reports, Power BI reports and Excel reports.
Power BI Service		The cloud-based service of Power BI (powerbi.com). The terms Power BI and Power BI Service are used interchangeably.
Power Pivot for Excel		A free add-in that extends the Excel capabilities to allow business users to implement personal BI models.
Power Pivot for SharePoint		Included in SQL Server 2012, PowerPivot for SharePoint extends the SharePoint capabilities to support PowerPivot models.
Power Query		A layer in Power BI Desktop and Excel for transforming and shaping data on which a data model is implemented.
Query		A DAX query allows external clients to query published data models.
Quick measure		A DAX measure that is implemented with a Power BI prepackaged formula.
Relationship		A physical or virtual join between two tables
Row context		Typically used in calculated columns, represents the "current" row.
Row-level Security	RLS	A security mechanism for ensuring restricted access to data.
Self-service BI		Same as Personal BI.
Semantic model		Layered between the data and users, the semantic model translates database structures into a user-friendly model that centralizes business calculations and security.
SQL Server Analysis Services	SSAS	A SQL Server add-on, Analysis Services provides analytical and data mining services. The Business Intelligence Semantic Model represents the analytical services.

SQL Server Integration Services	SSIS	A SQL Server add-on, Integration Services is a platform for implementing extraction, transformation, and loading (ETL) processes.
SQL Server Management Studio	SSMS	A management tool that's bundled with SQL Server that allows administrators to manage Database Engine, Analysis Services, Reporting Services and Integration Services instances.
SQL Server Reporting Services	SSRS	A SQL Server add-on, Reporting Services is a server-based reporting platform for the creation, management, and delivery of standard and ad hoc reports.
Snowflake schema		Unlike a star schema, a snowflake schema has some dimension tables that relate to other dimension tables and not directly to the fact table.
Star schema		A model schema where a fact table is surrounded by dimension tables and these dimension tables reference directly the fact table.
Tabular		Tabular is the second implementation path in Analysis Services that lets BI pros implement relational-like (tabular) semantic models.
Time intelligence		Type of analytics to analyze the data by time.
Variable		A DAX construct for refactoring certain parts of a formula to improve readability and performance.
Vertipaq Analyzer		A community tool for analyzing the model storage.
xVelocity		xVelocity is a columnar data engine that compresses and stores data in memory.

index

Increase your BI IQ!

Prologika offers consulting, implementation and training services that deliver immediate results and great ROI. Check our services, case studies, and training catalog at https://prologika.com and contact us today to improve and modernize your data analytics at info@prologika.com.

Currently, we offer these training courses that we can deliver onsite or remotely. Learn more at https://prologika.com/training/.

Applied Power BI

Power BI is a cloud-based business analytics service that gives you a single view of your most critical business data. Monitor the health of your business using a live dashboard...

Learn More >>

Applied DAX with Power BI

Power BI promotes rapid personal BI for essential data exploration and analysis. Chances are, however, that in real life you might need to go beyond just simple aggregations...

Learn More >>

Applied BI Semantic Model (Tabular and Multidimensional)

Targeting BI developers, this intensive 5-day class is designed to help you become proficient with Analysis Services Tabular and Multidimensional...

Learn More >>

Applied Microsoft Visualization Tools

Reporting is an essential feature of every business intelligence solution. One way to extract and disseminate the wealth of information is to author Reporting Services standard reports...

Learn More >>

Applied SQL Server Fundamentals

This 2-day instructor led course provides you with the necessary skills to query Microsoft SQL Server databases with Transact-SQL. It teaches novice users how to query data stored in SQL Server data structures.

Learn More >>

Applied MS BI End-to-End

This four-day class is designed to help you become proficient with the Microsoft BI toolset and acquire skills to implement an end-to-end organizational BI solution, including data warehouse, ETL processes, and a semantic model.

Learn More >>

Applied SQL Server Reporting Services

This intensive 4-day class is designed to help you become proficient with Microsoft SQL Server Reporting Services and acquire the necessary skills to author, manage, and deliver reports.

Learn More >>

Applied Master Data Management and Data Quality

Organizations that invest in master data management and improving the quality of their informational assets will be best positioned to reap ...

Learn More >>

Applied SQL Server Analysis Services (Multidimensional)

This intensive 4-day class is designed to help you become proficient with Analysis Services (Multidimensional) and acquire the necessary skills to implement OLAP and data mining solutions.

Learn More >>

Applied Excel and Analysis Services

This 1-day class is designed to help business users become proficient with using the Excel BI features to analyze corporate data in Analysis Services Multidimensional cubes or Tabular models.

Learn More >>

Applied Power BI with Excel

Power BI is a suite of products for personal business intelligence (BI). It brings the power of Microsoft's Business Intelligence platform to business users. At the same time, Power BI lets IT monitor and manage published...

Learn More >>

Customized classes per your requirements

Printed in Great Britain
by Amazon